CASS SERIES: STUDIES IN INTELLIGENCE
(Series Editors: Christopher Andrew and Michael I. Handel)

INTELLIGENCE INVESTIGATIONS

INTELLIGENCE INVESTIGATIONS

How Ultra Changed History

Collected Papers of
Ralph Bennett

FRANK CASS
LONDON • PORTLAND, OR

This collection first published in 1996 in Great Britain by
FRANK CASS & CO. LTD.
Newbury House, 900 Eastern Avenue
London IG2 7HH

and in the United States of America by
FRANK CASS
c/o ISBS, 5804 N.E. Hassalo Street
Portland, Oregon 97213-3644

Copyright ©1996 Ralph Bennett

British Library Cataloguing in Publication Data:

A catalogue record for this book is available from the British Library

Library of Congress Cataloging-in-Publication Data

Bennett, Ralph Francis.
    Intelligence investigations / Ralph Bennett.
        p.   cm. — (Cass series—studies in intelligence)
    Includes index.
    ISBN 0-7146-4742-X (cloth). — ISBN 0-7146-4300-9 (pbk.)
    1. World War, 1939–1945—Military intelligence. 2. World War,
1939–1945—Cryptography. I. Title. II. Series.
D810.S7B39   1996
940.54'85—dc20   96-31397

Permission to reprint the following has been gratefully received:

Chapters 1 and 6: Sage Publications, London.
Chapter 2: University of Exeter Press, Exeter.
Chapter 3: Brassey's (UK) Ltd., London.
Chapter 4: The Royal United Services Institute.
Chapter 10: The Director, National Army Museum, London.

Typeset by
Vitaset, Paddock Wood, Kent

Printed in Great Britain by
Bookcraft (Bath) Ltd, Midsomer Norton, Avon

Contents

Corrigenda

p. 19, line 2: for OPERATION, read Operation
p. 19, line 30: for nor the 90 PG, read nor 90 PG
p. 23, line 34: for Epsom, read EPSOM
p. 27, line 21: for comet, read COMET
p. 27, lines 21 and 22: for Market Garden, read MARKET GARDEN
p. 32, note 40: for Market Garden, read MARKET GARDEN
p. 33, note 46: for *Sichelschnitt* and *Wacht am Rhein*, read
SICHELSCHNITT and *WACHT AM RHEIN*
p. 59, line 1: for misjudgements Professor, read misjudgements of
Professor
p. 94, line 3: for Gymnast, read GYMNAST
p. 94, line 9: for Baytown, read BAYTOWN
p. 104, line 27: for SIGINT, read Sigint
p. 108, line 16: for Zitadelle, read ZITADELLE
p. 118, line 33: for Rösselsprung, read RÖSSELSPRUNG
p. 122, line 19: for Wacht am Rhein, read WACHT AM RHEIN
p. 123, line 6: for Elderly, read ELDERLY
p. 123, line 14: for Elderly, read ELDERLY
p. 128, line 12: for *MURGATROYD/WIEDERKAEUER,* read
MURGATROYD/WIEDERKAEUER
p. 186, line 5: for sup-posedly, read supposedly
p. 186, line 7: for imagi-nary, read imaginary
p. 186, line 8: for com-ponent, read component
p. 188, line 9: for Fortitude, read FORTITUDE
p. 190, note 16: for Fortitude, read FORTITUDE
p. 192. note 55: for Fortitude, read FORTITUDE
p. 203, note 1: for p. 196, read p. 202
p. 203, note 7: for addresses, read addressees

Introduction

Looking back, it is difficult now to believe that 'Ultra as history' is scarcely 20 years old, so firmly has it (in a rather inaccurate guise, it must be said) embedded itself in the public consciousness. Until 1974 all mention of 'Ultra as wartime intelligence' was forbidden, lest helpful cryptographic clues be accidentally given to potential enemies. The three following years might be branded as the – mercifully short – period of 'Ultra as legend': the inaccuracies of Winterbotham were quickly succeeded by the fictions of Cave Brown and *The Man Called Intrepid*, so that by 1977 Ultra seemed not a serious intelligence source but rather a kind of magic wand one wave of which solved all problems and won the war by itself.

Repelled, as a professional historian, by this travesty of material I had helped to produce, from the day in October 1977 on which the first Ultra documents were placed in the Public Record Office and 'Ultra as history' at last became possible, I set out to treat it as unemotionally as I had been used to treating medieval charters in pre-war Cambridge. I refrained from consulting men who had used it in the field, lest their fallible memories pollute the pure evidence of what had been written down 30 years before. *Ultra in the West* (1979) was the first book to treat Ultra with the critical respect due to a reputable historical source. Invitations to speak at intelligence conferences etc. followed, and the resultant papers, here reprinted, are in some sense a record of work in progress and a reminder of the way in which one man learned to weave a new form of intelligence into a campaign narrative, as the gradual release of more documents raised problems of interpretation and suggested new lines of inquiry. Against this steadily maturing body of knowledge and experience, conversations with senior wartime intelligence officers who had served in the field were no longer risky, and in *Ultra and*

1

Mediterranean Strategy (1989) I used their recollections, whether verbal or printed, to enrich the bald telegraphese of our signals by showing what it had meant to soldiers, sailors and airmen engaged in active operations.

The ten papers collected here fall naturally into two groups. The first five might be described as building blocks out of which a new style of history was being constructed. Never before had it been possible to document intelligence history so fully and so reliably: operational orders and reports intercepted currently and decrypted without much delay gave it a precision it had hitherto always lacked.

But this does not mean that the birth of 'Ultra as history' was either quick or easy, and a prominent feature of these essays is the light they shed on the way it came about and on the similarities and differences between intelligence history and 'ordinary' history. It is common to both types, for instance, but more dangerous to intelligence history, that the historian always tends to be on the winning side – the theme with which the first paper begins. To recognise this at once opens the door to thoughts about the need to shun hindsight and to avoid monocausal explanations (the result of blindness to other possible influences, caused by over-concentration upon one), and the seductions of what I think of as the 'must have been' delusion – that because A preceded B, then B 'must have been' caused by A.* This dilemma confronts the intelligence historian at every turn, and he can seldom find a completely convincing solution: so closely does the shape of the battle of Medenine conform to that of the preceding intercepts that in this case the influence of the one upon the other cannot be doubted, but there are examples where an element of uncertainty remains, moderated perhaps by some degree of probability.

Here we must lament the recent death of Sir Edgar ('Bill') Williams. Williams was Montgomery's chief intelligence officer from the August before Alamein right through to the surrender on Lüneburg Heath nearly three years later, and understood more about the interrelation of intelligence and operations than any other man. Regrettably, he never wrote down his reflections on what he knew, and historians will always

---

*In chapter 3 of *River Out of Eden* (London 1995), a study of the current state of Darwinian evolution theory, Richard Dawkins comprehensively refutes the fallacies of the 'must have been' argument with compelling scientific evidence. Historians should take note.

deplore the omission. By giving examples of situations in which preceding intelligence (whether from Ultra or another source) did or did
not lead to action, he could perhaps to some extent have calmed our
fears of constructing false cause/effect links. All we have, however, are
a short but informative paper composed in 1945 and the extensive tape-
recordings of interviews with him which buttress long passages in Nigel
Hamilton's *Monty*, but the commentary upon them is Hamilton's.
Williams never composed the wide-ranging appreciation which lay
uniquely within his power.

Two other themes of continuing interest arise from the early attempts
to assess the importance of Ultra as an influence on command decisions.
First, was that influence primarily tactical or primarily strategic? Most
early commentators were convinced that tactical significance pre-
dominated, but in recent years it has gradually become clear that it was
in strategic matters that Ultra excelled – front-line reliefs and local troop
movements could usually be as well or better monitored by the capture
of prisoners and the Y service.

The second theme is one which runs through all these first papers,
one which it is essential to bear in mind in any commentary on military
intelligence before Alamein: the hostile atmosphere in which intelligence officers often had to work and the initial inexperience of the
intelligence staffs themselves, the whole compounded by the casual way
in which they had been recruited in the first months of war and by sometimes bitter conflicts at the highest level.*

Translated decrypts of naval Ultra were passed from the Naval
Section at Bletchley Park to the Admiralty for action, whereas with effect
from March 1941 signals to commands abroad based on army and air
decrypts were composed and transmitted direct from Hut 3. Because I
knew in advance that Jürgen Rohwer and Patrick Beesly, who had
worked separately and together on naval Ultra, were to present jointly
their latest conclusions at a Symposium at Exeter University in
November 1985, I somewhat rashly decided to attempt a parallel study
by dissecting so far as I could the army information out of the
undifferentiated mass of army and air signals. The experiment was not
wholly successful, for until the originals can be consulted there is no
certain way of determining whether a given decrypt was of an army or
an air message. Out of it, however, came two worthwhile points. First,
an emphasis (shown by experience to be badly needed) on the necessity

---

*These conflicts have never been fully explained. Professor R.V. Jones has usefully added a contemporary
assessment of his own to the record, see *Intelligence and National Security* 9/1, pp.1–11.

of remembering that Ultra was not a single undifferentiated whole but as many-headed as the Hydra, both in the sense that it was subdivided within each branch of the armed services and in the sense that encipherment procedures might change twice or even three times a day, necessitating as many breaks; and secondly, an appreciation of the limitations of Ultra and of what it could and what it could not do – for instance, that it could tell little about conditions inside Germany because such information went by landline not by radio, an elementary fact forgetfulness of which helped to create the erroneous belief that Germany could be bombed into submission.

The same themes are uppermost in the review of the first ten years' work in Ultra-based intelligence history, published in 1987. It is remarkable how little that is vital the succeeding eight years have left to be added. There has still been no study of the part intelligence played in the discussion of the Chiefs of Staff Committee, where strategy was worked out and recommendations forwarded for government decisions – that is to say, the level at which the influence of Ultra was presumably most sensitively felt – and it is much to be hoped that the minutes of the Committee, now being gradually released, will go some way towards stilling fears that the Committee's conclusions were not as thoroughly digested or as impartially calculated as the complacency of the victor has hitherto supposed – given, of course, that besides intelligence other considerations (politics, supply, and the increasing preponderance of American material might, for instance) had always to be taken into consideration.[1]

Aside from such matters, historical writing has made lamentably little progress towards the integration of intelligence into the narrative of events, and the two are still usually studied in isolation: the former is still the missing dimension in the latter. Instead of attempting to remedy this, recent purveyors of 'historical revisions', preferring academically formulated abstractions to an effort to recreate in imagination the stresses of war, have allowed speculation to run profitlessly riot.

The 1987 review had nothing to say about Jugoslavia. Since then there have been a number of publications the existence of which must be noticed although they are almost worthless as history. With scarcely an exception, they are critical of British policy, in particular the 1943 decision to switch support from Mihailović to Tito. Reckless of evidence telling against their small knowledge and large prejudice, and urging their case with the passion of propagandists, the authors have so managed to capture the attention of the media that rational statements of alternative opinions have sometimes been suppressed.* Perhaps the passage of time will soon bring this unfortunate episode to an end.

The opening pages of the article on intelligence and strategy now seem marred by the choice of a once-popular American formulation as the starting-point. Nevertheless, they manage, I think, to carry further the discussion of key elements in the practice of intelligence in previous papers and to emphasise that secrecy is a *sine qua non* of a good intelligence service and not, as sometimes appears, the intrusion of evil and distortion into it. This last point, at any rate, is still of the greatest relevance today.

The rest of the article examines a series of wartime incidents which reveal the relation between foreknowledge and action, and cannot therefore avoid some repetition of what has been said before. Because it illustrates an argument, and because it sums up intelligence problems which were in the air before the collapse of the Soviet system, however, it retains some interest, even though conditions are now so different.

Insisting always that the practical utility of intelligence is alone worth serious study (because generalised, theoretical abstractions have little application to reality, whether in war or peace), my 1986 paper on 'Intelligence and Strategy in the Mediterranean' also necessarily involved some repetition. But in addition it framed the first comprehensive outline of the subject, which I developed later in *Ultra and Mediterranean Strategy*. A demonstration of the sudden and very marked improvement both in the provision and in the utilisation of intelligence about the middle of 1942 leads to an examination of the reasons for previous failures (largely the legacy of the mistaken attitude which prevailed in the 1930s) and of the resultant lessons for a more flexible and receptive future in which the anticipated volume of information might obscure the risk that excessive dependence on foreknowledge could lead 'our' action to become little more than reaction to what we knew of 'their' intentions, and hence to the loss of the initiative and perhaps of the chance of victory too. A little knowledge was certainly a dangerous thing in the summer of 1941, when Churchill was berating Wavell and Auchinleck on the basis of information which was a good

---

*It was with a view to countering this tendency that five of us published a short factual statement in *Intelligence and National Security* 10, pp.527–29.

deal less complete than he thought, but it is important not to underrate the risk that excess can lead to bewilderment, irresolution and delay.

The second group of papers offers a markedly different approach and has intrinsically a better claim to the title 'Intelligence Investigations'. Each paper tackles a topic where there is rich but imperfectly exploited Ultra information and presents research results on a scale large enough to do justice to the subject but in consequence too detailed to form part of a comprehensive campaign study.

From the middle of 1943 onwards decrypts of a number of Enigma keys used by German army and air headquarters large and small, widely disposed across Jugoslavia, poured into Hut 3 in such volume that they seemed only the scattered pieces of a maddening jigsaw puzzle until painstakingly reassembled into an intelligible pattern. The attack on Tito's HQ at Drvar on 25 May 1944 (ten days before the fall of Rome and 12 before D-Day) illustrates the problem they posed. It raised two questions: 'Did Ultra know about the raid in advance?' and, if so, 'Was any warning given to Tito?' The general, but unsubstantiated, belief that the answer to the first question was 'Yes' was reinforced by the publication of the third volume of *British Intelligence in the Second World War* in 1943, although my evidence, presented at a conference in the Imperial War Museum, had already given a decisive 'No' several months earlier.

The reasons why different conclusions were drawn from the same evidence are instructive. Intelligence received, however 'hot', can only serve to mislead unless it can be firmly fitted into a known context (the intelligence preliminaries to the battle of Kasserine are proof enough!). Messages intercepted as long as 48 hours before the attack did refer obliquely (no plain statement of German intentions was ever seen) to plans for a raid on Drvar, but there was nothing whatever at that moment to connect them with it more than with any one of a number of similar undertakings also in the planning stage in the same week. Only hindsight can connect them with Drvar, so there can be no question of foreknowledge. It follows that there can of course be no question of a warning. Since Tito and his staff seem to have paid insufficient heed to the suspiciously protracted attentions of reconnaissance aircraft, the raid gained complete surprise, and Tito escaped by the skin of his teeth.

It is in any case hard to see how a warning could have been issued even if intelligence had justified one, however. To have done so would have run counter to every known security rule and would have risked betraying the Ultra secret: by breaking Tito's code, the Germans sometimes discovered the light signals to be displayed round Partisan airfields when a supply drop was in prospect, but when Ultra revealed them our recipients were strictly forbidden to use their knowledge operationally.

An Italian committee which was planning to commemorate the Gothic Line in a volume to be published in 1984 invited me to contribute an article on the Ultra intelligence about it; an English version is printed here. It began with an outline sketch of Ultra, since I was writing for a public which might not know much about Sigint; the first three pages are therefore unoriginal, but it has seemed better not to truncate the article by excising them now.

On two occasions in April and May 1944 reports (the second unfortunately only fragmentary) by Kesselring's Chief Engineer on the current state of construction were intercepted. Since information of this kind was ill-suited for encipherment on the Enigma machine, it is to be supposed that it was only used when bombing or sabotage had temporarily cut telephone or teleprinter lines. The intelligence value of these intercepts derived partly from the fact that they long preceded the capture of documents giving similar but fuller information, and partly from the light they shed on the slowness with which construction was proceeding and on the differences between the readiness of different sectors of the fortifications. From them, and from air photographs, it was plain that Hitler's plans for the defence of northern Italy were not being pursued with the expected energy (despite the favourable mountainous location chosen, the Gothic Line could in reality be no more than second best in comparison with the withdrawal to the Alps which Rommel had advocated). Small wonder, then, that in June Hitler warned that while the Gothic Line was 'the final blocking position' to keep the Allies out of Lombardy, no one was to believe that a fortified position in the Apennines already existed or to forget that several months' labour was still needed to complete it.

This was obviously a piece of intelligence of the greatest moment, and its significance was enhanced by the realisation that the Adriatic sector, where the Allied offensive was to strike in August, was the weakest of all.

Hitler's message about the nature and purpose of the Gothic Line was a sign that the hitherto separate fronts were coming together as the war began to draw to a close in the spring of 1944, and may retrospectively be held a turning-point where Allied strategy failed – perhaps disastrously – to turn. The Italian campaign had begun as a reluctantly agreed Anglo-American device to attract as many German divisions as possible away from the Russian front and to prevent them from thickening up the defences of the Channel coast in readiness for D-Day. By the summer of 1944, however, Alexander was no longer willing to accept so subordinate a position, but wished for a share in the victory which was clearly in the making. He developed a plan to break the Gothic Line and to exploit success by striking through northern Jugoslavia to Vienna via the so-called 'Ljubljana gap'.

Although Roosevelt had given the idea (long nourished by Churchill) his provisional blessing at the Teheran conference in November 1943, it was calculated to rouse the worst suspicions of disreputable British Balkan scheming in American minds ('Say, where is this Ljubljana?' asked General Marshall dismissively. 'If it's in the Balkans we can't go there'). Even if Tito could have been relied on to protect its southern flank, and even on the supposition that Kesselring's armies would disintegrate as soon as the Gothic Line was breached, the strategic prospects of so deep an advance into enemy territory were always questionable.

On the other hand, evidence that the Germans feared something of the kind accumulated during the summer of 1944. As they painfully withdrew from Greece through Bosnia, it became more and more essential for them to retain a firm hold on the head of the Adriatic and to protect the coastline against Allied intervention. A hostile landing was regarded as a real and dangerous possibility. But fear does not guarantee the means to avert the danger which causes it. From the Allied point of view, the opportunity for 'the Vienna alternative' existed.

Such an operation never took place, and the pros and cons have seldom been investigated since. Risky it would certainly have been, but it was not just a wild fantasy. It was cut from the same cloth as Market Garden, with Ljubljana standing in for Arnhem and Vienna for the Ruhr. Either might perhaps have ended the war six months early; neither did.

Fifty years on, it is tempting to extend this kind of thought and see the Vienna plan as a way to stem the Russian advance towards western Europe and as the first hint of the Cold War that was to come. The temptation must be resisted. Due attention to chronology and strategy prove such a thesis untenable. In its heyday, Alexander conceived the

Vienna alternative in purely military terms as part of the tripartite alliance to win the war, without the least admixture of politics; only in its death-throes, when it had already been discarded as a military option, did Churchill begin to see it as a means to restrain Russian power.

The article on FORTITUDE which follows was an attempt to solve a puzzle which is still without a solution. It posed a simple question: by what means, and with what success, was Ultra intelligence from Abwehr sources which bore on FORTITUDE made available to 21 Army Group? An astonishing silence hangs over this single stage in an intelligence process which has been common knowledge since the 1970s. The official *British Intelligence History* studiously avoids it, and so does Sir Michael Howard's *Strategic Deception*, even tantalisingly quoting in footnotes documents not available in the Public Record Office. The (unpublished) *History of Strategic Deception*, compiled directly after the war by a man through whose hands all the relevant information had passed, is reticent, obscure, even misleading, at key points in the narrative, and arrives at some questionable conclusions. When I approached them, several of the personalities involved at the time either could not, or would not, answer my questions.[2]

Why this continuing secrecy over Abwehr material and over the way it was used in operations? The names of the double agents, much of what they 'discovered', and their contacts in Germany have long been known and discussed. What is gained by an embargo (for one presumably exists) on how the information they procured was utilised?

Whatever the reasons for it, secrecy over these matters does a great disservice to history. Deception had long been part of Allied strategy in the Middle East, but never before had it been so deliberately and so closely geared into operational plans or designed to distort German reactions at the highest level. It would not be too much to say that the success of OVERLORD depended on it. Eisenhower and Montgomery needed to know as soon as possible whether the deception plan was having the desired effect or not. Wehrmacht Ultra could tell them, for instance, that in the first days after the landing two or three panzer divisions were being held back in the Calais area, but not whether this was merely because OKW was playing safe for a moment, or whether it was because the famous GARBO message had been believed. Historians are therefore forced back once more on the lame 'must have been' explanation for first-rate phenomena, yet certainty (or something very near it) could presumably be established without difficulty from Abwehr documents which exist but are hidden from view. These documents should be released while the few still living men who handled them could, if only they were allowed, breathe life into them from their fading memories.

The National Army Museum proposed to mark the fiftieth anniversary of the Battle of Crete by holding a Study Day, and invited me to take part in its deliberations. These included a debate between Mr Anthony Beevor, whose *Crete: the Battle and the Resistance* had just been published, and myself. I spoke from notes, which I have reconstituted into a piece of continuous prose for the present purpose.

Mr Beevor took much the same general line as most of those who had written about Crete before him – that is to say, he severely criticised Freyberg's handling of the island's defence – but had thought to buttress his arguments by making lavish use of Ultra, which had not been open to his predecessors. To my mind, most of the criticisms do not hold water, and Ultra certainly does not support them. As well as demolishing Mr Beevor's arguments to the best of my ability, I sought to make several points which have a permanent value for the study of intelligence in the Second World War.

The chronology of these early days is of vital importance for an understanding of the place of intelligence in the defence of Crete. The first Ultra signals were sent from Hut 3 at Bletchley Park on 13 March 1941. Ultra first showed a German intention to attack Crete on 6 May, only six weeks later and only a fortnight before the attack was launched on 20 May. Because of the scandalous neglect of military intelligence between the wars and because, until the impossible was achieved on 22 May 1940, only a few mathematicians believed that the 'unbreakable' Enigma cipher could be broken, there were no trained intelligence officers to compose or receive the Crete signals. Not surprisingly, some of our signals lacked desirable precision, and the security rules governing the use of Ultra were far from clear. But they, and still more a superficial reading of them, do not provide a firm enough basis for a hindsighted attack on Freyberg. Freyberg made mistakes but, given the unprecedented conditions and the extraordinary instructions under which he was compelled to operate, most of his actions were sound in the circumstances as he was able to see them.

The loss of Crete was sadly disillusioning as British fortunes declined in the Middle East, but it could hardly have been prevented with the resources available at the time: Egyptian airfields were too far from Crete for the planes based on them to protect the island, Wavell had no tanks to spare for Crete, the troops forming the garrison were tired and ill-equipped after their hasty withdrawal from Greece. The unexpected Ultra warning of peril encouraged a surely vain hope that Crete could be protected more than temporarily against an enemy who held all the cards and could in reality never have been prevented from winning. There are lessons here for the relationship between intelligence and its operational usefulness.

Does 20 years' work on the most informative intelligence source yet known, by more minds than were ever before devoted to such a task, offer any useful conclusions about the practice of intelligence in war or the use of it in writing military history?

Several suggest themselves, and some have figured in the preceding pages, but general concepts distil so reluctantly from a mass of particulars that none is readily reducible to a formula. The advent of radio intelligence on the scale on which it was practised between 1940 and 1945 so completely transformed the part which knowledge about the enemy could play in operations against him that the anomaly thereby created was for the moment obscured. The proper analysis and interpretation of the new-style material required the disciplines of academic scholarship, yet the results had to be applied by men whose actions were necessarily governed by other and coarser laws and in conditions where the emergencies of the moment might demand quick decisions and preclude lengthy reflection. 'In battle, the light of reason is refracted in a manner quite different from that which is normal in academic speculation', wrote Clausewitz; Sir Edgar Williams, one of the chief channels along which Ultra passed into the battle arena, is more succinct. Speed was often preferable to absolute accuracy, he pointed out: 'In battle we deal not with the true but with the likely. Better the best half-truth in time than the whole truth too late'.*

A disjuncture was thus created between academically analysed intelligence and the form in which alone it could be used in the rough-and-tumble of battle. No means of bridging the gap existed. Hitler's mistake in moving his *Schwerpunkt* from west to east and south-east in 1941–42 gave the British time to acquire the new techniques needed for

---

*Williams was prominent among a number of young Oxford and Cambridge graduates, many just embarking upon an academic career, who in the years following 1940 became leading practitioners of the new style of intelligence, adapting themselves either to producing it or to discovering how best to apply it in the field.

the purpose and to forge them into a new and sharp weapon of war. So much time is not likely to be granted again, nor such an escape repeated. A possible lesson to be learned is the need to train intelligence officers in the latest techniques in advance and to teach commanders to listen to what they have to say and use it appropriately.

The intelligence officers who learned these new techniques in 1941–42 were dealing with a novelty. The Enigma and *Geheimschreiber* ciphers were broken gradually, not at a single stroke. We worked up to maximum capacity with equal gradualness, and though intensely busy from 1943 onwards were never unbearably overloaded. Can the balance be retained in future? Unless it can, the need for training is still more urgent, in order to avert, as far as possible, the deadening influence of excess upon discrimination and judgement.

On the other hand, simple excess of decrypted information may not turn out to be a serious problem. The historian must always bear in mind that the 1940–45 situation was peculiar to itself and may never be repeated. Enigma was believed unbreakable – still more the digital *Geheimschreiber* cipher – so that the Germans felt no necessity to seed their messages with disinformation. Ultra could always be taken as true; the only problem was to understand it correctly. More precautions by cipher users, and the compulsion to regard every bit of information as potentially misleading, have changed the situation beyond measure.

An equally complete change has come over the preservation of secrecy. 'If I thought my coat knew my plans, I would take it off and burn it', said Frederick the Great; his attitude was mirrored a century later by Stonewall Jackson ('If I can deceive my friends, I can make certain of deceiving my enemies') and a wholesome respect for the keeping of secrets still prevailed about 1940. It was taken for granted that one would preserve with the utmost care any secret with which war service made one familiar. Many thousands at Bletchley Park and in the field knew the Ultra secret and none betrayed it. An almost opposite situation prevails now. The wave of horror which greeted the revelation, by an MP during the Falklands war that we were reading Argentine signals would scarcely be repeated today: a 'leak' of some sort would probably have made the 'secret' public already by a news-hungry Press which cares little for anything but the latest 'sensation'.

That a positive cause/effect link, as well as temporal priority, has to be established between two events before one can safely be labelled the consequence of the other seems obvious, but to ensure it is an obligation too often disregarded by historians. Frequently, it must be admitted, this is because conclusive evidence to fulfil it is lacking, particularly in the study of long-past centuries. Radio intelligence on the scale on which Ultra was available from 1943 onwards has made fulfilment more possible than ever before in one particular field,* but the risk of 'must have been' conclusions still remains. To insist too strictly on an exact observance of the rule enunciated at the beginning of this paragraph risks pedantry, of course, but it is a standard every historian ought to maintain if he can and to admit the reason for failure specially if he cannot. As a medieval historian in origin and by continuing commitment (and therefore accustomed to the lack of absolutely conclusive evidence), I feel that an enhanced regard for logical proof is the greatest gain work in intelligence and on intelligence history has brought me.

*To the purist this is an overstatement. Signals logs were destroyed long ago, so it is impossible to know exactly when a given Ultra signal reached its designated recipient, and therefore to know for certain whether it could or could not have played any part in his subsequent decisions. Again, whereas Montgomery gave Williams permission to disturb him at any hour of the day or night if the news warranted, many American commanders restricted their Ultra officers' access to one or two specified times a day.

NOTES

1. But meanwhile see Noel Annan: *Changing Enemies* (London 1995) 59–82.
2. An article in the *Sunday Times Magazine* for 12 May 1996 about the current rebuilding of 'Colossus' (urged with persuasive evidence to have been the world's first computer), the machine which decrypted the *Geheimschreiber* (Lorenz) cipher, argues that this was the means by which the Allies became aware of the *Abwehr* reaction to their D-Day deception plans.

1

Ultra and Some
Command Decisions

'The historian is a natural snob. He sides with the gods against Cato and applauds the winning side', wrote Dean Inge half a century ago. *Victrix causa diis placuit, sed victa Catoni.*[1] It may seem strange to begin a discussion of Second World War intelligence with a classical tag and the 'gloomy dean' of the 1930s, but his remark neatly points up a familiar historiographical problem which has a double relevance to the task of assessing the place of Ultra in the making of command decisions. Since Ultra was perhaps the largest[2] and certainly the most reliable single source of intelligence about the enemy available to the Allies from the spring of 1941 onwards, it would clearly be useful to discover how much influence it had upon their conduct of the war. As this paper will show, however, no more than a partial and provisional estimate can yet be made. For the present* at least, all talk of 'completely rewriting the history of the war' in the light of Ultra must be discounted, and even the eventual release of all the surviving Ultra material is unlikely to compel so drastic a revision.

By 1945, the Allies were the winning side. When the secret that the Enigma code had been broken was first let out[3] six years ago, there was an immediate tendency to attribute too great a responsibility for victory to it alone. This chimed in with – was perhaps really part of – a natural change in historical fashion a generation after 1945. The new fashion wanted to depose the heroes of the past and to replace the story of five years' uphill struggle with an insistence that the economic balance was so heavily weighted in favour of Britain, Russia and the United States that they were always bound to win, and with the assertion that the Allies

* Written in 1980.

14

should rather be blamed for the foolishness or timidity which (it was alleged) prevented them from gaining a quicker victory than praised for the determination which enabled them to triumph in the end. The chief recent sign of this fashion is John Grigg's 1943: *The Victory that Never Was,* and it may also be discerned in Mr Julian Amery's letter to *The Times* of 21 June 1980 about the proposed Anglo-French union of 1940.

In the present state of our knowledge, Ultra can probably contribute little towards tackling broad strategic questions such as are here raised, for scarcely half, even of the signals sent from Bletchley to field commands, have been released. A proper assessment of Ultra's strategic value will only be possible when the whole corpus has been thoroughly studied and compared with information obtained from other sources, notably the Y-service, prisoners of war and low-grade codes. (At this distance of time, it is not by any means easy to discover from which of these sources a field commander derived a particular item of intelligence, since most of the operational histories were written before the existence of Ultra could be publicly admitted.) Meanwhile, it is safe to assume that Ultra's best work was usually done at a level slightly below that of grand strategy, although it made periodical highly successful excursions into battlefield tactics.[4]

However, there is at any rate one exception to this general rule. The breaking of Triton[5] by the Naval Section at Bletchley Park in March 1943 brought the U-boats under control at last and so changed the balance of power in the Atlantic that the whole future course of the war in Europe may have hung upon it. The war at sea is outside my direct knowledge, however, and this paper is concerned solely with the land battle and the air above it, which alone were my business as a member of Hut 3 at Bletchley.

There is a second sense in which Dean Inge's warning may apply. The road to final victory lay through many lesser successes and several set-backs. In some of them, the value of Ultra to the field commanders is quite plain, in others – for a variety of reasons, some of which are obscure – it is strangely difficult to determine. But the need for caution in deciding Ultra's usefulness or otherwise is as great in the short term as in the long, and in almost every case demands a more detailed examination than has yet been undertaken. The contribution of a source unique in the history of warfare can only be measured the hard way. To say this is not to denigrate the importance of Ultra, but rather to plead that so exact a source demands an equivalent exactness of the historian, and to point out that Ultra's quality and quantity draw attention to something which, though by no means confined to this particular historical source, is a peculiar handicap in the evaluation of it. We know remarkably little about what the fighting commanders thought of Ultra and how it affected their decisions. Nor, so far as I am aware, are we likely to learn much more in future. As consumers, their appetites were rapacious, but they seldom explained their taste-preferences, and it is too late now for much market research. Exceptions, like the account Professor R. V. Jones has given of how Bletchley decodes helped to beat the beams and delay the V-weapons, are likely to remain exceptions.[6] The Ultra historian is therefore often compelled to guess in spite of the risks entailed, and to rely on inference where he longs for certainty; he must nevertheless hold fast to an austere resolve never to pass one off as the other.

Medievalists probably have to brave pitfalls of this sort more often than modernists, but we have not been conspicuously successful in avoiding them. Was the growth in the power of the twelfth-century French monarchy the result of conscious and deliberate policy on the part of a succession of Capetian kings, or was it accidental? What was in the mind of their contemporary, Frederick Barbarossa, when he asserted the Emperor's rights in Italy by force? The answers profoundly affect one's interpretation of several critical themes in the history of medieval Europe, but there is practically no positive evidence to provide them – despite which, reputable scholars have confidently presented pages and pages of inference as fact, and have explained actions as if the purposes behind them were as plain as the events themselves. Most of the explanations have taken the plausible but unsatisfactory form 'since this was the result, that must have been the cause' – the argument of the winning side. A practising medievalist, accustomed to demolishing arguments like these, therefore, comes to modern military history with a ready-made scepticism of anything but conclusive proof of the relation between cause and effect, and with an innate distrust of any generalisation which is not properly supported. The links between knowledge and action, between event and explanation, have to be demonstrated beyond all reasonable doubt. In the case of Ultra there is a real danger of an easy and uncritical descent into 'must have been', and the path is already well trodden.

Even granted this necessary caution, a great deal more Ultra will have to reach the Public Record Office before the chief command decisions of the war can be classified with any certainty according to the part Ultra played in them. All that can be done at present is to indicate a few types and suggest some reasons why they differ. One differential, the incidence of which has not been much discussed but which will probably have a considerable bearing on the final conclusion, is variations in intercept policy. The progressive switch of resources from the Mediterranean to the west in the spring of 1944, for instance, is apparent from the most superficial comparison of the signals to the two theatres, but it is not so easy to see whether this is the reason why the value of Mediterranean Ultra seems to fall off that same spring. The theatre itself was deliberately downgraded, particularly after the capture of Rome, and it may be that with consequently reduced resources it was not always possible to determine which radio links were likely to give the best yield of high-grade intelligence or to monitor them regularly. Again, it is fair to surmise that coverage was never so complete anywhere as in Africa between the Gazala battles of June 1942 and the German surrender on Cape Bon a year later, but also to suppose that there was severe competition with the navy for intercept sets and that the military yield was reduced from time to time by the refractoriness of the army keys. Variations in the volume and value of Ultra depended mainly on three things: variations in intercept policy (about which little information is forthcoming),[6a] the success of the code-breakers (which advanced fairly steadily from early 1942 onwards), and the German use of landlines (which for practical purposes debarred Ultra from access to northwest Europe until the spring of 1944).

They also depended in the early days on the purveyors' and the consumers' inexperience of the medium, combined with a security consciousness which was sometimes misplaced – notably the fiction which represented Ultra information as the work of a super-agent who could be in several places at once, with the result that some recipients (no doubt conditioned by their military training to distrust all intelligence not derived from battle contact anyhow) at first dismissed it altogether. Some of the 1941 signals, when we see them, will probably seem amateurish and clumsily drafted beside those of the summer before Alamein.[7] Both parties gradually became more sophisticated and began to settle into an easier relationship, but the 2000 miles which separated them were a distinct obstacle to mutual understanding and sometimes caused a dialogue of the deaf until exchange visits began in the spring of 1942. Things were already very much better by the time I went to Cairo in October to join another officer in signalling one easily broken army/air cooperation key on the spot.

Because the signals cannot yet be inspected, comment on Ultra's influence on command decisions in the desert and Tunisia, in Sicily and at Salerno can be nothing but speculation at present.[8] It is, however, a safe reflection that some of these decisions will look very different when we see the evidence. One rediscovery to which I am particularly looking forward myself is the date of the Ultra signal which gave away Rommel's intentions at Alam Halfa, for this should settle the dispute whether Montgomery's defence plan was inherited from his predecessor or suggested to him by his opponent. The frequency with which we decoded and passed on the Africa Corps' tank strength returns is another. If, as memory suggests – but memory is not to be trusted – we did so regularly and often, then 8 Army must be supposed usually to have known pretty accurately where the balance of mobility and fire-power lay, but not always to have taken this knowledge into proper account. This in turn is likely to sharpen criticism of its conduct in some of the desert battles.

The Anzio landing (22 January 1944) is the first major action for which full Ultra coverage is yet available. Ultra can have played little if any part in planning, but in three respects it was evidently of great assistance during the weeks immediately before the operation. Kesselring told Jodl[9] early in January 1944 that he had no fear of an Allied landing, and Canaris (whom Kesselring subsequently blamed for giving him bad advice) shortly reassured his Chief of Staff, Westphal, that such a thing was out of the question for a month or six weeks.[10] Ultra had no access to either opinion, but by keeping touch with every German division in Italy and confirming that none of them was being shifted to coastal defence it arrived, if negatively, at the same conclusion as OKW – that between the Cassino front and mouth of the Tiber 'the coast was to all intents and purposes unguarded'.[11] That this should be so was the more remarkable in view of the number of Ultra reports by other authorities about expected landings on both coasts of Italy.[12] (Only one of them was anywhere near the mark: on 14 January Kesselring sent a single battalion of the Hermann Goering Division to watch the seaward approaches behind 94 Division's front.) Its effect was enhanced by what were admitted to be 'inconclusive' air reconnaissance reports which failed to spot anything sinister right down to the last day,[13] as well as by repeated misinterpretations of Allied shipping movements – the arrival of aircraft carriers in the eastern Mediterranean was taken to be a way of reinforcing land-based fighters, for instance, and no alarm was shown at the disappearance of landing-craft from Bizerta harbour.[14] Even the 10th Italian human torpedo flotilla, whose operational orders and after-action reports the Naval Section regularly intercepted at this time, saw nothing to awaken its suspicions off Gaeta or in the bay of Naples.[15]

As D-Day for OPERATION SHINGLE approached, Ultra performed a third priceless service by letting General Mark Clark know that his plan to press his attack on the Gustav Line hard enough to attract German reserves away from the neighbourhood of Anzio had succeeded. The GOC XIV Panzer Corps, General von Senger und Etterlin, phoned Kesselring on 18 January to ask for reinforcements to prevent his front from collapsing; after some hesitation Kesselring, believing that he had no reason to fear a landing behind it, ordered 29 and 90 Panzergrenadier Divisions up to 10 Army from Rome.[16] Barely 24 hours later, Ultra was reporting elements of 29 PG moving south,[17] with more unspecified reinforcements also on the way to von Senger's hard-pressed 94 Division, and by 0300 on the 20th it had discovered that 29 PG was to take over a section of 94 Division's front.[18] Both signals were of course sent with the highest priority. As the first troops went ashore on the 22nd, it became known that the unspecified reinforcements were 90 PG and that the staff of I Parachute Corps had come from Frascati to direct all three divisions.[19] Thus through Ultra the Allied command knew in advance that surprise was almost certain and that initial resistance would be light because the nearest reserves had been diverted elsewhere and were consequently not available to counterattack the beach-head during its vulnerable first hours. Even if Anzio was in some respects a misbegotten scheme, this realisation must add one more reason for regret that its early success was not more immediately and powerfully exploited.

However, we must not forget that Lucas, in command of the landing, did not receive Ultra because he was only a corps commander. Mark Clark did receive it, of course, at 5 Army headquarters, but security regulations forbade him to pass it on except under heavy disguise. Since apparently neither 29 nor the 90 PG had been identified by contact on the Cassino front before 22 January, it is hard to imagine how, without betraying Ultra, Clark could have informed Lucas that both these divisions were by that time heavily engaged in the Gustav Line and therefore could not counter-attack him in the immediate future. Whether the knowledge that the road to Rome was open and the city almost unguarded would have been enough to stop Lucas feeling that the whole affair had 'a strong odour of Gallipoli'[20] and to prevent him from taking refuge behind ambiguous orders and refraining from a quick advance cannot be known. In any case, the German reaction to SHINGLE was only below expectation on the first day. By the afternoon of the 23rd it was more or less what had been foreseen, and Kesselring was quick to read Lucas's surprising passivity to mean that a large-scale expansion[21] of the beach-head was no longer imminent.

Information derived from Ultra offered better prospects of success than the landings achieved, then, but the reasons why the operation first stalled and then became hopelessly (if heroically) bogged down are to be found not in the performance of any source of intelligence but in the lack of an unequivocal definition of primary objectives and in the psychology of a tired commander. By way of contrast, Ultra provided little of high operational value to General Alexander for the offensive (DIADEM) of 11 May 1944 which broke the Gustav Line, joined up with the Anzio beach-head at last, captured Rome and took the Allies as far as Lake Trasimene before it petered out. DIADEM is memorable not so much for what Ultra did as for what it has been wrongly credited with doing.

But first, its positive contribution to DIADEM. A clutch of reports[22] from Kesselring and his senior subordinates in May and June repeatedly stressed the problems of supply and transport which plagued them. These reports confirmed to the Allied commanders that, once prised out of their fortifications, the German armies would find it immensely difficult to conduct mobile warfare on their way back to another pre-pared position, and no doubt thereby encouraged them to feel that one more big push might topple Kesselring's house of cards altogether and open the way not only to the Lombard plain but perhaps even to Austria as well. Until all the Italian signals can be studied in proper sequence it would be premature to attempt to assess whether, and if so how much, Ultra was responsible for Alexander's dream of advancing through the Ljubljana Gap into Hitler's homeland, but inasmuch as its gloomy reports about supply and transport were a regular feature of the Italian campaign it is safe to say that they probably fostered the belief that if only an Allied offensive could achieve enough momentum it might make it impossible for the Germans to stop anywhere south of the Alps.

To return to DIADEM. On 8 May Kesselring 'once again' called upon the naval authorities in Italy to carry a larger proportion of the supplies he needed, since railways and roads were so frequently interrupted by air attack, and reiterated his conviction that the Italian front was 'decisive for the conduct of the war'.[23] By early June he was persuaded that the situation would improve only if more fighters and ground-attack aircraft could be allotted to the *Luftwaffe* in Italy.[24] (On only eight days during the previous four weeks of heavy fighting had *Luftflotte 2* managed more than a hundred sorties of all types of aircraft, and had averaged about 70.[25] Ultra only missed its daily returns of total effort on four days in the month.) Recurring complaints of ammunition shortage are still more illuminating. By 11 June Kesselring had been forced to conclude that shortage of ammunition had deepened every successive crisis in the fighting, and he ordered corps and divisional commanders to adopt 'the most ruthless means' to overcome it, even to the closure of roads to all other traffic; he had evidently forgotten that less than a month earlier the chief quartermaster of 10 Army had pointed out that this was just what the units and formations for which he was responsible could not do, because they had too few lorries of their own to fetch supplies for themselves.[26]

Ammunition was not the only thing in short supply. On 6 May OKH curtly told the Hermann Goering Division that because fewer and fewer tanks and assault guns were coming out of the factories the division would have to lose the privileged status which OKL had granted it during the winter and that its establishment of weapons would be reduced to the same level as that of the *Wehrmacht* and SS divisions.[27] Next day Kesselring circulated an order from Hitler which drew attention to the 'excessively strained German manpower situation'.[28] After a fortnight's fighting Mackensen at 14 Army complained about low morale and almost everything else: the fighting power of his divisions had declined shockingly, partly through attrition and partly because there were not enough good NCOs; tanks and lorries often broke down on long journeys, he had too few anti-tank guns and he was 20 per cent under strength in radio operators.[29]

Just as before Anzio, there were enough divergent reports of expected new Allied landings to show that in this respect at least German intelligence was wildly inaccurate – or very gullible, for several of these rumours, notably those suggesting Civita Vecchia as the target, had been put about as part of the deception-plan known as Nunton.[30]

All in all, Ultra gave Alexander a good deal of useful information about the enemy as he planned and launched his offensive. Though very encouraging, it can hardly have been decisive for the success or failure of his operation. DIADEM is therefore one of the cases where Ultra is unlikely to enforce the rewriting of history. It did, however, provide a curious forewarning of the future. In the course of it, the German rank-and-file fought with a skill and determination which gave the lie to what generals like Mackensen had been saying about them in Enigma messages. If this had been remembered 18 months later, it might have served as a useful corrective to the facile conclusion, drawn by so many after the Falaise pocket battle and subsequently the source of so much error, that the war was over bar the shouting because the Germans could fight no longer.

Contrary to what has just been said, readers of Group Captain Winterbotham's *The Ultra Secret* have been led to expect that the DIADEM battle narrative needs a great deal of revision. In four or five pages of his book Winterbotham claimed to quote (from memory, of course) from a dozen or more signals, most of them emanating from Kesselring or Hitler, in which every important reaction of the Germans to DIADEM was starkly revealed. There appears to be no Ultra warrant for most of his claims.[31] Moreover, there was an interval of twenty-four hours or more between German and British times of origin on most days at this period – presumably a reflection of decoding difficulties or of delays in the retransmission to England of Mediterranean intercepts – which would, of course, have reduced the operational value of Ultra significantly.[32]

It would serve no good purpose to dwell upon every case where *The Ultra Secret is* misleading over DIADEM, but a few examples may be quoted. While it is certainly true that Ultra showed that Kesselring was quite unable to decide where and when the Allies would strike next, the files contain no signal of 10 May to that express effect. Nor is there a signal of 13 May revealing that he had committed all his reserves by then, though it might have been possible to deduce as much from a close scrutiny of the many recent signals conveying corps and divisional locations. There is no sign of an order from Kesselring for a general withdrawal from the Liri valley shortly afterwards, nor of his asking and receiving permission to move back to the Caesar Line just in front of Rome. A signal of 3 June[33] does, however, by implication support the claim that Ultra showed Hitler agreeing to the evacuation of Rome; but it also says a great deal more, for it orders the formation of a new front as far south as possible – and Hut 3 could not despatch this signal until 9 June, by which time the whole world had heard about the Americans' triumphal entry into Rome!

The point that Winterbotham's book is completely unreliable as an Ultra source need not be laboured further, and indeed would scarcely be worth mentioning at all were it not for the fact that the contagion has spread. A volume of the United States official history (E. F. Fisher: *Cassino to the Alps*) was published three years after *The Ultra Secret*. Mr

Fisher quotes the latter as his authority on a dozen occasions[34] – usually, it must be admitted, in the most general terms. But in so doing he has cast over its inaccuracies the cloak of respectability which belongs to an official publication, and has very likely given further currency to errors which it would have been better to scotch at once, among them the legend that Bletchley could intercept, decode, and translate a German text and retransmit an English equivalent 'within minutes' of the original going on the air. (Between two and two-and-a-half hours was the best Hut 3 could manage.) Gresham's Law applies to history as well as to coinage. The task of correctly assessing the usefulness of Ultra intelligence will be longer and more difficult unless the circulation of false coin can first be prevented.

Ultra played no part in the greatest command decision in the west – the choice of time and place for the invasion of Europe – and its chief value before 6 June 1944 was surely confined to revealing the dispositions the GAF intended to make in an emergency and to serving as an absolutely reliable check upon other intelligence about the order of battle of the German army. It was best on the panzer divisions (all of which it identified) and weakest on locations – for instance, it missed the late move to Caen of 21 Panzer, whose counter-attack on the first afternoon might have cut the bridgehead in two. Once the invaders were securely ashore, however, Ultra began to offer them a series of opportunities which could have been given by no other source. In several of these cases the cause-effect relationship between knowledge and action can be demonstrated quite convincingly if not positively proved.[35]

The air strike on 10 June which paralysed Panzergruppe West for a fortnight was the earliest and most spectacular of these cases, and the snuffing out of 17 SS's attack at Carentan three days later (also clearly the result of an Ultra warning) was decisive for the capture of Cherbourg by 1 US Army. By now Hitler had become sufficiently alarmed to order II SS Panzer Corps across from the Russian front to dislodge the invaders. There was no hint of this for several days, but ample Ultra evidence of it accumulated in time to enable Montgomery to prevent the new arrivals from interfering with Epsom, the battle for the crossings of the river Odon, and in particular to bring an attack by 9 SS Panzer Division to an abrupt halt on 9 July. In all three cases Ultra clearly prompted actions which had a most important bearing on the progress of the campaign. As the scale of operations grew greater during the following weeks, so did the scale of Ultra's contribution. A close scrutiny of the signals passed to western commands during COBRA, the

American breakout at the end of July, and in the early days of what became the Falaise pocket, shows beyond reasonable doubt that Ultra was behind some of the most important decisions taken at this time.

All through the three weeks before COBRA the German commanders opposite 1 US Army were continually complaining about the heavy casualties they were suffering and about the material superiority of the Americans; more than one of them predicted that if (as they expected) an offensive soon opened on this part of the front it was bound to break through their fragile defence lines. The only serious effort von Kluge could make to support them was to transfer the Panzer Lehr armoured division from Caen to St Lô. Ultra knew of his decision within 12 hours of his making it on the evening of 7 July and 36 hours before the first tanks reached their destination; this, and the four hours' notice we gave of an order for the division to attack directly it arrived, was enough to ensure that Panzer Lehr came up against prepared defences and scarcely disturbed 1 US Army's equanimity at all.[36] By the time COBRA opened, then, Bradley had good reason to anticipate a victory almost as rapid and complete as he achieved, because he knew in advance that morale was low on the other side of the hill and that the enemy expected to be beaten.

The COBRA plan did not originally call for immediate exploitation eastwards, and Patton's first orders were to clear Brittany, not advance up the Loire valley. No very precise explanation seems to have been given of the reasons which led Bradley to abandon his more modest original intention on 8 August in favour of a bolder course, although there was still only a very narrow supply corridor through Avranches, but it is hard to escape the conclusion that he did so partly at least because he already knew from Ultra of the first moves in what we now call Hitler's Mortain offensive and was confident that he could ride it out and convert it into a chance to annihilate the German armies in France. There is no positive proof, but the evidence is persuasive enough to silence the sceptic. The first clear signs that a counter-attack was in the wind became available on 5 August (hindsight can now even detect them on the third) with the withdrawal of 2 SS Pz and 116 Pz from the line to concentrate under XLVII Pz Corps north of Mortain. Conclusive evidence for it was signalled during the evening of 6 August, and details of objective and troops engaged shortly after midnight. The attack was a little delayed, the warning was enough and the American lines held – but the enemy showed no signs of retreat. When Bradley took his momentous decision on 8 August, therefore, Ultra and the previous

24

day's experience combined to counsel boldness rather than caution, for he could foresee that Hitler's foolish gamble would compound his own advantage and therefore already envisaged the destruction of Army Group B. This was surely the supreme moment of Ultra in the west, for if it was responsible for a stroke upon which we can now see that the triumphant progress of the next few weeks largely depended, then its contribution to victory was great indeed. Bradley's judgement was soon proved right by the signal forecasting a renewal of the attack on 11 August, but if he had hesitated after the first phase there might never have been a Falaise pocket and the swift advance across northern France in the next three weeks.[37]

The weakness at the western end of the front which opened the way for COBRA showed how successfully the German command had been induced to believe that the main Allied thrust would come in the east. To the obvious topographical considerations which suggested this there had been added the repeated British attacks round Caen, and some of the most useful Ultra signals during the first six weeks were no doubt those which showed the panzer divisions concentrating in the same area to counter them, together with intelligence appreciations which revealed the intensity of Rundstedt's fear that they presaged a deadly thrust from Caen towards Paris. The other half of the deception plan sought to propagate the notion that a large Anglo-American army group in southeast England was preparing to pounce on Calais as soon as the Normandy landings had distracted the attention of OB West sufficiently. Signals like the group in late June which showed 116 Pz being kept away from Normandy to meet this threat are therefore likely to have been taken into account when command decisions were made. Another and very much larger group – German digests of deductions drawn from their Y-service intercepts and intelligence appreciations based upon them, which make up a considerable proportion of the signals issued during the middle six months of 1944 – proved the success of the deception plan still more convincingly. In other respects these signals may now be of mainly academic interest, but this cannot be established until they have been properly investigated. Because I did not know either the real or the notional Allied order of battle, *Ultra in the West*[38] touches only lightly upon this group of signals; Mr Cruickshank, who is familiar with both, did not make much use of Ultra when he wrote *Deception in World War II*. The official history of deception which is now being prepared will presumably show whether the Germans' errors were ever of such a size or kind that they could directly affect an operational decision by the Allies – and will perhaps also reveal how many of the breaches of signals security which gave the Y service its chances were deliberate and how many culpable.

Thus until the liberation of Paris, the receipt of all major items of Ultra intelligence in the field was followed by action so evidently dependent on it that the relationship cannot be doubted, and there are no examples to the contrary. From the moment when the great advance came to a halt in early September, however, striking instances of the disregard of Ultra on matters of first-rate importance begin to accumulate. On 1 September Eisenhower took over the duties of Land Force Commander, directly controlling operations in a way he had not done before; SHAEF itself was similarly without experience of operational command. That the one change accounts for the other would be a more tempting hypothesis if it fitted all the facts, was not obviously an oversimplification, and did not involve thinking the unthinkable – a 21 Army Group commander without a will of his own. There is some support for the theory that after Falaise many at all levels of authority believed the war to all intents and purposes already won, and therefore suddenly relapsed into a state of euphoria. A collective fit of midsummer madness which lasted long enough to explain why the significance of some Ultra items was overlooked in November is scarcely credible, but there appears to be no acceptable alternative.

The contrast between the two periods is sharp and sudden. After Mortain, the influence of Ultra can still be traced in the early stages of the Germans' efforts to escape from the pocket, but then gradually fades from view in the fortnight's mobile warfare which followed (a great many signals were sent at this time, but the speed of the advance probably meant that most were out of date by the time they were delivered). On 5 September, the day after the capture of Antwerp docks, came an item so obvious (it now seems) that hindsight can scarcely believe that the news that Hitler planned to render Antwerp useless to the Allies by holding on to both banks of the Scheldt was even needed to prompt the measures necessary to foil him.[39] Yet this explicit warning – repeated two days later in an even more swiftly decoded instruction from Hitler to 15 Army in Holland – was completely disregarded, with the consequence that a pardonable momentary oversight by an armoured division exhilarated but exhausted by its long drive across France and Belgium was soon converted into a strategic mistake of such magnitude that its repercussions were felt almost until the end of the war. Montgomery's dream of an immediate advance to the Ruhr or Berlin in force great enough to kill the German bull with a toreador's thrust before it could turn at bay in its homeland was militarily feasible only if his 40 divisions could be supplied through Antwerp.[40] Yet for ten days he made no effort to ensure that he could use the port, and by then it was too late. If, in all the flurry and excitement of seeming victory, ordinary logistical prudence deserted the planners, Ultra was there to remind them in good time. Why its warning went unheeded is incomprehensible. Both Montgomery and Eisenhower continued to issue orders which either directly stated or indirectly implied that the approaches to the port were of only secondary importance, although both friend and foe (Ramsay and Hitler) had pointed out their error.[41] Within a few days the defence of Breskens and Walcheren had been organised and the Allies condemned to an autumn and winter of impotence and frustration.

Whatever the reason for the aberration – and it plainly had a great deal to do with the sudden emergence of a plethora of strategic options and the necessity to readjust sights from the short range of the bridgehead battle to the far longer range of a final victory on German soil – the atmosphere in which the mistake over Antwerp was made was to all intents and purposes still the same at the time of the decision about Arnhem: Comet (the lesser operation out of which Market Garden grew) was first contemplated on 3 September, when 11 Armoured Division was still racing towards Antwerp. The similarity extends into the field of Ultra. The main distinction is simply that the evidence was a shade less compelling in the later case, but the process of thought which could dismiss as unimportant the confirmation which Ultra's strong hints that 9 and 10 SS Panzer Divisions were near Arnhem gave to Dutch Resistance reports and to one probable interpretation of air photographs was surely very much the same as that which paid no heed to Hitler's explicit declaration of intent about Antwerp.[42] The evidence for the movements of 9 and 10 SS was not conclusive, mainly because it was not right up to date when 1 Airborne Division was briefed, but the authority of Army Group B was behind some of it. Unless there had been a very recent high-level change of plan – which was improbable now that Student and 1 Para Army had managed to stabilise the front – the Ultra evidence was therefore not likely to be misleading. MARKET GARDEN was not an operation planned entirely in relation to tactical opportunities and intelligence about the enemy, however. There are slightly sinister undertones of excessive haste, Anglo-American rivalry and even desperation about it; the possibility that there were tanks at

Arnhem was the one awkward fact that would not fit the desired pattern, so the best thing was to sweep it under the carpet.

This hypothesis, unappealing in itself, has at least the merit of partly explaining away the problem the Ultra historian has to face over Antwerp, Arnhem and the Ardennes – that almost all the officers who received Hut 3 signals were by this time thoroughly experienced at their job and had in the very recent past shown themselves fully capable of estimating accurately the value of every item of intelligence that came their way. Only one of them, Strong, is known to have demurred at MARKET GARDEN,[43] but it is inconceivable that others did not do the same. Their masters overrode them, as they were fully entitled to do, but their masters were at fault when they allowed both their subordinates and posterity to believe that the tanks at Arnhem were a surprise.

Browning, in command of the airborne troops, was on the Ultra list and may have had the Ultra evidence about 9 and 10 SS in mind when he told Montgomery, 'I think we might be going a bridge too far', on 10 September, for most of it had been transmitted by the sixth. He was evidently no longer paying any heed to it two or three days later, for he advised Major Urquhart 'not to trouble himself'[44] about the air photographs. Montgomery had reacted in the same way to Strong's and Bedell Smith's warnings on the twelfth. Wisdom after the event must not misconceive the way military decisions are made by demanding that an operation of this size, from which immense strategic advantage could be expected if all went well, should have been cancelled because of a single piece of intelligence. It is entitled to suggest, however, that because tanks could so easily overrun unprotected infantry and because without the last bridge the whole operation was pointless, this single piece of intelligence clearly held the key to success or failure, and therefore deserved much more serious consideration than it received.

The same four weeks of rapid advance and abrupt check saw the broad front strategy applied for the first time, and this offers a kind of inverse parallel to Arnhem on a larger scale. Some of the British objections to ANVIL/DRAGOON, the most extreme example of it, were proved sound by Hitler's prompt[45] order to evacuate the south of France (reported at once by Ultra) and by the Americans' failure to cut off significant elements of 19 Army although Ultra revealed the intended timetable of its laborious march up the Rhone valley. More importance, however, attaches to the signals which show that it was not only Blaskowitz (commanding Army Group G) who was nervous about his escape route through the Vosges, but that others were equally concerned about the immediately adjacent area to the northward – from Trier and the Mosel valley to Dijon, the rendezvous for the columns retreating from the south-west, and Belfort, where 19 Army reached comparative safety on 6 September. Thus the very area where Patton was pressing forward with or without permission as far as his artificially restricted resources allowed was shown by Ultra to be even more sensitive than south Holland or Aachen, where the sacred soil of the Reich was just coming under attack. Rundstedt admitted it when, even before the fall of Paris, he transferred XLVII Panzer Corps thither straight from Mortain and the pocket, and Hitler demonstrated the competition for scarce reserves between two widely separated danger-spots when he moved 1 Parachute Army to the Albert Canal over much the same route in the opposite direction shortly afterwards. At this moment Patton was a greater menace than Montgomery. It was no doubt as politically impossible to give the Americans a monopoly of petrol and glory as the British, and the logistical problem entailed by a switch of direction from north to south would have been formidable; but simply from the point of view of intelligence about the enemy it was evident throughout September that the southern part of the front might yield more quickly to pressure than the northern and that it would be easier to 'bounce' a Rhine crossing up the Mosel or through the Saarland than at Arnhem.

The first of Ultra's many hints of a forthcoming offensive in the Ardennes came in late September,[46] but all were overlooked. None was explicit, and there was almost no indication of date, but cumulatively they amounted to a long series of reminders that something large and unexplained was going on. The length of the time-scale – just three months elapsed between the decoding of the order for the setting-up of 6 SS Panzer Army and the launching of the offensive – was perhaps the biggest handicap to the elucidation of what should have presented itself as a mystery demanding solution, for it required the evidence to be pieced together after the fashion of a PhD thesis rather than that of a normal military intelligence task. The clearest indications were of place, and it is astonishing (particularly in view of Eisenhower's reported remark that Allied lines were so stretched south of Aachen that 'we may get a nasty little Kasserine if the enemy concentrates in one place')[47] that the arrival of so much armour opposite the weakly held Ardennes front and the constant air reconnaissance of the area behind it was not seen to contradict the prevailing theory that the Germans would counter-attack further north and then only when the Allies struck out for the Rhine.

The mythology of the Ardennes, like that of Arnhem, took shape long before Ultra could be mentioned openly. Nor is it easy today to superimpose Ultra upon analyses of the intelligence digests of the period before 16 December like Pogue's,[48] which could not mention it. In this mythology only Strong (whose account does not carry much conviction) at SHAEF and 'Monk' Dickson, the G-2 of 1 US Army, are held to have foreseen the attack. Colonel Dickson came quite near the truth in November but veered away from it later, and his opinion is in any case said to have been discounted partly because of an alleged reputation as an alarmist and partly because he was on bad terms personally with his superiors. But Dickson had been receiving Ultra since the Tunisian campaign of 1942, and in cooperation with Bradley had become skilled in the operational use of it. How much did Ultra shape his opinions and add steel to his expression of them? Alternatively, why did it not do both of these things to greater effect? Were there really no other Ultra officers, apart from these two, who saw anything from any intelligence source to jolt them out of their equanimity? And what was the real reason why the commanders did not listen to such warnings as they received? It can hardly be put down simply to cocksureness, and they were all experienced enough by Christmas 1944 to distinguish the one risk it was too dangerous to run from the many which had to be accepted if all action was not to be paralysed. These are questions which it may already be impossible to answer because few of those who could do so are still alive, and if this is the case then the release of the Ultra signals has made the mystery of the Ardennes more rather than less difficult to understand.

This reflection throws into sharp relief the chief obstacle confronting any retrospective Ultra criticism of the conduct of the war: namely, that the historian's temper is vastly different from that of the man of action, and that the passage of time makes it even harder for him to recreate in imagination the circumstances in which a commander's decisions have to be made and the sense of urgency which propels most of them. A commander always has to take calculated risks, but his calculations can never be exact and it is all too easy for the historian to expose the looseness of his arithmetic afterwards. Out of fairness to those who bore tremendous responsibilities in the past, the historian must never forget this. This said, however, there do appear to be several occasions during the Second World War when Ultra was culpably neglected with unfortunate results. It is almost certain that the release of more signals will show up new cases in the desert in 1941 and 1942. Inexperience in the handling of Ultra and a failure to comprehend fully either its peculiar nature or its potentially decisive value may perhaps explain some of the earlier cases – as, on a favourable construction, it does Pound's behaviour over Convoy PQ17, for instance – but the mistakes made in the last six or nine months of the war are not so easy to pardon.

NOTES

This paper was presented to the Anglo-American Conference on the History of the Second World War held at the Imperial War Museum, London, 28–31 July 1980.

1. W. R. Inge, *Outspoken Essays* (second series 1922), 169; Lucan, *Bellum Civile,* i, 126.
2. Working from the slight statistical evidence available and from our recollections, Mr Peter Calvocoressi *(Top Secret Ultra,* 6 and note) and I arrived independently at the figure of not less than half a million separate items produced between spring 1941 and the end of the war. My own service in Hut 3 covered just the same period.
3. By Group Captain Winterbotham in *The Ultra Secret* (1974), which was published before any Ultra documents had been released and was therefore written from memory.
4. Some examples are given below on p. 124.
5. See P. Beesly, *Very Special Intelligence* (1977), 152–185.
6. R. V. Jones, *Most Secret War* (1978).
6a. But now see Aileen Clayton, *The Enemy is Listening,* which was published after this paper was written.
7. Cf. F. H. Hinsley, E. E. Thomas, etc., *British Intelligence in the Second World War,* i, 393–394, 420.
8. When the signals become available, I hope to publish a study of Ultra in the Mediterranean .
9. P. E. Schramm, *Kriegstagebuch des OKW*, iv, 122.
10. M. Blumenson, *Salerno to Cassino,* 319.
11. Schramm, op. cit., iv, 124–125.
12. Public Record Office, DEFE 3/129 etc., VLs, 3531, 3624, 3771, 3805, 3855, 3925, 4423, 4427, 4255.
13. VLs 3857, 3863.
14. VLs 3540, 4161, 4441.
15. VLs 4072, 4129, 4158, 4213, 4240, 4379, 4400, 4430, 4434.
16. Blumenson, op. cit., 318–319.
17. 18/1 VL 4302 1904/19. (This formula means that a German message which originated on 18 January was transmitted at 1904 hours on 19 January as VL 4302. The same formula, sometimes with a more precise time of origin, is also used in later footnotes.) On 29 PG, see also VL 4308.
18. 2300/ 19 V L 4331 0304/ 20.
19. 20/ 1 VL 4464 0159/22, VL 4476, 1300/21 VL 4506 1802/22.

20. Blumenson, op. cit., 355, 426.
21. Ibid., 365 (23 January).
22. KVs 3451, 3886, 4328, 4370, 4652, all dated between 3 and 18 May.
23. KV 3378.
24. KV 6745.
25. KVs 3291, 3391, 3514, 3715, 3854, etc. At the same time, the Allied air forces in Italy were flying an average of 435 sorties every 24 hours (excluding anti-shipping operations and attacks on ports). (C. J. C. Molony, *The Mediterranean and Middle East*, v. 689.)
26. KVs 7965, 4328.
27. KV 3623.
28. KV 3482.
29. KVs 5761, 5796.
30. KVs 3652, 3791, 3884, 4424.
31. *The Ultra Secret*, 113–118. Similar misapprehensions can easily multiply. Mr. Nicolson interviewed General Mark Clark in 1970 (Nigel Nicolson, *Alex*, 233). Clark told him, 'We had broken the German code and read the messages from Hitler to "drive us into the sea and drown us".' What code? Clark did not say. When Mr. Lewin quoted this passage *(Ultra goes to War*, 285), he took the code to be Ultra. So did I – until recently I sought in vain for a remotely similar signal in Ultra. However, there was a Hitler order timed 0045 on 26 January to mount a counter-attack and 'break the bridgehead into bits and throw the enemy into the sea' (Schramm, op. cit., iv, 132). This order may have been transmitted in another code broken by the Allies; alternatively, Clark may have seen it as a captured document after the war and have come by 1970 to believe that he had seen it as a decode in 1944.
32. See, for instance, KVs 3652, 3693, 3720, 3791, 3886, 3951, 3960, 4365, etc.
33. June KV 7169 2039/9.
34. E.g. on pp.20, 42, 541.
35. Full references for this and the next two paragraphs will be found in my *Ultra in the West*, Chaps. 2, 3 and 4.
36. 2300/7 XL 1196 0654/8, 0215/10 XL 1492 1403/10. Compare Blumenson, *Breakout and Pursuit*, 137–138.
37. The Ultra battle-narrative is in *Ultra in the West*, 112–122. For Bradley's decision, see Omar Bradley, *A Soldier's Story*, 372–376. Bradley represents the decision as his own, but, of course, as Land Force Commander, Montgomery was still technically; his superior, although he and Bradley had both commanded Army Groups since 1 August.
38. Pp. 52–53.
39. P.m./3 September XLs 9219, 9248 1835/5; *Ultra in the West*, 141–143.
40. It has been suggested that either Amsterdam and Rotterdam or Hamburg were 21 Army Group's real objectives, and that this explains the neglect of Antwerp. Neither suggestion is at all convincing; both depend, for instance, upon a successful outcome to Market Garden (which was then still in the first stages of planning), for all three cities are east of the Rhine.
41. See, for instance, L. F. Ellis, *Victory in the West*, ii, 21–27; J. Ehrman, *Grand Strategy*, v, 524–529.
42. The Ultra evidence about Arnhem is set out in *Ultra in the West*, 143–151.

43. K. W. D. Strong, *Intelligence at the Top,* 149; C. Ryan, A *Bridge too Far,* 139–141.
44. Ryan, op. cit., 142.
45. 0940/17 August, XLs 6753, 6919 1408/17.
46. 18 September HP 1378 1626/27; *Ultra in the West,* 180–190. The parallels with 1940 can be pursued in extraordinary detail. Not only was Corap's 9 Army as ill-advisedly weak as Hodges' 1 US Army in 1944, but long before *Sicheischnitt,* the GAF had regularly reconnoitred the same Meuse crossings in the Ardennes as they did later before *Wacht am Rhein,* and the French Deuxième Bureau knew in March 1940 of German troop concentrations in the same part of the Rhineland as SHAEF knew from Ultra in November 1944 (Alistair Horne, *To Lose a Battle,* 198, 233). But since it is unlikely that anyone in authority at SHAEF in 1944 had also been at GHQ four years earlier (or would have noticed the parallels if he had!), these can only be items in a historian's collection of curiosities.
47. Forrest C. Pogue, *The Supreme Command,* 295; Strong, 153–154.
48. Pogue, op. cit., 361–372.

2

Army Ultra in the Mediterranean Theatre: Darkness and Light

The simple metaphor of my title represents a feature of Ultra intelligence which deserves more attention than it has yet received. We still tend to speak of Ultra as if it were an abstract, uniform concept of unvarying consistency, instead of a bundle of awkward practical realities which varied both in quality and quantity of content and also over time. To think of it as a smooth unchanging abstraction is dangerous, for it can mislead interpretation and distort a historical judgement of Ultra's strategic worth. Those of us who helped to make Ultra what it became grew familiar through experience with the sometimes capricious and unpredictable variations in the material from which Ultra was compiled, and I doubt whether anyone who did not serve in Hut 3 at Bletchley Park could gain an equal familiarity now simply by studying the documents in the Public Record Office. Therein lies a certain risk that Ultra may in future be seen as a constant ingredient in intelligence rather than as the living and evolving creature which it really was.

Perhaps it would help if we were in the habit of speaking of Ultras not Ultra. The Ultra of the week in June 1944 which saw the capture of Rome and the D-Day landings was very different from the Ultra of the corresponding week in 1941, for instance, and any attempt to assess its influence on the war must take account of the difference. The change over the intervening three years in the quality and quantity of its content is fundamental to such an assessment; so too is the complete contrast between the ways in which Ultra intelligence was received, appreciated and utilised by operational commands at each of these two periods. In no field were these changes more marked than in that of army Ultra.

Attempting to explain the number and variety of Ultras to an unsophisticated audience, I have sometimes likened Wehrmacht Enigma keys

34

to three sisters each with a brood of children. The naval sister was the least fertile; her first-born was long in gestation (no naval key was broken until August 1941) and never had many siblings, but one of them was the source of Ultra's single greatest contribution to victory: Ultra-based knowledge of U-boat movements combined with new means of locating and destroying them to win the battle of the Atlantic in May 1943. Luftwaffe Enigma was the first to lose its virginity (if I may labour my metaphor) and later became the most prolific bearer of children. The GAF general key yielded to the cryptographers early in 1940 and was decrypted almost every day for the rest of the war; in addition, progressively smaller and smaller air commands were given their own key, all of which were broken in due course, though not all of them all the time.

By contrast, Army Ultra was late to appear and smaller in volume. Its lateness (the first breaks were not until September 1941, and thereafter Army keys were only read intermittently until April 1942, and even then somewhat discontinuously and often several days late) and its irregularity (the officers who used Army Enigma and the operators who enciphered their messages observed such strict security that their transmissions were hard to break) frequently posed problems of interpretation. The security-consciousness of the *Heeresnachrichtenwesen* was expressed in the warning its head, Fellgiebel, gave to his staff in 1939: *Funken ist Landesverrat (To use the radio is to commit treason)*, and strikingly demonstrated by the fact that scarcely one even of the covernames for large military operations was mentioned in radio messages in army keys. These two features – drawbacks from our point of view – could not however prevent the weight of intelligence conveyed by Army Enigma and the authoritative provenance of so much of it from outstripping Luftwaffe Enigma in intelligence value once Army Ultra was available in quantity. This was partly, of course, because the Luftwaffe was in decline from mid-1942, though Tedder's and Coningham's tactics had wrested air superiority over the desert from *Fliegerfuehrer Afrika* much earlier – Siegfried Westphal, Rommel's operations officer, complained that even in 1941 the via Balbia was only safe at the RAF's mealtimes. But in any case a *Panzerlage* (a return of the number of tanks serviceable each day, the number under repair and the estimated length of their stay in the workshops, each head broken down under the several types of tank)[1] was worth more than *Fliegerfuehrer's* (or *Fliegerkorps II's* or *X's*) equivalent daily strength returns, which were more common, because it was *Panzerarmee Afrika* which captured Tobruk and had to be prevented from breaking through at Alamein, not any part of the German air force. For the same reason, but with a far higher intelligence rating, *Panzerarmee's Tagesabschlussmeldungen* were usually of greater value than *Luftflotte 2's* parallel evening reports of operations carried out and intentions for the following day.

Forty years ago, there was no difficulty in identifying Army Ultra – the difficulty was to decrypt it. Today things are different. There is now no absolutely certain way of knowing whether a particular signal in the Public Record Office was derived from Army Ultra or not. There are two reasons: in the first place, whereas the whole of the Naval Section's output came from Naval Ultra, Hut 3 dealt in army and air material indifferently. Unless, therefore, a given signal bears unmistakable marks of its origin upon its face ('Strength return *Fliegerfuehrer* tenth June', for instance, or 'Day report *Panzerarmee . . . '),* conclusive evidence to distinguish between army and air material is now lacking in a great many cases, and evidence to distinguish between keys in almost all. Common-sense suffices in a number (plainly, a tank return will not have been transmitted in a Luftwaffe key), and the lists in the appendices to *British Intelligence* in others; but while the lists prevent gross error by giving the dates of the first breaks of each key, they are not precise enough to elucidate individual instances. Secondly, the office copies of the teleprints underlying each signal carried a note of the key involved in each case, but we are not allowed to see the teleprints. This is another example of the extraordinary and seemingly indefensible security measures from which historians of the Second World War suffer: since we are allowed to talk openly about intercepts and decrypts today, why may we not trace each message to its source? Until we can do so, a historical analysis such as I am attempting here cannot be carried to a proper conclusion, and I am bound to admit this limitation upon what follows. (It is of course a matter for even greater regret that the publication of an official account of how the decrypting was done is still forbidden; this condemned the late Gordon Welchman to write *The Hut Six Story* from an inevitably faulty memory and without access to documents, with the natural but infinitely regrettable result that his book contains nearly as many errors as Winterbotham's does on the intelligence side, and probably more omissions.)

To sum up: there is now no absolutely certain way of identifying particular signals as derived from Army Enigma. Past acquaintance with them may, I hope, serve to reduce my mistakes to a minimum. Having read all the signals when they were first issued and shared in the composition of many of them, and having now, 40 years later, read all 100,000 of them again, I feel fairly sure of my ground. It seemed only right to admit, however, that I cannot be quite as confident as Professor Rohwer and Mr Beesly of the provenance of my material.

Some dates are now necessary. The general-purpose Luftwaffe key, and another air key for use in the Mediterranean, were both being read currently at the beginning of 1941. Rommel landed in Tripoli on 12 February, advanced into Cyrenaica early in April and reached the Egyptian frontier by the end of the month. Direct signalling from Hut 3 to Cairo (later to other headquarters as well) began on 13 March. No army decrypts were read until 17 September, and only irregularly to start with: for a few weeks until mid-October, again for most of November, but then no more until April 1942. Thus Rommel's spectacular drive across Cyrenaica, which outwitted his opponents and nullified all the gains of O'Connor's winter rout of the Italians, BREVITY and BATTLEAXE (the first two abortive British counter-attacks) and the latter part of CRUSADER, the British autumn offensive – all these passed without benefit of Army Ultra. Luftwaffe decrypts told what Froehlich's and Geissler's aircraft were up to, but Rommel's tanks were the danger, and there was no news of them at all. Army officers like myself, forced to sit idly by while our RAF colleagues composed signal after signal without any apparent influence on the fighting, were keenly aware of the prevailing imbalance in Ultra, but it seems to have passed unremarked elsewhere. Most importantly, it did not deter Churchill from goading first Wavell and later Auchinleck to the attack, although neither knew much of the enemy's situation and both professed themselves far from ready to take the initiative.

Churchill was Ultra's first and greatest friend, and nothing can detract from his wartime leadership, but in these months he was so anxious for a victory to set off against Dunkirk, Crete and Singapore that he overplayed his hand and inadvertently associated Ultra too closely with setbacks in the desert. He took one or two signals[2] – they showed that Rommel had been ordered to rest on his laurels or even draw back a little – at face value and ordered the generals to press on regardless. Disasters followed. There are several explanations; one in particular is relevant here. Neither Churchill nor anyone else seems to have realised that the virtues of the new intelligence tool, Ultra, were matched by corresponding vices: it was as yet unbalanced, for the reasons just given, and an understanding of it called for more than just a translation of the German words. Of course no one possessed all the requisite skills in

1941, but no one stopped even to wonder whether Ultra could really solve all problems so easily, whether there was not a catch somewhere. There was. Without Army Ultra, nothing could show whether or not Rommel had the resources to attack supposing, however improbably, that he chose to defy German military tradition and disobey the orders of Halder and OKH; but there seems to have been no attempt to estimate whether he had the petrol and tanks to push on if he were disposed to take the risk. It was not grasped that the encouraging (from the British point of view) evidence lacked a sufficient background against which it could be set in perspective and properly assessed. Still worse: throughout this period – it included the time of Force K's ascendancy in the central Mediterranean – air Ultra was providing evidence of German shortages and betraying the movements of convoys so frequently that the RAF and the navy were taking a heavy toll of Axis supplies. A lot was known about ships, but little about what they carried and nothing at all about that part of their cargoes consigned to the Afrika Korps. Ultra told nothing about the number of tanks reaching Libya or about the performance (it was excellent) of the tank repair workshops. Yet it was the tanks (and the 88s [88mm anti-tank guns] upon which I will not dwell, although there is much to say about them too) which mattered. They mattered supremely on one occasion. As Rommel slowly retreated in December, it was lightly concluded in Cairo that he had few tanks left. No one looked carefully at the hint – it was no more, but it was a plain hint – in Ultra that there might possibly have been tanks on the last ship to dock at Benghazi before the Germans evacuated the port. There were, and it was with them that Rommel counter-attacked on 21 January 1942, regaining in a few days what CRUSADER had stutteringly conquered in six weeks and at great cost. (The *Ankara,* the ship that carried the tanks, became a *bête-noire* to the British; she made countless transits of the Mediterranean and it took over a year to sink her.)

The episode has another disquieting aspect. The whole British intelligence system was in a very poor way in 1939, as Dr Andrew has just shown in unprecedented but regrettably still incomplete (because of more inexplicable security black-outs) detail.[3] British army intelligence scarcely existed. It was given no prominence at Sandhurst or Camberley. The Intelligence Corps had been abolished after the First World War. Field Marshal Gerald Templer later had the well-deserved reputation of knowing a lot about military intelligence, but there is singularly little evidence in John Cloake's new biography to prove it for the pre-1939 period.[4] To stay long in intelligence imperilled an officer's chances of promotion and thus his whole career. Ill-founded optimism prevailed in Cairo at the time of CRUSADER, and in retrospect the mistake over the *Ankara* is unsurprising though still grievous. It follows that even if more Ultra had been available it is unlikely that it would have been used to much advantage. This is only speculation, but it may serve as a reminder that an army (or navy, or air force) is only as good as its commanders' intelligence (in both senses of the word) and armament when the two are put to combined use; a failure of either leads to ruin. By how little did 8th Army escape that ruin in 1941–42!

Shafts of light began to pierce the gloom during the spring of 1942 – for instance, the first *Panzerlagen* were decrypted and soon became frequent enough to banish for good miscalculations like that of January – and they were not much dimmed even by the loss of Tobruk in June and the headlong retreat to Alamein, where a front was at last stabilised in late July. Changes of organisation and personnel at both ends of the Ultra delivery line made for improved drafting of signals and a fuller appreciation of them at the same time as new cryptographic successes were providing a greater depth and variety of intelligence and this was gradually being brought into a closer relationship with the direction of operations. It is important to stress the range of this development both at Bletchley and in the Cairo and desert headquarters during these months. Though beaten and temporarily discouraged, 8th Army was not demoralised but ready for another fight when Montgomery took over in mid-August, and this applied particularly to the intelligence staff. With Rommel poised for the final push which would take him into the Delta and begin the dissolution of British authority in the Middle East, there was a crying need to know what he planned to do and still more how he planned to do it. Ultra was able to provide the answers in good time, and the intelligence officers whom Montgomery inherited were able to convince him of its value in a way their predecessors had never managed to convince him. Montgomery used Ultra with resounding success at once and thereby founded in the public mind (and, less fortunately perhaps, in his own as well) the legend that he alone had the secret of victory. Army Ultra came into its own in August 1942, and retained for the rest of the war the intimate connection with operations which it had lacked before and which it now thoroughly deserved.

Alamein at the end of October has been regarded as a turning point ever since Churchill's victory speech; from the intelligence angle, Alam Halfa, where Rommel shot his last bolt at the end of August, deserves the title even more. There are two extreme views of this battle, one represented by Mr Correlli Barnett's myopic determination to denigrate everything Montgomery did, even to the extent of mistakenly quoting Ultra as evidence for the prosecution, and the other by Mr Hamilton's account, which was written before criticism began occasionally to oust hero-worship from his narrative. Did or did not Montgomery take over an existing plan for the defence of the Alam Halfa ridge and steal the credit when he thwarted Rommel's attack and forced him to turn tail for the first time? The argument has nothing to do with Ultra, but an appreciation addressed by Rommel to OKH and OKW, which was decrypted from an army key on 17 August,[5] sheds more light on one part of it than has yet been fully realised. Montgomery had taken certain actions on 13 August, the day he assumed command of 8th Army; he had not seen the existing plan when he did so, and his actions departed widely from the plan. Four days later – the time interval is important[6] – Ultra showed that these actions were absolutely correct, for they had provided a strong defence at the point where Rommel intended to attack. Armed with the confidence that his judgement was a hundred per cent right, Montgomery could relax and enjoy the crucial defensive battle, certain that the brave and inspiring words with which he had addressed 8th Army officers when he took over were about to be justified by events.

Ultra's chief contribution to victory at Alamein was to throttle Rommel's petrol supply line by what Italian historians have called 'the hecatomb of the tankers', but this was the work of Italian naval and German air force decrypts. Army material was for the moment necessarily tactical, like the whole battle (because there was no room for manoeuvre behind a short front with ends sharply defined by the sea and Qattara Depression; by contrast, Alam Halfa had strategic overtones) and tactics was Army Ultra's weakest point since it could seldom deliver its results in time to keep up with a fluid battle – here it differed markedly from naval Ultra at its best – and the Y Service was often quicker: Ultra reported the move north of 21 Panzer Division which created the opportunity for Montgomery's decisive thrust on 3 November,[7] but the Y Service had done so already.

After the brilliant intelligence successes of the past three months, it is sad that much good Ultra was wasted between Alamein and Tripoli, between November 1942 and January 1943. Ultra told how few weapons the Afrika Korps had carried away from the battlefield (eleven tanks and 29 anti-tank guns), and week by week throughout Rommel's retreat it showed how little petrol there was for his tanks and transport vehicles: only enough for 150 kilometres on the morrow of Alamein, so little that the Afrika Korps was delayed twenty-four hours in moving out of Benghazi, supply lorries stranded with empty tanks for days on end between Buerat and Tripoli.[8] Rommel called the situation 'catastrophic', partly because he knew that a torch had been lit behind him which might burn down the Tunisian refuge towards which he was straining with painful slowness before he could reach it. When on top of all this Ultra revealed that Rommel had told Hitler and Mussolini that they must 'face the probable annihilation of what was left of Panzer Army',[9] surely Montgomery should have cast aside his groundless fear that Rommel could still strike back and his apprehensions over the mutual distrust of infantry and armour, made light of the undoubted difficulties of a lengthening supply line, and risked a bold stroke to cut Panzer Army off and destroy it before it could reach Tunisia? Intelligence alone does not win battles, but here was as good a chance as any to find the exception to the rule.

Even the intelligence-directed battle of Medenine could not atone for this neglect. After the shock Rommel administered to the Americans, from Eisenhower down to the unfledged Combat Commands, at Kasserine in February, it was obvious that his next move would probably be to use his interior lines to throw the whole weight of his armour against the British 8th Army. He joined 10th Panzer Division from Tunisia with the old desert hands of 15th and 21st Panzer; 31,000 men and 135 tanks advanced eastwards, and Army Ultra followed their every move closely. Rommel's Chief Quartermaster let out the date on which they planned to attack – 6 March or sooner – and by the third the whole force was under orders to move along two thrust-lines which pointed directly at Medenine.[10] Amply forewarned, Montgomery dug 600 anti-tank guns into the ground and awaited developments with more than his usual equanimity. The German armour recoiled, and soon the ground was littered with burning tanks. 'The Marshal had made a balls of it. I shall write letters', said Montgomery when he saw them.[11] In fact, Rommel had not been there at all. His desert veterans were humiliated under the command of a mere Italian, General Messe. Rommel, a sick as well as a disappointed man, left Africa for good almost at once.

Army Ultra played a great part in the immediately succeeding battles of Mareth and the Wadi Akarit. It showed that Messe foresaw the shape of the coming British attack but got its timing wrong,[12] and that he was ready to retreat because he believed himself to be weaker than the

Anglo-American forces converging on his escape route from two directions. It revealed the strength of the Mareth defences (in spite of which a costly frontal assault was made on them to distract attention from the New Zealanders' 'left hook' through the hills), was particularly up-to-date with exceptionally frequent tank strength returns, and betrayed von Arnim's cry to Kesselring on the morrow of defeat that the situation was desperate, so short was he of petrol and ammunition.[13] By mid-April the Axis bridgehead was no more than the outer defences of Tunis and Bizerta; in a relatively built-up area the Wehrmacht could use land-lines in preference to radio, and Ultra of all types diminished considerably in the last weeks before the surrender on Cape Bon on 13 May.

Inter-allied differences about closing down the Mediterranean theatre after the conquest of Tunisia were temporarily stilled at Casablanca in January 1943 by the decision to invade Sicily but not necessarily to go any further. The target was too obvious for comfort, and an attempt to throw dust in Axis eyes was made at the end of April by Operation MINCEMEAT ('The Man Who Never Was'), which suggested that the obvious was being used as a cover for genuine landings in Sardinia and the Balkans.

Deception plans, particularly plans as ingenious as MINCEMEAT, are fascinating and intellectually persuasive: but how to discover whether they are succeeding in their purpose of deluding the intended victim? The most skilful agent could hardly penetrate the highest councils of the enemy and send his report of their discussions out in time and without being detected. Here Ultra now performed a service which could scarcely have been thought of by those who broke Enigma in 1940. It performed a similar service to even greater effect a year later, when it proved that the elaborately structured illusion that the 'real' OVERLORD would hit the Pas de Calais in July was believed not only on D-Day, as intended, but for another month or more as well, with incalculable benefit to the invaders. On this occasion the critical intercept was the formal warning sent on 12 May by OKW to OB South and OB South-East.[14] It began: 'According to a source which may be regarded as absolutely reliable, large-scale landings in the eastern and western Mediterranean are projected in the near future ... the cover-name is HUSKY', and it went on to specify points on the coasts of Greece and the Aegean islands which were particularly vulnerable and therefore in need of special protection. The two theatre commanders and their subordinates began at once to demand extra aircraft and troops to meet the supposed threat. The RAF's raids on Sardinian ports and airfields were interpreted as part of a softening-up process preceding the landing, the garrisons of Sardinia and Corsica were strengthened (notably by an SS Brigade) rather than that of Sicily, but the most convincing sign that MINCEMEAT was being swallowed was the immediate transfer of 1 Panzer Division (then probably the best armoured formation in the German army) from Brittany to Greece, where it arrived on 14 June, still almost a month before HUSKY struck Sicily. At least a hundred tanks, which could have thrown the landing parties off the Sicilian beaches, were thus shown by Ultra to have gone off elsewhere on a wild goose chase. This calmed the fears of Eisenhower, who had asked permission to call the assault off if he had reason to think that the garrison of Sicily had been strongly reinforced, and significantly contributed to the success of HUSKY, which was none too well planned (because the responsible commanders were still engaged in Tunisia at the planning stage and so scattered all over the Mediterranean that it had been difficult to bring them together to discuss ways and means) and none too well executed (because there had been too little time to train the troops in the novel techniques required for a combined operation on this scale).

The longer term importance of this intelligence was to confirm the view which the British Chiefs of Staff were to urge with increasing conviction throughout the next 12 months of debate – that pressure in the Mediterranean could and would relieve the Russians by attracting divisions away from the German eastern front and at the same time weaken the prospective opposition to OVERLORD, then still a year away. At no time was this more comprehensively manifested than in the third quarter of 1943 in a series of Army Ultra intercepts of outstanding value. There had already been vague hints that the Germans were taking advance precautions against the possibility that the Italians might desert the Axis, and the name of Rommel had been associated with them. Just after the middle of August – that is, soon after the fall of Mussolini on 25 July – the scope of these precautions was suddenly revealed. Army Group B, it appeared, commanded by Rommel, was controlling three corps and nine divisions (two of them armoured, one being the *Leibstandarte Adolf Hitler,* a recent expansion of the Fuehrer's bodyguard) and 200 tanks, half of them the new Tigers and Panthers with formidably thick armour and tremendous hitting power; its purpose was to keep open the Brenner supply route and secure control of northern Italy.[15] The likely maximum scale of the German reaction to an Italian surrender – which in the event was announced to coincide with the Salerno landing (AVALANCHE) on 9 September – was thus known well beforehand. It was followed by a series of reports by II SS Corps (one of the three corps in Army Group B) detailing over the next week or two the strong-arm methods by which Lombardy was being 'pacified'. The strategic significance of all this is beyond doubt: all that was missing was an Allied force strong enough to overrun the sketchy defence which was all the Germans had yet been able to prepare south of the Lombard Plain, and an inkling of Hitler's future intentions (he did not know them himself yet): would he fight for the whole peninsula or retire to the safety of the mountains in the north?

In view of Hitler's lengthening record of 'stand fast' orders, it was to be expected that he would follow the same policy now, although plain strategic sense, backed by Rommel's reputation and persistent advocacy, suggested that it would be preferable to conserve resources by abandoning the Italian mainland in favour of a more easily and more economically defensible line either across the northern Apennines from Genoa to Rimini or along the Alpine foothills. Had Hitler accepted Rommel's advice (and the second alternative would have served also as the southern wall of the Alpine Redoubt of which later rumour spoke), he would of course have disappointed the Allied Chiefs of Staff, who counted on Italy to hold as many divisions as possible away from Normandy and Russia, but he would have avoided the compulsion to permit Army Group B's infantry (though not its panzers) to be drawn bit by bit into the cauldron of Cassino – to be followed by others from both the other theatres under the stress of later emergency – with nothing to show for his pains but a slight slowing down of the Allied advance towards the Lombard plain. The first sign that Hitler would once more settle for 'No retreat' came in early October with an order to Kesselring to that effect.[16] It was quickly followed by a series of moves south by Army Group B's divisions[17] and in the course of time by others from every corner of the overblown Reich. On the German side, therefore, the strategic decision that there was to be an Italian campaign was taken within a month of AVALANCHE, but Hitler dithered for a further month before appointing Kesselring *Oberbefehlshaber (OB) Südwest* and sending Rommel off to improve the Channel defences.

With the front static on the Winter Line, the Anzio landing (SHINGLE) was laid on in late January 1944 in the hope of breaking the deadlock. Army Ultra gave the undertaking a kind of blessing by demonstrating that 5th Army's immediately preceding offensive on the main front had drawn 3, 29 and 90 Panzergrenadier Divisions away from the landing area and down to the Garigliano[18] but a combination of insufficient force, imprecise orders and timid leadership ruled out the advance on Rome which was its ostensible but problematical purpose. A few weeks later, heroic resistance saved the constricted beachhead from Kesselring's set-piece counter-attack (FISCHFANG), and the defensive battle was materially assisted by Ultra-based foreknowledge not only of Kesselring's whole plan (with his boast that he could 'throw the Allies back into the sea') and its timing, but also of its likely strength in tanks and infantry.[19]

With the failure of FISCHFANG, Kesselring set out his alternative – a series of defensive lines to protect Rome.[20] Allied planning, which had already begun, for the DIADEM offensive in May could thus take account of these in good time, and it was further aided by a succession of tank returns which showed that Kesselring disposed of slightly more than 300 tanks and 600 anti-tank guns;[21] an additional bonus was that the returns were set out under divisional headings so that, since the air liaison officers reported (in a Luftwaffe key) the locations of their divisions and corps almost daily, it was usually possible to tell the distribution of heavy weapons over the whole front at a glance.

In a short sketch like this, the piling up of apparently repetitive detail may easily become tedious, but one or two examples of a rather different kind from those already cited may be of interest. Directly after the capture of Rome on 4 June 1944, Alexander's allied Armies in Italy, which had already lost several of their best divisions to OVERLORD, were milked of more in preparation for the ill-considered and militarily unnecessary ANVIL/DRAGOON landing in the south of France, and the Mediterranean was relegated to the status of the second-class theatre. This ought to have meant that well-fortified defence lines would serve the German purpose now even better than at Cassino, while conversely it seemed to present the Allies with a more difficult task than before if (as was the case) Alexander refused to accept second-class status but determined to continue the advance in spite of his diminished resources. How could Ultra help him to escape from a kind of poverty trap?

During his short tenure as GOC-in-C Army Group B, and as part of his advocacy of withdrawal from peninsular Italy, Rommel sent Hitler a map of a proposed 'Apennine position' and issued orders for the construction of defences in the Lower Alps.[22] No word of this reached the Allied commanders through Ultra until the New Year, when the establishment of a new authority, *Armeegruppe von Zangen,* was reported; its duty was 'to develop the Apennine position with the greatest energy'.[23] Precise details of the whereabouts of this 'Apennine position' and an insight into the nature of the defences under construction came in an extremely long report from Kesselring's Chief Engineer in mid-April.[24] It revealed that far more labour and materials were being devoted to the two coastal sectors (the Serchio valley in the west, and the Foglia valley down to Pesaro in the east) than to the mountain stretch between them, and that the Adriatic coastal plain – where 8th Army broke through the following autumn – was the less well protected of the two. Still later, at the end of June, a Hitler directive,[25] the purpose of which was to speed up construction, gave away information of the greatest significance. So little had been done to date, Hitler complained, that it was essential that the 'common misconception' that there already was a fortified Apennine position should be 'scotched once and for all', in spite of the fact that it was intended to be the final defence line to prevent the 'incalculable military and political consequences' of an Allied penetration into the plain of Lombardy. Unhappily, the long and at times bitter disputes about the desirability or otherwise of ANVIL had come to an end shortly before this illuminating piece of intelligence (which among other things finally killed the theory that the Germans might withdraw of their own volition) could be used to show that a powerful blow delivered at once in Italy might reach the Alps and open the Riviera approach to the Rhone valley more quickly and effectively than a landing on the coast of France. Alexander lost several more experienced divisions. But he nevertheless assaulted the Gothic Line in August, delivering his main stroke on the Adriatic, where Ultra had shown it to be weakest. A succession of river obstacles, the slower progress of 5th Army over the fearful obstacle of the mountains in the centre, and the lateness of the season unfortunately prevented the complete breakthrough which Hitler had feared.

Army Ultra paved the way for the final offensive in the spring 1945 and assisted materially in its execution. Eight tank returns, the last of them a conveniently short time before the offensive, showed that the wastage of the autumn and winter fighting was barely being made good, for the total number of Army Group C's tanks remained almost constant from January to March, without significant increase. The strictest economy in the use of ammunition was enjoined by OKW – only essential targets were to be engaged, and even the current ration of six (!) howitzer rounds a day could no longer be justified – and after

Christmas OKH issued a warning that the February allocation would be reduced by 30 per cent. Petrol was just as short. Berlin threatened to cut the monthly quota if the situation on the eastern front deteriorated, and Jodl peremptorily ordered OB Southwest and OB Southeast to limit the scope of their operations 'ruthlessly' in view of the general fuel shortage.[26] The scarcity of petrol was shown up in other ways too. Because Allied air raids repeatedly blocked the Brenner route, it took 715th Division (on its way to help stem the Russian advance into Hungary) a whole month to cover the 150 miles from southern Lombardy to the Austrian side of the pass, but the constant breaks in rail communications also curtailed the inflow of petrol so drastically that Kesselring could not avoid stooping to complain to OKW that he had not received proper compensation for petrol used in moving this single division to railhead,[27] and in April his successor had to remind Berlin that his petrol supply would last scarcely a fortnight at current rates of consumption but for a far shorter time if he had to make tactical moves in such a hurry that 'improvised means (ox-drawn vehicles)' were ruled out.[28]

By careful attention to the time and place of real and simulated operations the Allied command exploited this tactical handicap to the full, taking advantage of the Germans' known nervousness on both flanks to lead their armoured and mechanised formations a sorry dance from side to side of the front to meet illusory threats, thus compelling them to burn up precious petrol which could have been put to better use and to wear out tank tracks, which were hard to replace. A small attack in the mountains, principally designed to improve 5th Army's start-line for its attack on Bologna, for instance, drew 29th *Panzergrenadier* (PG) away from Liguria (where it had gone to forestall a rumoured coastal landing which the Allies were not intending to make). Soon the division was lured right across to the east coast by the trick of playing on enemy fears (which Ultra had repeatedly disclosed in recent months) of a landing at the head of the Adriatic to join up with Tito's forces in Bosnia and Croatia. It was possible, through Ultra, to track 29th PG from its new position behind Bologna by stages through Mantua and Padua to the area north of Venice and on into Istria, whence it hurried back (minus several tanks) too late to stop British commandos round Lake Commachio from opening 8th Army's route to break through the Argenta gap and burst into the enemy's rear. Much the same story, but with less local colour, could be told of 90th PG and 26 Panzer Division. The bulk of the German armour and motor transport had long been confined to these three and only one or two other formations, which were thus first lured out of the way and then side-stepped when feigned operations gave way to real.

One of the longest messages ever intercepted (it ran to almost a thousand words in translation) gives a fine impression of what Army Ultra could do in the last year of the war, and at the same time it offers an unsurpassable tribute to the strategy of Alexander and Mark Clark, for it is an admission of defeat from the mouth of their principal opponent. On 14 April von Vietinghoff (who had become OB Southwest when Kesselring took over as OB West at the beginning of March) gloomily surveyed the first five days of 8th Army's offensive.[29] The fury of the Allied attack, especially from the air, he wrote, confirmed the Allies' intention to destroy the German armies in Italy before the end of hostilities in the rest of Europe. Severe damage to signals communications was making control of operations impossible, and every attempt at movement was smashed as it started. Four divisions had been almost completely wiped out, and every new line of defence was penetrated as soon as it was manned. Parts of the front would have to be given up voluntarily in order to free even the smallest reserves to meet the expected American attack west of Bologna. Unless the British could be halted north-west of Lake Commachio, they would break through to the Po. If OKW wished to keep the Allies away from the 'Reich fortress' for as long as possible, the Army Group would have to begin retiring towards the Ticino soon, for it would take a fortnight to execute so elaborate a movement.

Depleted though their strength had been through a political decision, their enemy recognised, three weeks before he surrendered, that the Allied armies in Italy had won a total victory.

In time of war it is essential to distinguish intelligence that is useful from that which is merely interesting and to classify it by source in so far as that helps to grade it by degree of reliability; but it is open to question whether, when peace has returned, it is profitable to separate the different elements and to scrutinise them a second time in isolation from each other, thus divorcing in the study items which in the field were treated as parts of a single though variegated whole. Again, military intelligence is by its nature ephemeral, a means to an end not an end in itself. The historian of intelligence dare not fall into the academicism of his colleagues in constitutional or economic history. By studying in minute detail the structure of government, society and wealth in fourteenth- and fifteenth-century England and France, for instance, the medieval historian may even now discover new clues to explain why Edward III and Henry V, ruling over a thinly-populated offshore island, were able to win Crécy, Poitiers and Agincourt and dominate a larger and wealthier country for so long. The significance of the battles themselves, however – and that of Alamein – remains quite unaffected by the most profound study of the intelligence which led up to them. We ought always to bear this in mind, lest we claim too much for our subject.

Is a study of Army Ultra on its own of little value, then, even though it was an important part of a larger whole which for more than half the 1939–45 war provided almost all the Allies knew about the enemy and furnished information on a scale unapproached by any previous intelligence source? Manifestly, a study so artificially restricted cannot avoid distorting truth. There was no place in it for an examination of the damage done by aircraft and warships to trans-Mediterranean supply traffic in 1941 and 1942, for example, and for the tremendous strategic influence a shortage of petrol and ammunition exercised on the defeat of Rommel, for all the intelligence which made it possible came from air and naval keys. Yet its chief consequence was to limit the mobility and firepower of the Afrika Korps.

On the other hand, two advantages can certainly be claimed for such a study, though their value will diminish or disappear entirely when, in the course of time, the place of Ultra in the history of the Second World War becomes clearer and more precisely definable than it is today. The first drives home the point that Ultra was not a constant but that its content was subject to apparently random fluctuation from month to month, even from day to day. The case of the Gothic Line illustrates this. The information quoted above came from two very long messages, one in April and one in May. Neither was much more than a list of figures under a number of headings, therefore slow and tedious to encipher on a machine on which every figure had to be spelled out as a word. What accident caused them to be transmitted by radio in Enigma? Did chance bombs cut teleprinter lines, or was there a simple electrical failure? Why did the accidental interruption of more natural methods of communicating complex data about the construction of wire and concrete defences happen twice at an interval of five or six weeks, and never again? – for it is unthinkable that no more progress-reports were rendered between the end of May and the assault on the Gothic Line in August and September. These questions have no answer, but they are still worth asking if they induce a more realistic appraisal of the source and a better appreciation of the fortuitous way in which it imparted information even of the highest strategic significance.

Secondly, if a deliberate but momentary concentration on one aspect of intelligence throws its unpredictable variability into sharper relief, then it will usefully discourage hasty judgements on the contribution of Ultra to victory. We are indeed nearer a final verdict today than could have been foreseen ten years ago, but we have not yet got beyond the stage of establishing the facts and thereby agreeing on the foundations upon which a final verdict may one day be based.

NOTES

A more complete set of references will be given in my forthcoming book *Ultra and Mediterranean Strategy*.

1. At some periods – the Tunisian campaign was one of them – the Y Service decrypted similar returns in lower-grade ciphers, but there seems to be no record of how regularly this was done.
2. OL 211. Ultra signals quoted in this paper were prefixed OL, MKA, QT, VM, ML, JP VL, KV, BT, KO. All are in the Public Record Office.
3. C. Andrew: *Secret Service: The Making of the British Intelligence Community* (London, 1985).
4. John Cloake: *Templer, Tiger of Malaya* (London, 1985), esp. pp. 64–7.
5. MKAs 2094, 2095.
6. Sir Edgar Williams, Montgomery's chief Intelligence Officer, has twice recently (Nigel Hamilton: *Monty, The Making of a General 1887–1942* (London, 1981), pp. 652–3; T. E. B. Howarth (ed.), *Monty at Close Quarters* (London, 1985), pp. 21, 22 stated that it was on 15 or 16 August – i.e. before he could have seen Rommel's appreciation – that he gave Montgomery the decisive account of Ultra intelligence. He does not expressly refer to the 17 August signal, yet seems plainly to imply it.
7. QT 4958.
8. QTs 5794, 5977, 5877, 5893, 5959, 6374, 9177, 9681.
9. QT 6859.
10. VMs 5605, 5620.
11. N. Hamilton: *Monty, Master of the Battlefield 1942–44* (London, 1983), p. 169.
12. VM 6984.
13. VMs 7823, 7841.
14. ML 1955.
15. JPs 1487, 1512, 2911, 2952, 3080.
16. JP 6045.
17. JPs 6545, 6578, etc.
18. VLs 4302, 4331, 4546.
19. VLs 4559, 5359, 5449, 5594.
20. VL 8072.
21. VL 3190.

22. Oberkommando der Wehrmacht, *Kriegstagebuch 1940–1945* ed. P. E. Schramm (Frankfurt, 1961–65), iii, p. 1141, iv, p. 591.
23. VLs 5359, 5381. The Apennine position became the 'Gothic Line' in April and was rechristened 'Green Line' in June. Fuller details about Ultra knowledge of the fortifications may be found in a paper I presented to an international congress in Pesaro in 1984, the proceedings of which have been published under the title *Linea Gotica 1944* (Milan 1986). See pp. 125–42.
24. KV 1578.
25. KV 9843.
26. BTs 2635, 2879, 3367, 4854, 5510.
27. BT 6125.
28. KOs 555, 586, 588.
29. KOs 496, 529.

3

World War II Intelligence: The Last Ten Years' Work Reviewed

Intelligence is gathered in order to be used. Intelligence which is not used is of little significance – this is where the study of intelligence differs from other historical studies – and scarcely deserves to be called intelligence at all. Intelligence is not an end in itself, nor is the means by which it is gathered: both serve a greater end, the securing of political advantage in peacetime or victory over an enemy in war.

These pedestrian platitudes, baldly expressing what might be supposed self-evident truths, have unhappily often been lost from sight in writings about intelligence and the Second World War. Two recent trends have been responsible. In the first place, so much attention has been focussed on the intelligence-gathering institutions – which are singularly uninteresting in themselves, and about which it is government policy in Britain, at least, still to deny access to a great deal of information without which no complete and absolutely reliable account can be written – that distortion has occurred and the producer has stolen the limelight from the product. Particularly since the unmasking of Blunt and the publication of Andrew Boyle's *Climate of Treason*[1] (the two coincided in time), the peculiar British fascination with spies and moles has increased the public appetite for scandal. Nigel West's *MI5* and *MI6*,[2] for instance, supplied easily marketable produce without much indication of provenance or guarantee of quality. More recently, Christopher Andrew's agreeably anecdotal narrative[3] has covered the same ground and much more besides. Repeatedly pointing to the generally accepted conclusion that defective analysis, not inadequate collection, was the cause of most intelligence failures, his amusing demonstration of the ramshackle methods, casual recruitment and general ineffectiveness of the SIS (Secret Intelligence Service) up to the outbreak of war and before the emergence of Ultra, throws new light on the undervaluation of intelligence as a whole, a facet of Britain's vulnerability in 1939 which has not always been taken sufficiently into account. The book nevertheless concentrates attention on the workman rather than on his wares. The upshot in every case is a somewhat condescending denigration of British intelligence in the past which scarcely promotes useful reflections on the nature of intelligence or the purposes for which it is gathered.

Secondly, admirable narratives abound, but little serious effort has been made to weave wartime intelligence into accounts of the debates at Chiefs of Staff level and above at which Grand Strategy was hammered out, or even into assessments of the ways in which intelligence determined strategic or operational decisions in a theatre of war, or tactical moves on the battlefield itself. Instead, there has been an increasingly academic approach, in part the consequence of the admission of military history to a prominent place in university curricula (rightly, because no aspect of western life since the 1930s can be properly studied in isolation from the rise of belligerent Nazism or the menace of Russia) as official documents have been progressively released to the public, and in part the result of the increased employment in government service and its ancillary agencies of academically trained men and women as career professionals rather than as temporary and strictly amateur 'professor-type' recruits like those enlisted by GCHQ in 1939 and 1940. Both these trends have encouraged the pursuit of intellectual abstraction instead of practical inquiry into the use of intelligence in a given case: titles like 'Intelligence and surprise' are more likely to be met with today than (for example) 'The role of intelligence and surprise in the battle for Rome, May 1944.'

In one way or another, therefore, attention, has been diverted away from what should be the primary purpose of any study of intelligence: how far, and in what ways, did knowledge of the actions and intentions of foreign powers and their armed forces affect what was thought and done by governments or commanders-in-chief, their immediate fighting subordinates and their respective staffs? A brief look at what has been written about intelligence and the Second World War during the last decade or so will make this clear.[4]

Radio communications became an important source of intelligence as early as 1914, when the British intercepted and decrypted German naval signals; and, by the middle of the Second World War, signals intelligence (SIGINT) had become the major provider of high-grade information, almost completely replacing human agents, details of whose contributions are in any case for the most part secret. Apart from the Oslo report, the interrogation of prisoners about the technicalities of beam-bombing, and the information about V1s and V2s which came out of occupied Europe, little front-rank intelligence was derived from any other source.[5] Any review of recent intelligence literature must, therefore, for practical purposes be confined to considering what has been written about SIGINT. My own limitations will restrict this review still further: little will be said here about the war with Japan; and the compartmentalisation which prevailed at Bletchley Park – and the rigorous application of the 'need to know' principle – meant that, although I worked on German Enigma for almost the whole of the war, I scarcely even knew the meaning of Magic and Purple and am still not qualified to appraise them.

Ground rules for the application of intelligence to modern military purposes were laid down 20 years ago by Roberta Wohlstetter, whose study[6] of the reasons why SIGINT warnings of the Japanese raid on Pearl Harbour were disregarded made current the now standard distinction between 'signals' and 'noise', and later by Donald MacLachlan, who distilled the essence of his wartime experience in naval intelligence into a book[7] which retains its value today, even though its author could not reveal the Ultra foundations on which it rested. Pointing out the obstacles (including the maldistribution of intelligence) which in 1941 stood in the way of an overall assessment of the danger from Japan, Mrs Wohlstetter concluded that (in the words of Thomas Schelling's foreword to her book) 'It was not our warning that was at fault, but our strategic analysis. We were so busy thinking through some "obvious" Japanese moves that we neglected to hedge against the choice they actually made' – the same trap into which western intelligence was seen, when the relevant Ultra could be examined, to have fallen when it failed to foresee the German Ardennes offensive exactly 3 years later.

Subsequent studies have repeatedly emphasised the lesson that the humans who use it are the weak link in the intelligence chain, not the raw material they receive – for example, the belief that British tank armour was superior to German was 'an article of faith, not a matter of evidence' at the War Office in 1940 and 1941, or the Air Ministry so completely shared the widespread belief in a 'knockout blow' by the Luftwaffe that it was for a long time blind to evidence that the German bombing force was solely designed to give a close support to the army.[8] However, the lesson has proved easier to deduce than to assimilate: why else should successive writers repeat their own newly-gained experience that unconsciously held preconceptions are the intelligence officer's chief handicap? Here, at any rate, is one way in which increased attention to intelligence and its uses has greatly benefited the historiography of the last five decades. Wesley Wark's vivid and enlightening analysis[9] would scarcely have been subtitled 'British Intelligence and Nazi Germany 1933–49' had it been written 10 or 15 years ago, when it would probably have been conceived as another study in the politics of appeasement; nor would it have laid so much valuable stress on the erroneous preconceptions which shaped the thinking of the service ministries in accordance with changing current assumptions or on those other beguilements, mirror-imaging and the 'not invented here' syndrome, which persisted in crediting Hitler with a rationality they professed themselves and which was still obstructing Allied relations as late as the last summer of the war.

The first two attempts to assess the significance of the newly revealed source after Winterbotham's hindsighted and often misleading feat of memory in 1974[10] both wear remarkably well, considering how much more has become known in the 10 years since they were published. Given that he had never been privy to Ultra and depended almost entirely on the recollections of others, Ronald Lewin's *Ultra Goes to War*[11] presented a lively and fairly faithful (if occasionally too light-hearted) account of Bletchley Park and its work, which is deservedly becoming the standard version. We are not now likely to get one from an insider,[12] and the comparable chapters of Nigel West's *GCHQ*[13] are markedly inferior. It has to be borne in mind, however, that only a few hundred Ultra signals had reached the PRO (Public Record Office) when Lewin sent his manuscript to press, and that it was three more years before all 100,000 army/air signals and the half-million translations of naval decrypts were released.

Probably the greatest service of the conference on the role of signals intelligence which was held at Bad Godesberg and Stuttgart in November 1978[14] was to find a remedy for the fever of historical revisionism which was already widespread in the wake of books[15] now best forgotten. Led by Jürgen Rohwer, the convener of the conference, influential British and American figures who had helped create Ultra roundly condemned the hasty conclusion that existing histories would have to be rewritten. Another 20 years would be needed to establish the facts securely, urged Edward Thomas, Harry Hinsley's chief collaborator on the official history of British Intelligence; only then would it be safe to draw conclusions.[16] Just over a year later Peter Calvocoressi, a former member of Hut 3 at Bletchley Park and one of those who had attended the conference, wrote in similar terms.[17] Quite lately there has been a hint that in journalistic quarters the usual cycle of change in historical fashion is beginning to turn too fast and too far: after a great deal of ill-informed nonsense, Philip Knightley rashly proclaims that 'Ultra has been given an importance it does not deserve.'[18]

With the obvious exception of the British Grand Strategy series,[19] the official histories on both sides of the Atlantic made little direct reference to intelligence of any kind. The British authors appear to have known about Ultra, although they did not include it; the Americans seem at first to have been denied knowledge even of its existence.[20] The most recent British volume on the Mediterranean campaigns,[21] however, follows Ultra closely on crucial occasions[22] but does not explicitly refer to it; one American volume[23] is marred by some unfortunate references to Winterbotham on matters where he was mistaken. Similarly, there is little about intelligence in general histories like that of General Sir William Jackson – indispensable until the official series is complete – or in biographies like Nigel Nicolson's of Alexander, all of which were published before the release of Ultra.[24]

With the operational background thus fully delineated and initial over-excitement about Ultra giving way to caution, it might have been expected that a trend towards integrating intelligence and operations historically would become apparent. Unfortunately, progress towards this end has been slow. Few of the many highly regarded books published in the last 10 years (some of them by men who, serving in senior staff posts during the war, helped to plan Allied operations in the light of current intelligence, and some by young postwar historians) have done full justice to both aspects.

David Belchem, who was Montgomery's operations officer for the last 18 months of the war, was content to recount his own experiences and to narrate events with scarcely a mention of the intelligence which sometimes shaped them. It was he who propagated Winterbotham's entirely baseless legend that there was 'virtually no signals intelligence' before the Ardennes offensive.[25] John Keegan summarily but fairly described Ultra as playing 'perhaps a decisive part in the battle for Normandy', but gave only two brief illustrations and did not enquire whether it affected planning in general or only battlefield tactics.[26] More than either of these, Carlo d'Este recognised the part played by intelligence throughout, but curiously regarded Ultra as an entirely British affair and faltered in his account of its bearing on Hitler's Mortain offensive.[27] His misplaced criticism of Montgomery does not rest mainly on the use of intelligence.

Flashback by General Sir Charles Richardson, Belchem's predecessor as Montgomery's chief operations officer and later head of plans at 21 Army Group, is one of the few soldiers' books to make intelligence a leading ingredient of its narrative; but the illustrations of Ultra are intermittent and some of the details are inaccurate.[28] It is strange that Field Marshal Lord Carver did not make the largely ineffective use of intelligence the main theme of his 'New Look at the Libyan Campaign, 1940–1942'[29] – except of course, that it would have weakened rather than strengthened the defence of Ritchie's memory, which was his chief purpose. Nevertheless, Carver accorded Ultra full credit as a general proposition, but did not investigate it in detail. Dominic Graham and Shelford Bidwell's *Tug of War. The Battle for Italy, 1943–5*,[30] only mentions Ultra three times, never with particular emphasis. These examples are enough to show how far apart intelligence and operations are still usually being kept.

There have been distinguished exceptions to this general rule, the most striking of which concern the war at sea. The three volumes of Stephen Roskill's classic work,[31] like their army counterparts, were published before reference could be made to Ultra, but many pages of Roskill's masterly exposition betray its influence; although based on Ultra, Alberto Santoni's sometimes frenetic *Il Vero Traditore*[32] is less reliable, for instance, as a guide to the losses inflicted on Rommel's trans-Mediterranean supply lines. The first author to be able to use the new materials, in the shape of the Ultra-based signals issued by the Admiralty's Operational Intelligence Centre – in which he had served for the whole of the war – was Patrick Beesly. His death six months ago (1986) was a great sorrow to his friends and an irreparable loss to naval scholarship. His *Very Special Intelligence*[33] showed how the fortunes of the Allies in the Battle of the Atlantic fluctuated with Bletchley's ability to decrypt German naval signals at some periods and not at others, and was won when decryption coincided with the provision of new means of locating and destroying U-boats with very long range aircraft, support groups, and so on. Intelligence and Operations were in fruitful daily contact in the OIC; history was exemplarily illustrated and made rounded and complete by their renewed juxtaposition in Beesly's book. His example was followed and his work expanded by the naval chapters in *British Intelligence,* the two chief authors of which had been prominent members of Bletchley's Naval Section, when the translated decrypts which underlay OIC's signals were opened to view and much more detail could be added to the story. In later years Beesly collaborated with Jürgen Rohwer, a former German naval officer, whose *Geleitzug Schlachten im März 1943*[34] described some of the critical convoy battles from the German side.

An as yet unpublished paper of Beesly's[35] discussed with great restraint and sensitivity a controversial instance of a central problem in the use of intelligence in war: how far should the responsible commander – almost inevitably a regular soldier, sailor or airman of some age and seniority – defer to the judgement, however well grounded in experience of interpreting the peculiarities and uncertainties of intelligence sources, of an officer almost certainly many years his junior, much lower in rank, and very likely a 'hostilities only' recruit from civilian life? Was Admiral Pound right to disregard the advice of his intelligence officers, Paymaster Commanders Denning and Winn, and take his (as it proved) disastrous decision to order convoy PQ17 to scatter – given that he believed, but they did not, that there was a threat from heavy German surface ships to the convoy and the supplies it was carrying to Russia? After meticulously examining all the circumstances and taking into account the pressures upon everyone concerned, Beesly felt that Pound was wrong to give the order and concluded that this was 'one more example of the folly of allowing Operations to dominate Intelligence.' The two propositions do not necessarily stand or fall together. Perhaps the latter was too starkly phrased, but it will continue to be of crucial importance as long as decisions of a similar kind have to be taken. Neither an American President, with his finger on the atomic button, nor a NATO commander in a theatre of operations, can ever possess the special ability to interpret intelligence which is less than conclusive but upon which irreversible decisions have to be taken.

Alternatively, if Operations should not dominate Intelligence, neither must Intelligence presume to dictate to Operations. How can the intelligence officer, even though he possesses special ability, shoulder the responsibility of taking decisions for which neither his training nor his experience have prepared him? The two dangers are equal and opposite. Ill consequences followed when Major-General Kenneth Strong, Eisenhower's Chief Intelligence Officer, persuaded his commander in the autumn of 1944 that no danger was to be anticipated from the Ardennes, and in spring 1945 that the so-called 'Alpine Redoubt' was a worthwhile military objective. Moreover, the misjudgements Professor Lindemann, fortunately exposed in time by the then Dr R. V. Jones,[36] showed that the expert can easily convince himself that he knows more than he really does.

The inescapable dilemma of command in these examples admits of no easy solution, but a close examination of the examples themselves may point in the right direction: lessons deduced from the past may help to clear a path through the many obstacles to communication between intelligence and operations which exist nowadays.

Maritime affairs should perhaps be regarded as a special case, because the time-scale is usually so short. PQ17's supply ships were sunk soon after they scattered, *Bismarck* was lost, found again and destroyed in a week, the OIC's efforts to route Atlantic convoys away from U-boat packs either succeeded or failed quite quickly, whereas on land Medenine and Alam Halfa, which lasted 1 and 6 days respectively, were untypical. The relation of intelligence to land operations is looser, particularly where the broad outlines of grand strategy are concerned. General Sir David Fraser, drawing on far more material for his enlightening biography of Alanbrooke[37] than Sir Arthur Bryant could use for *The Turn of the Tide* and *Triumph in the West*,[38] could still identify only a very few examples of the direct influence of one upon the other.

Brooke's chief concern was always to match the conditions in which allied troops would have to fight with the resources and capabilities they would have at the given time, not to take opportunistic advantage of German mistakes revealed by intelligence. The clearest of these examples occurred in Italy. In agreement with Churchill, Brooke urged the benefits to be won from enticing the Germans to disperse their dwindling manpower by reinforcing Italy at the expense of the Russian front and their preparations to resist a landing on the Channel coast. Signs of the movement of individual divisions out of reserve or between theatres were almost routine – order of battle was a staple of all intelligence sources – but on occasion Ultra eavesdropped on strategic appreciations by Hitler and OKW, and confirmed Brooke's views by demonstrating that the enemy planned to do exactly what he had prophesied and play into Allied hands by fighting a stubborn rearguard action all the way up the Italian peninsula.

On the rare occasions when this sort of thing happened, an individual item of intelligence might reach Chiefs of Staff level in its original form, but ordinarily everything was first considered by their handmaid, the Joint Intelligence Committee (JIC), and passed upwards later as part of a summary. The JIC records are therefore an essential key to a correct estimate of the effect of intelligence received upon strategic decisions taken, and the withholding of them from view is probably the single largest remaining obstacle impeding World War II historiography. References to the JIC and its chairman, Victor Cavendish-Bentinck, have usually been respectful but very generalised. *British Intelligence* attempts no thoroughgoing estimate of its work but speaks of the committee's 'increasing effectiveness' after the reorganisation which took place in the summer of 1941. Yet the same authority later quotes a number of instances where the JIC's forecasts proved lamentably wide of the mark: it believed, for example, in June 1942, and repeated in December, that a decline in civilian morale might bring about a German collapse 'with startling rapidity'; expected that Kesselring would withdraw his armies to the Alps right up to the moment when Ultra showed the contrary; and repeatedly based its predictions on the assumptions that Hitler would conduct his strategy according to rational principles.[39]

If these illustrations are typical of its work as a whole, it is less surprising that even after his complaints led to the 1941 JIC reorganisation, Churchill still insisted on seeing Ultra in the raw, and consequently tended to make the same sort of mistakes as Pound, thereby forcing Brooke to spend long hours restraining him. Was the JIC as much of a help to the Chiefs of Staff as it ought to have been? A central body to consider intelligence from all sources – the Foreign Office, the three armed services and the Ministry of Economic Warfare – so that the Chiefs of Staff should receive a single interpretation and not several conflicting opinions, was a logical and sensible innovation on the face of it. But so also was the OKW, yet it served the German cause ill, and the Allies did not suffer significantly from having no centralised Defence Department. Logic is not all: 'For forms of government let fools contest, Whate'er is best administered is best.' Would some different arrangement have cleared the way for speedier decision-making? Did the addition of one more tier to the hierarchy of committees mean that differences were rubbed down into bland formulae? We do not yet know enough to say, but in view of the prevailing obscurity it is the more to be regretted that Patrick Howarth's recent biography of Cavendish-Bentinck[40] makes no attempt to answer these and similar questions, or to assess the contribution of the JIC and its chairman critically. This gap in our knowledge urgently needs repair.

The obligation laid upon Montgomery to wring victory out of defeat in Egypt and then to oversee the greatest opposed landing in history –

failure in either these enterprises could, he knew, affect the outcome of the war disastrously – might have been expected to induce him to squeeze the maximum advantage out of any information which could make his task easier. Strangely, it is still not clear whether he did or did not do so. He himself always wrote as if he drew up his famous 'master-plans' unaided, yet in all his campaigns he kept his Chief Intelligence Officer, Sir Edgar Williams, close by his side. Nigel Hamilton's three-volume biography[41] makes due reference to Ultra – though scarcely to any other intelligence source – and abounds in lengthy extracts from interviews with Williams and other surviving members of Montgomery's staff, but does not advance the 40-year-old debate noticeably. Montgomery did not 'follow the fruits of Ultra' (whatever precisely that may mean) – Hamilton even denies that Medenine was in any sense Ultra's victory, although a signal showing Rommel's intended thrust-lines had in fact reached Montgomery 24 hours before the battle – and writes that problems only arose when intelligence 'contradicted his genius for tactical decision-making', as at Alamein and Arnhem, but does not attempt to resolve the conflict. The remark that in March 1945 it was *obvious* from Ultra' (my italics) that Bradley should take certain actions similarly overlooks all the delicate weighing-up of probable meanings and interpretations which is the intelligence officer's daily task. For longer than any of his predecessors in high command, Montgomery enjoyed, and could utilise or not as he chose, better intelligence than any of them had received. What use did he make of this bounty? Shortly before D-day he said that future historians would 'dither over a thousand particulars – Mulberries, Ultra intelligence and the like – losing sight of the things that *really* matter.' Can intelligence always be so safely ignored?

The absence of a close enough link between Intelligence and Operations is a disappointing feature of the two volumes of Martin Gilbert's biography of Churchill which deal with the war years. Gilbert makes ritual gestures of respect towards 'the primacy of the Enigma decrypts'[42] in keeping Rommel's trans-Mediterranean supply routes under constant attack during CRUSADER in November 1941, for instance, and in providing ammunition for the broadsides Churchill fired at Wavell and Auchinleck for their reluctance to take the offensive, as well as in his accounts of the retreat from Tobruk in June 1942 and in the preparations for Alamein. But his handling of intelligence matters is often clumsy and he sometimes reports the timing of Ultra signals wrongly – even though it was often the timing which determined their value. His account of PQ17[43] does not touch on the Intelligence/ Operations dilemma discussed above, and his narratives of the battle for Rome in May and June 1944, and of the breaching of the Gothic Line later on, show no appreciation of the part played by intelligence in either. Very strangely, Churchill managed to give an account of the way the Chiefs of Staff committee did its work[44] without specifically mentioning intelligence, but it is difficult not to feel that some comment on it was required and that these two massive volumes (severe pruning of their almost 2000 pages would have increased their impact) have done less than justice to the part played by intelligence in military affairs in comparison with other elements in the decision-making process to which they give coverage – the pressures exerted by allies abroad and parliamentary critics at home, the problem of dividing exiguous resources and inadequate manpower between competing theatres of war to the best advantage, and so on. Gilbert looks more often to the 'what' than to the 'why' of Churchill's actions, and in consequence has produced an over-elaborate narrative rather than a mature and critical study: a proper appraisal of intelligence about the enemy has fallen victim to his choice of method.

Nothing could have been more welcome, from the standpoint adopted here, than *British Intelligence in the Second World War,* had the promise of its subtitle, 'Its influence on strategy and operations', been fulfilled. Indispensable though it will always remain as a work of reference, the official history is too compressed and too indifferent to literary style to make easy reading even for scholars. The chief impression it leaves on the mind is that of massive weight and often tedious detail amid which breadth of vision and overview become lost to sight. It would be churlish not to recognise the enormous amount of material which the editors have consulted and summarised, and the immense labour this must have entailed, but since no one else has had (or is likely to have in the near future) access to all the sources open to them, their conclusions would have been as instructive as their digest of information. There is little to show how they judge the intelligence from the various theatres as an aid to strategic and operational planning at different stages in the war, or to explain whether they think it was properly utilised or not. The progressively larger flow of Ultra decrypts, the improving quality of intelligence-servicing they were given at home and in the field, and the readiness of commanders to take notice, all pass without the attention they deserve. The gradual conversion of the British – and later the American – armed forces from near-contempt of intelligence into users so avid for it that on occasion they relied on it too much was in the long run at least as important a feature as the development and manufacture of more and better weapons. Whereas in 1940 and 1941 too little intelligence was available to answer even some of the simplest and most fundamental questions, by 1944 the modern phenomenon of a superfluity was already apparent, and with it the need to discover new ways of ensuring that channels of communication did not become blocked and that its true essence reached the top.

The naval chapters of *British Intelligence* are less open to these objections than those concerned with land operations, whose thicker texture was more awkward to handle. This may be why in the treatment of the latter there can sometimes be detected a blurring of judgement and a reluctance to draw possibly embarrassing conclusions which it would have been desirable to avoid. The events of the Alamein summer and the Kasserine crisis are cases in point. So are occasions when a final verdict must depend on the files which the official historians have been able to consult, but which the rest of us cannot see. No attempt is made, for instance, to suggest whether the frequent quotations from JIC papers which have not been released do or do not show the Committee giving helpful guidance to the Chiefs of Staff. Again it is not made clear – perhaps deliberately? – whether some crucial parts of the account of relations with Jugoslavia are left vague because there is now no evidence to fill gaps properly, or whether the evidence exists but is still suppressed. To marry an account of what intelligence was provided during the war with what happened operationally is perhaps too complex a task to tackle satisfactorily except at the cost of inordinate length. *British Intelligence* has set out in the right direction, but it has not got as close to its stated goal as could be wished.

The Missing Dimension,[45] edited three years ago by Christopher Andrew and David Dilks, took its title from Cadogan's remark that secret intelligence is 'the missing dimension in most diplomatic history', and makes good its claim to widen the meaning of the phrase to embrace political and military history as well in a series of original essays which draws upon British, American, French, Irish and Japanese records. Few would now dispute the claim, and the material assembled in these essays confirms it beyond all doubt. They have done an admirably pioneering service, but the matter cannot be allowed to rest here. The new discoveries must not be left lying parallel with the old familiar accounts, mute witnesses to their insufficiency, but must modify them where appropriate and assist in the creation of a new norm. In the field of military history, it is plain that the process has hardly begun.

Although he wrote it in an autobiographical form with himself as the central point of reference, Professor R. V. Jones's *Most Secret War*[46] is in fact an isolated example of the happy accomplishment of this ideal. The imaginative employment of special scientific knowledge was indispensable to successful defence against the imminent and alarming threats to the civilian population inherent in the beam-bombing of 1940–41 and the V-weapons of 1944–45, and Jones's privilege of access to Churchill enabled him to call upon authority to neutralise opposition and overcome delays. His impatience with 'the hierarchical attenuation of information' is unbounded.[47] In this special field, where conditions favoured it and where the novelty and urgency of the threat demanded instant action, intelligence and operations had to be combined at once if anything at all was to be done. The partnership is plain to see in Jones's fascinating and authoritative account of how successful defence measures were improvised. On the larger scale of military operations in a whole theatre of war no single individual could be both intelligence officer and land force commander, and separation unavoidably attenuates the relationship; but it is bound to exist, and can be described.

Air intelligence is more loosely linked to operations than that of the other two services, except on the immediate tactical plane, and this explains why so much less has been written about it. The most recent history[48] shows how the RAF's greatest single innovation of the war years – army/air co-operation, against which the Air Ministry had set its face before 1939 – was developed by Tedder in the Middle East with little reference to intelligence about the enemy and much to practical necessity. SIGINT could give useful warnings of the enemy's intended strikes, provided that decryption was quick enough and that security could be protected, and suggest targets for our own, but the pattern was repetitive and there were few lessons to be learned. At the other extreme, air intelligence before and during the war is most notable for case-histories in the evil influence of preconceived ideas. Strategic bombing had always been regarded as the prime way to destroy German manufacturing capacity, and no amount of photographic evidence that the bombers were missing their targets more often than they hit them availed to shake the Air Staff's confidence. Portal thought that the air offensive was 'beginning to have great results' at the same moment as he was creating the Pathfinder Force because it was not doing so, and

'Bomber' Harris's conviction that his Lancasters could themselves compel Germany to surrender by New Year 1944 led him to condemn Coastal Command as 'merely an obstacle to victory' while the part it played in winning the Battle of the Atlantic was becoming plainer to see every day.[49] Because there were no agents in Germany, and internal German reports of bomb damage went by land-line until almost the end of the war, there was no Ultra to show him his mistake.

At the cost of a digression from the main theme, mention must be made of two related matters. First, how it was that Enigma came to be decrypted is still not clear in every particular. Shortly before he died in 1985 Gordon Welchman corrected and valuably amplified his previous account.[50] In spite of the B-Dienst, there was no true German equivalent, but the story of the W/T Listening Company which provided Rommel with the intelligence from which his victories sprang until it was overrun at Alamein in June 1942 has recently been told by one of his intelligence officers.[51] Secondly, the relation of intelligence and diplomacy has been explored in a collection of essays edited by Richard Langhorne,[52] and Correlli Barnett's *Audit of War*[53] has controversially exposed the weak social and industrial foundations of wartime and postwar Britain, and shed an oblique, but revealing, light upon the way superior intelligence almost accidentally saved us from disaster. Gordon Welchman's reiterated 'We were lucky' takes on a new meaning and warns against complacency over the success of Allied intelligence in World War II.[54]

Another warning against complacency is implicit in recent theoretical writings about intelligence. These have mainly been American, and their authors mostly men who have served the government in some capacity which has given them experience of how intelligence is actually handled in practice and of the extent to which it is allowed to influence policy. The authors draw upon later evidence – Korea, Vietnam, and their acquaintance with the corridors of power in Washington in peace and war – as well as upon the Second World War. All come to the depressing conclusion that there is very little chance of intelligence being used objectively or of commensurate benefit being derived from the millions of dollars and man-hours invested in the production of intelligence ostensibly for just these purposes. They focus on the two chief obstacles which in their opinion bar the way – a glut of information, and their superiors' preconceived ideas.

Both these obstacles were described forcefully 10 years ago in a disillusioning paper by Thomas L. Hughes entitled 'The Fate of Facts in the World of Men',[55] which every intelligence officer seeking a career in government should be compelled to read. Remarking on the difference between 'the clear picture seen by the convinced policymakers and the cloudy picture usually seen by intelligence', and noting that 'the quantity of current intelligence conspicuously exceeds the audience's capacity for absorption', he points to the temptation open to the politician – intelligence tells but politics decides, and no man can wear both hats at once – to seize randomly upon a single striking bit of information from the mass in front of him. As for ideas – 'Politics is personalities with ideas more or less casually attached', and facts may be either 'accommodated to the preconceived ideas of opinionated men', 'emptied into the sieves of mindless consumers to be left to dribble out into inconsequentiality', or 'poured into re-usable bottles labelled with vintage views'.

Richard K. Betts proceeds in similar vein:[56] 'a glut of ambiguous data' creates 'the problem of overload' from which there is no escape but which may result in the political chief being offered so many half-digested courses to choose from that he will simply select the one which 'accords with his own predisposition'. In consequence 'there is no guaranteed prophylaxis against intelligence failures' and we must steel ourselves for the 'most outrageously fatalistic of all solutions: tolerance or disaster'.

Under present-day intelligence-gathering conditions 'all that exists is noise'.[57] The wider the range of material, the narrower the range of vision: 'like people growing older, governments may have been acquiring more and more powerful glasses but nevertheless becoming able to see less and less' because, bewildered by excess, they take refuge behind the shutters of their predispositions.[58] Yet 'there is no conclusive evidence that "open-minded" officials avoid disasters better than rigid ones',[59] and no imaginable institutional change is likely to remedy this deplorable state of affairs.[60]

Disturbing though all this may be as a portrait of the present or a vision of the future, how relevant is it to intelligence in World War II as this recedes into the remoter historical past? Surely, in several respects. No comparable set of reflections could have been composed in Britain or America in the years before 1939: intelligence was not highly regarded in the armed services or elsewhere (witness Churchill's struggle to secure a hearing for unwelcome intelligence about Nazi Germany) and there were no ready-made intelligence staffs.[61] It was 18 months or 2 years before – the air defence of Great Britain apart – either country needed to deploy large forces on land, sea or air; in the interval, soldiers could be trained, weapons manufactured, and civilians recruited for intelligence outlets. Had there been no interval, none of these things could have been accomplished in time. World War II intelligence must always be appraised against this background of improvisation and haste – a totally different background from that of today.

Once the drawbacks of this slow start had been overcome, by the autumn of 1942, there were no obstacles in the way of sound intelligence penetrating to the highest decision-making levels of the kind so much lamented by modern commentators. Ultra information was unhesitatingly accepted as true and reliable, though of course in need of interpretation because of its usually piecemeal nature. Its strategic usefulness depended on those who handled it in Whitehall or Washington. Fortunately, the relationship of Operations and Intelligence in the field was by this time a usually smooth and happy one, and awareness of this should sharpen interest in the conditions of 40 years ago – that is to say, in the various bodies concerned, from the JIC down, and including related authorities like SOE and the deception staffs. The focus of attention needs to shift from the product to the process of consumption. Finally, one essential difference between intelligence then and now prevents a fair comparison between them. Ultra was an almost unrepeatable phenomenon. Ultra was 'signals' devoid of any intermixture of 'noise'; modern SIGINT, certainly in peacetime, and presumably also in war, contains an unquantifiable amount of 'noise'. Disinformation was a technique practised by Goebbels and the Reich Propaganda Ministry, but mercifully not by the Wehrmacht. The modern problem is different and no doubt more difficult.

NOTES

1. A. Boyle, *The Climate of Treason.* Hutchinson, London (1979).
2. N. West, *MI5. British Security Service Operations, 1909–45.* Bodley Head, London (1981); N. West: *MI6. British Secret Intelligence Operations 1909–45.* Weidenfeld & Nicolson, London (1983).
3. C. Andrew, *Secret Service. The Making of the British Intelligence Community.* Heinemann, London (1985).
4. G. C. Constantinides' shrewd comments in *Intelligence and Espionage: An Analytical Bibliography* [Westview Press, Boulder (1983)] are a valuable guide down to 1982, but many important books have been published since it went to press.
5. The legend that Canaris supplied Menzies with information secretly has recently been authoritatively contradicted by Robert Cecil in *Intelligence and National Security* 1, 182.

6. R. Wohlstetter, *Pearl Harbor. Warning and Decision*. Stanford University Press, Stanford, CA (1962).
7. D. MacLachlan, *Room 39, Naval Intelligence in Action, 1939–45*. Weidenfeld & Nicolson, London (1968).
8. F. H. Hinsley with E. E. Thomas, C. F. G. Ranson and R. C. Knight, *British Intelligence in the Second World War*. HMSO, London (1979–1984) in three volumes, one to come. The quotation is from Vol. i, p. 77. See also W. K. Wark, *The Ultimate Enemy: British Intelligence and Nazi Germany, 1933–39*. Cornell University Press, Ithaca (1985).
9. Wark, *ibid.*
10. F. W. Winterbotham, *The Ultra Secret*. Weidenfeld & Nicolson, London (1974).
11. R. Lewin, *Ultra goes to War. The Secret Story*. Hutchinson, London (1978).
12. Peter Calvocoressi's book (see note 17) is only in part an internal history.
13. N. West, *GCHQ. The Secret Wireless War 1900–86*. Weidenfeld & Nicolson, London (1986).
14. J. Rohwer and E. Jäckel, *Die Funkaufklärung und ihre Rolle im Zweiten Weltkrieg*. Motorbuch, Stuttgart (1979).
15. For instance A. Cave Brown, *Bodyguard of Lies. The Vital Role of Deception Strategy in World War II*. W. H. Allen, London (1976); W. H. Stevenson, *A Man Called Intrepid*. Harcourt Brace Jovanovich, New York (1976).
16. Rohwer and Jäckel, *op. cit.*, pp. 390–392.
17. P. Calvocoressi, *Top Secret Ultra*. Cassell, London (1980).
18. P. Knightley, *The Second Oldest Profession. The Spy as Bureaucrat, Patriot, Fantasist and Whore*, p. 175. André Deutsch, London (1986).
19. HMSO, *Grand Strategy*. Five volumes, published between 1956 and 1972. The two narrative series (The Mediterranean and Middle East, and Victory in the West), of six and two volumes, respectively, have the same publisher and similar dates. (The five-volume American series was published in Washington between 1958 and 1977.)
20. Forrest Pogue in Rohwer and Jäckel, *op cit.*, pp. 376–378. Also d'Este (see note 27), p. 416.
21. W. G. F. Jackson, *The Mediterranean and Middle East*, Vol. VI/1. HMSO, London (1984).
22. *Ibid.* See, for example, Chap VI, on the ANVIL debates.
23. E. F. Fisher, *Cassino to the Alps*. Washington (1977).
24. W. G. F. Jackson, *The North African Campaign 1940–43*. Batsford, London (1975); *The Battle for Italy*. London (1967); *The Battle for Rome*. London (1971); *Alexander of Tunis as Military Commander*. Batsford, London (1971); N. Nicolson, *Alex*. Weidenfeld & Nicolson, London (1971).
25. D. Belchem, *All in the Day's March*. Collins, London (1978).
26. J. Keegan, *Six Armies in Normandy*. Cape, London (1982).
27. C. d'Este, *Decision in Normandy. The Unwritten Story of Montgomery and the Allied Campaign*. Collins, London (1983).
28. C. Richardson, *Flashback*. Kimber, London (1985).
29. M. Carver, *Dilemmas of the Desert*. Batsford, London (1986).
30. D. Graham and S. Bidwell, *Tug of War; the Battle for Italy 1943–5*. Hodder & Stoughton, London (1986).
31. S. W. Roskill, *The War at Sea*. HMSO, London (1954–1961). Three volumes.

32. A. Santoni, *Il Vero Traditore*. Mursia (1981).
33. P. Beesly, *Very Special Intelligence*. Hamish Hamilton, London (1977).
34. J. Rohwer, *Geleitzug Schlachten im März* 1943. Motorbuch, Stuttgart (1972).
35. Prepared for a conference at the U.S. Army War College in April 1986, it is shortly to be published in the conference proceedings.
36. R. V. Jones, *Most Secret War*. Hamish Hamilton, London (1978).
37. D. Fraser, *Alanbrooke*. Collins, London (1982).
38. A. Bryant, *The Turn of the Tide*. Collins, London (1957); *Triumph in the West*. Collins, London (1957) .
39. *British Intelligence,* Vol. i, p. 299; Vol. ii, p. 114, Vol. iii, pp. 4–6, 14 and 43. See also E. Thomas, The evolution of the JIC system during the World War II, in *The Proceedings of the Medlicott Symposium on Intelligence and International Relations,* 1900–45, at Exeter University in 1985, which are shortly to be published. Other opinions are equally divided: his experiences led R. V. Jones, who abhorred committees, to a low estimate of the JIC, see his *Most Secret War,* pp. 205 and 365–366. Donald MacLachlan had a much higher opinion; see his *Room 39*, pp. 240–269.
40. P. Howarth, *Intelligence Chief Extraordinary. The Life of the Ninth Duke of Portland*. Bodley Head, London (1986).
41. N. Hamilton, *Monty. The Making of a General,* Vol. 1. Hamish Hamilton, London (1981); *Monty. Master of the Battlefield,* Vol. 2. Hamish Hamilton, London (1983); *Monty. The Field Marshal,* Vol. 3. Hamish Hamilton, London (1986). The quotations are from Vol. 2, pp. 125 and 153; Vol. 1, p. 654; Vol. 3, p. 550, respectively.
42. M. Gilbert, *Winston S. Churchill,* Vols vi and vii. Heinemann, London (1983, 1986). The quotation is from Vol. vi, p. 1244.
43. Gilbert, Vol. vii, pp. 141–142.
44. Gilbert, Vol. vii, p. 139.
45. C. Andrew and D. Dilks, *The Missing Dimension. Governments and Intelligence Communities in the Twentieth Century*. Macmillan, London (1984).
46. Jones, *op. cit.*
47. *Ibid.,* p. 419.
48. J. Terraine, *The Right of the Line. The Royal Air Force in the European War*. Hodder & Stoughton, London (1985).
49. *Ibid.,* pp. 503 and 426.
50. G. Welchman, *The Hut Six Story*. Allen Lane, Harmondsworth (1982). See also, G. Welchman, 'From Polish Bomba to British Bombe: The Birth of Ultra', *Intelligence and National Security 1,* 71–110.
51. H.-O. Behrendt, *Rommel's Intelligence in the Desert Campaign*. Kimber, London (1985).
52. R. Langhorne, ed., *Diplomacy and Intelligence in the Second World War*. Cambridge University Press, Cambridge (1985).
53. C. Barnett, *The Audit of War*. Macmillan, London (1986).
54. G. Welchman, *The Hut Six Story,* p. 169; G. Welchman, 'The birth of Ultra'. *Intelligence and National Security 1,* 107.
55. T. L. Hughes, 'The Fate of Facts in the World of Men', in *Foreign Policy Association Headline Series,* No. 223, pp. 58, 19, 40, 11 and 10, respectively.
56. R. K. Betts, 'Analysis, war and decision. Why intelligence failures are inevitable'.

World Politics 31, 64, 69, 76, 84 and 89 (1978).

57. M. I. Handel, 'Intelligence and the problem of strategic surprise', *Journal of Strategic Studies* VII, 237.

58. E. R. May, *Knowing One's Enemies. Intelligence Assessments before the Two World Wars,* pp. 532 and 537. Princeton University Press, Princeton, NJ (1984).

59. R. K. Betts, *Surprise Attack. Lessons for Defence Planning,* pp. 122–123. Brookings Institution, Washington, DC (1982).

60. R. K. Betts, 'Analysis, war and decision', p. 64; R. K. Betts, *Surprise Attack,* p. 174; W. Laqueur, *World of Secrets. The Uses and Limits of Intelligence.* London (1985).

61. The reasons why authority was deaf to several voices raised in warning against the risks of unpreparedness are explained in J. Haswell, *British Military Intelligence.* Weidenfeld & Nicolson, London (1973).

4

Intelligence and Strategy in World War II

The fashion in spy stories. which began with Ian Fleming 30 years ago and has since changed only in the complexity of detail woven by his successors, has distorted the popular view of intelligence in war. Sir John Masterman's *Double Cross System* did not help when it linked secret agents with some of the critical events of 1939–45, and the myriad 'revelations' of recent years have kept the ball rolling in the wrong direction. The cumulative effect has been to spread a romantic but erroneous idea of the way in which intelligence is obtained and how it can affect action. When the existence of Ultra – no spy indeed, but a highly secret and unsuspected source – was first revealed in 1974, there were some who said that the whole history of the war would have to be rewritten. and their cries are only now dying down. Underlying all has sometimes been the assumption that one side has only to discover the other side's intentions in order to thwart them – that is to say, that intelligence is the main, if not the sole, determinant of military action. It is a grave error.[1] So too is another, which often accompanies it. Intelligence-gathering is not, as this line of thought assumes, the sudden discovery of a single all-revealing item, but in most cases the laborious piecing together of maddeningly irreconcilable fragments.

Past practice and present theory of intelligence (if current American writing be taken as representative of the latter)[2] diverge widely in several important respects. The two grew up in such different circumstances – one in war, the other during an uneasy peace; one therefore exclusively military, the other mainly political – that they could not be expected to coincide exactly. The differences between them nevertheless call for investigation in order to bring out the particular qualities of military intelligence during World War II.

71

To begin with an obvious difference. There was no time, in those days, to expound theory, distinguish categories or consider concepts for that would have been a distraction from the all-important task of collecting information quickly, extracting the maximum amount of useful intelligence from it, analysing this and passing the gist of it on to those who could use it to prosecute the war. If peace-time conditions are really more leisurely (a questionable proposition in the days of Superpowers armed with weapons of total destruction), then fine distinctions may be useful so long as they do not become hair-splitting and thus distract from the main purpose, the discovery of the potential enemy's intentions. Forty years ago, there was little time to think about such things, but both historical accident – for example, the way in which the production and assessment of Ultra was grafted on to existing institutions at a time when neither its value nor its future volume could be foreseen – and practical convenience led to some differentiation of function and responsibility. One consequence of this, to the importance of which every account of the higher direction of the war bears witness, is completely at variance with the definition of intelligence used by Professor Godson and others.[3] They include action resulting from intelligence within the definition of intelligence itself.[4] In contrast, the experience of 40 years ago shows that such a broad definition is not only logically confused (reflective analysis and decisive action are distinct – even contrary – concepts) but capable of being dangerous (those in the Ultra secret were forbidden, on security grounds, to risk capture by the enemy, for example; and there was repeated friction between SIS and SOE when the latter claimed intelligence-gathering – the SIS's job – among its own functions).

During World War II the process of gathering and analysing intelligence was kept completely separate from the (subsequent) use of intelligence to guide operations. Neither the Secret Service (agents) nor the Ultra staff at Bletchley Park (high-grade Sigint) nor the Chief Intelligence Officers at field commands (who received information from both sources as well as the results of prisoner interrogation and other intelligence gained at the front) had any hand in the formulation of strategy or tactics. Ultra was delivered to authorised recipients without any gloss (save what was required to elucidate meaning) and unaccompanied by any operational deductions or proposals for action, and the duty of Chief Intelligence Officers was limited to presenting a clear. accurate and up-to-date intelligence picture of the enemy as often as required.[5] In the light of all the information at their disposal – the state of their own troops and the quantity of petrol and ammunition available, for instance, as well as the intelligence picture – the field commanders then decided upon their course of action; at the highest level the Chiefs of Staff planned Grand Strategy in the same way.[6] The danger that results from planning operations in the light of Intelligence alone was more than once unhappily demonstrated during 1941, when Churchill badgered Wavell and Auchinleck in turn to begin an offensive in spite of their logistical and other misgivings because he mistakenly believed that Ultra guaranteed success.[7] Under war-time conditions, at any rate, the dangers that result from confusing intelligence-gathering with consequent action are multiplied tenfold when covert action is included as part of intelligence,[8] for the qualities of intellect and judgement required for the cool and balanced appraisal of evidence are seldom allied with a bent for the solitary and adventurous life for which covert action on hostile territory calls. The histories of the British SOE and the American OSS provide many illustrations, not to speak of some notorious cases of ill-judged political intervention by American intelligence agents in more recent years.

The slight emphasis upon secrecy and security[9] is another reason for supposing Professor Godson's definition of intelligence inadequate in an important respect. Failure to observe security regulations cost the lives of several British agents in Holland between 1941 and 1943, for instance.[10] A far less flagrant breach could have lost Ultra at almost any time,[11] for even a single military action which the enemy could only understand on the supposition that an Enigma message had been deciphered would have been as certain to lose the source altogether as when the Russians changed their commercial code after Baldwin read the text of decrypts to the House of Commons in 1927 in order to explain the Arcos raid.[12] To prevent inadvertent action from giving away the secret of Ultra and leading to changes which might make Enigma unreadable, the dissemination of Ultra was narrowly restricted and its operational use severely controlled by precise security regulations.[13] Forty years on, security is almost a dirty word. Lip-service is paid to the need for it, but 'leaks' are common (in the recent Ponting case, a senior British civil servant passed Ministry of Defence documents to an unauthorised recipient), the United States has a Freedom of Information Act and many in Britain demand the same. All the emphasis is on open government, and secrecy is pilloried as the first step towards submission to tyranny. Yet intelligence perishes without secrecy, and high-grade Sigint, the provider of the best intelligence, needs the most careful protection of all. Forty years ago, the security and discretion of those who knew military secrets[14] could be relied on; now it cannot. The social atmosphere surrounding intelligence has changed as constraints which seemed natural and acceptable in war-time have faded from the public memory. But this makes it more, rather than less, essential to insist on the paramount importance of security in any definition of intelligence.

Another great difference between the two sets of historical circumstance and the regard paid to intelligence in each derives from a point made earlier – that during the war Intelligence officers were farther removed from the making of strategy or policy than they seem to be now. Not only was there clear evidence, very early in the career of Ultra, that intelligence alone could not always determine strategic decisions,[15] but the separation of function already outlined made it well-nigh impossible for the problem which apparently bedevils intelligence communities in today's more peaceful conditions to occur at all. From 1942, when the proven value of Ultra established intelligence in its rightful place, admirals, generals and air marshals were usually prepared to pay proper attention to it. There was no temptation for intelligence officers to tailor their material to suit the preconceptions of their superiors, after the fashion bitterly complained of by a former Director of the United States Defense Intelligence Agency,[16] and it was unthinkable for anything to occur which remotely resembled General Westmoreland's refusal to transmit a new and unfavourable estimate of Vietcong numbers to Washington because it would be unwelcome to the President.[17] The failure to foresee the German offensive in the Ardennes in December 1944 is not to be explained in this way, but rather by a sudden and astonishing inability on the part of all concerned, intelligence officers included, to rid their minds of preconceptions before examining the evidence.[18]

The risk that prejudice and a closed mind may unbalance judgement belong to the human condition and cannot be entirely banished, but the reasons why it was so much less prominent 40 years ago than today may once more serve to show that although intelligence cannot be the same in war and in peace there are enough similarities between the two for war-time experience to provide warning and guidance today. Intelligence is no longer intelligence if it is not as objective as the human mind can make it; a desire to please can destroy its value as quickly as an intention to deceive.

A final difference, even though it may seem too obvious to mention, contains a caution for present-day historians of World War II and perhaps even for senior serving officers. Age has now removed from positions of authority in the three services all those who fought in that war; by the end of 1985 all the British Chiefs of Staff were men who were too young to wear uniform then.[19] The same will be true of active historians before long.

He who has not drawn up orders on the battlefield or devised strategic plans in time of war is compelled instead to imagine the conditions under which these things are done. A similar enforced substitution of imagination for experience may handicap the historian of intelligence more than other kinds of historian, particularly if he makes the academic's common mistake of overrating matters of the intellect and supposes that knowledge must always be the spring of rational action. He may then too easily conclude that a commander acted as he did because he possessed a particular piece of intelligence, when in fact his motives were quite different. For several months in 1942, for instance, intercepts told Rommel a great deal about British intentions,[20] but neither this nor his superiority in tactical thought and speed of manoeuvre, nor his more powerful tanks and guns, could prevent his scope from being tightly restricted by the vulnerability of the sea-routes from Italy and the Aegean along which his supplies had to come, and by the fuel consumption of the lorries which brought petrol for his tanks more than a thousand miles along the Via Balbia from Tripoli because there was no other adequate port in north Africa. (The history of 1941/42 might have been very different if there had been a railway across the Western Desert as there already was across the American prairies, the Siberian steppes and the Nullarbor Plain.) Again, one of the reasons for the prolongation of the Italian campaign into 1944, in addition to Allied knowledge of German intentions to defend the peninsula and Anglo-American differences over policy, was the lack of sufficient ships to bring more divisions back to England for OVERLORD. None of the Allies' invasion-sites of 1943/44 was chosen for intelligence reasons, but because of the limited range of the aircraft which would have to protect the landings and because the beaches were suitable for tanks.

The role of intelligence in strategy was in fact very small until the recent past, and it became larger in World War II for special reasons. Political rather than military strategy inspired Marlborough's 250-mile march to the Danube, for example, and it was his unusual talent for organisation and logistics, rather than intelligence about the enemy, which enabled him to use his tactical skill to win a victory at Blenheim and justify the immense risks he had taken to get there. Nelson spent many weeks vainly seeking the French in the empty spaces of the Atlantic, caught them up almost by accident in Aboukir Bay and beat them because he handled the fleet, and his captains their ships, better than the French. The whole conduct of the Crimean War is a denial of the value – even of the possibility – of military intelligence, whether with a large or a small initial letter.

By the middle of the nineteenth century, however, the invention of the electric telegraph was clearing the way for intelligence to play a greater part in determining strategy. The new railways were beginning to make rapid mobilisation and strategic deployment possible even before a declaration of war, but by the Austro-Prussian War of 1866 the telegraph could prevent so large a movement of troops from being carried out secretly enough to gain strategic surprise for the aggressor, because news could now travel faster than even the newly mobile armies, and incomparably faster in relation to troop movement than in any previous age.[21] A generation later Marconi freed the telegraph from its bonds of copper wire and presented intelligence-gathering with an enormously widened scope. The opportunities radio offered to both user and eavesdropper were immense – the rapid and secret conversion of intention into action by means of orders transmitted over long distances on the one hand, and on the other the gathering, through code-breaking, of intelligence about enemy intentions which would have been quite beyond the power of the cleverest agent. For the first time intelligence was made capable of influencing strategy in a big way, but at a cost which General Erich Fellgiebel, head of the *Heeresnach-richtenwesen,* recognised when he told his staff to remember always that 'Funken ist Landesverrat' ('To use the radio is to betray the country').[22] (If OKW had borne this more prominently in mind there might have been no Ultra.) Some small advantage was taken of the new opportunities during Allenby's 1917 campaign in Palestine,[23] but the real curtain-raiser to the revolution – the great folly of 31 May 1916, which prevented Jutland from being a decisive British victory[24] – was highly inauspicious. Thus World War II was the first real test of the strategic and tactical usefulness of the new opportunities, and the novelty of the situation may go a little way to account for the indifferent use which was made of them at first.

The rest of this chapter will deal mainly with Ultra (but from 1941/42 onwards what other source of military intelligence was capable of influencing strategy?), particularly with that part of it which was derived from decrypts of army and air messages touching Europe and the Mediterranean, with which I was chiefly concerned at the time.

The history of intelligence in its relation to strategy in this area can be divided into three periods: from the outbreak of war to the winter of 1941/42; from then until the late summer of 1944; and the last nine months.

**

Intelligence was woefully inadequate to start with, and it had a minimal influence on strategy during the greater part of the first period. The enemy was both overrated and misunderstood, and it was a political decision to give a guarantee to Poland which it was impossible to honour militarily. No sense of realism disturbed the 'Phoney War' and although intelligence played a part in the Battle of Britain[25] and Ultra intelligence a larger part in defeating the beam-bombers,[26] both were self-contained episodes which could teach few lessons outside their own time and territory. Political miscalculation veneered over by a sort of moral obligation led to the disastrous intervention in Greece in March 1941 contrary to every rule of military prudence, in defiance of such Intelligence as there was, and in total disregard of the contingent risk of losing Cyrenaica. Crete, in May, was the first occasion on which Ultra discovered the enemy's battle-plans in advance,[27] but the island's accidental garrison of tired troops evacuated from Greece under fire was unable to make effective use of it.

There was by now a regular flow of Ultra decrypts from North Africa, but most of them recorded the movements of Geissler's and Froehlich's aircraft not Rommel's tanks, yet Rommel was by far the greater danger. It was this unfortunate imbalance which Churchill overlooked when – too eager to use what he almost regarded as his private intelligence source to gain a victory striking enough to offset the lengthening list of British defeats – he tried to browbeat first Wavell and then Auchinleck into premature offensives. It was doubly unfortunate that one of Ultra's first big coups – General Paulus' report to Halder in May 1941 of the instructions he had given Rommel[28] – was more representative of OKH's thinking than of Rommel's action, and therefore proved strategically misleading.

Ultra was exceptionally well informed about the movements of the Axis supply-ships (though sadly not yet of their cargoes) by now, and in combination with aerial reconnaissance it served as the basis from which an intelligence-directed assault was mounted against trans-Mediterranean traffic by the RAF. When a strong naval squadron was briefly added in the autumn of 1941 very severe damage was done, and the combined operation even relieved pressure in the Atlantic (though this was not of course its primary purpose) by causing Hitler to divert a significant proportion of his U-Boat fleet to the Mediterranean. However, although the strategic role of intelligence was prominent in this instance, and although the sinking-rate achieved was high enough to cause the Axis considerable inconvenience, (the annihilation of the 'Duisburg' convoy on 9 November 1941 and the reduction of the Luftwaffe's petrol stocks in Libya by 90 per cent in four months are particularly noteworthy)[29] there remains a puzzle. On the one hand, had Axis supplies not been thus restricted, 8 Army would probably not have won CRUSADER at Christmas. On the other, why were more ships not sunk – plenty more routes and timings were reported – and Axis supplies strangled altogether? There seems to be no written record of contemporary complaint that more should have been done, nor any surviving memory of grumbling by the soldiers. Only the most painstaking reconstruction (which the disappearance of records has no doubt made impossible) of strengths and locations could determine whether sufficient strike forces were available for additional action during the winter of 1941/42, or whether all additional air strikes were ruled out for security reasons (though this is improbable, for the regulations about preliminary reconnaissance in order to avoid compromising the source were by this time well understood and observed). It may be that there were simply not enough suitable aircraft (the U-Boats had driven the Navy's Force K away by this time), but another plausible explanation is that the operational use of intelligence, and its potentially wide repercussions, had not yet been fully appreciated. There was certainly a good deal of incomprehension both in the highest quarters in London and among the military in Cairo. Churchill urged Auchinleck to the attack because Rommel's army 'was having the greatest difficulty in so much as existing'[30] – which was uncritically to take at face value the clamour of complaint over shortages which Ultra was now supplying – and the over-confidence in Cairo before CRUSADER (which was planned without reference to intelligence) rested partly on gross miscalculations of the Afrika Korps' tank strength, miscalculations which had grave consequences in January 1942, when the possibility that Rommel had received a consignment of new tanks at Benghazi in the course of his retreat was discounted in spite of pointers to the contrary from both Ultra and the front line.[31] It was with these tanks, of course, that Rommel recaptured Cyrenaica up to the Gazala line almost at once.

Professional soldiers received no training in intelligence before 1939, and so were disinclined to ascribe much value to it. They were, therefore, not at all well prepared to make proper use of the remarkable new source of information suddenly available to them. However, some allowance must in fairness be made for the severe security regulations which denied even senior intelligence officers the knowledge that it was derived from decrypting *Wehrmacht* signals; they could hardly be expected to take an anonymous source seriously, since the credibility of news depends on its provenance. Add to all this the well-known tactical and command shortcomings of the British Army of 1941, and the inadequate use of intelligence is explained. Ultra itself had not yet reached its fullest unfolding, moreover; it had very little to say, for instance, about HERKULES, the plan to attack Malta which Hitler unwisely cancelled, and although it did predict correctly the timing of Rommel's offensive of May 1942, it did not discover where the blow would fall, with the result that 8 Army's dispositions were faulty and paved the way for the further mistakes which led to the loss of Tobruk and the retreat to Alamein.

Two developments during the spring and early summer of 1942 transformed the relationship between intelligence and operations and marked the boundary between my first two periods. The cryptographers finally mastered the army keys (they had been broken briefly in the autumn, but then lost again), and these now provided types of information (notably logistical) which had hitherto been lacking and which could give a context and a background to make the misunderstanding of occasional striking signals much less likely than in the past. At the same time. changes in organisation at the production end at Bletchley and of personnel at the receiving end in Cairo and the desert made the assessment of the practical intelligence value of Ultra signals far more exact than hitherto and thereby (in the words of Sir Edgar Williams, who joined the Middle East intelligence staff that spring and rose to be Montgomery's Chief Intelligence Officer in Africa and Europe) 'put Intelligence on the map'.[32] Ultra was at last ready to become a really powerful instrument of war.

Dramatic proof of this came quickly. Auchinleck had stabilised the front at the end of July, but by the time Alexander and Montgomery took over in mid-August there was already talk of a new Axis offensive, which in fact materialised a fortnight later at Alam Halfa. We need not consider the rather absurd dispute[33] as to whether Montgomery inherited his defence plan or devised it himself; the essential point is that he had already made defensive preparations, which later proved decisive, before 17 August when a decrypt[34] showed them to be exactly what was required to counter Rommel's intentions. This was less extraordinary than it seems, because it can be argued that the topography of the area dictates the only possible lines of attack and defence, but within a few weeks the battle of Alam Halfa was in public the foundation of Montgomery's reputation for winning victories, while in private it demonstrated the usefulness of Ultra to generals. Alam Halfa is also, of course, a striking illustration of the point that successful generalship does not necessarily depend on foreknowledge of the enemy's plans.

The larger volume of logistical material and the more thorough analysis it was now receiving had already formed the basis of a renewed assault on Axis supply ships at sea and on lorries carrying stores from port to front line. This proved its operational value when Ultra showed, for instance, that a single large tanker was carrying more petrol than the entire stock on Libyan soil that day, that Rommel's army was living such a hand-to-mouth existence that the Alam Halfa attack had to be delayed for nearly a week until sufficient fuel arrived, and that even then the Afrika Korps became stranded, a sitting target in the open, because it had run out of petrol.[35]

The assault on Axis shipping continued relentlessly, and so did regular reports of its consequences. But neither this nor any other form of intelligence could affect the immediate situation strategically. The unbroken line of minefields and wire from the sea to the Qattara Depression made a frontal attack at Alamein unavoidable; only tactical surprise could therefore be expected, and although the Y Service's almost hourly tracking of the Panzer divisions' movements (frequently confirmed during the following night by Ultra's rendering of Panzer Army's evening report) sometimes had immense tactical value, it was without strategic significance.

On the other hand, the regular Ultra reports of supply shortages, particularly of petrol, opened up strategic vistas by making it clear that, once his line was breached, Rommel would not be able to withdraw more than a fraction of his army nor retain enough freedom of movement to regroup and fight again until he was many hundreds of perilous miles nearer his base at Tripoli. This was already plain long before the battle began on 23 October, and was repeatedly confirmed right up to the fall of Tripoli in January 1943.

Montgomery has often been criticised for the sluggishness of his pursuit, but these repeated Ultra reports seem to justify far sharper condemnation than he has yet received. A single illustration must suffice. Towards the end of November he believed, says Montgomery in *From Alamein to the Sangro*,[36] that Rommel (then briefly resting behind the Agheila defences) had a hundred tanks and plenty of anti-tank guns. To write this was to suppress the clearest evidence to the contrary; Ultra was, of course, still secret when he published his book, but he had no business to contradict it so blatantly. It had shown that the Afrika Korps was down to eleven tanks on 9 November, and by 26 November Montgomery knew that it had only managed to creep back to 35 (or 43; Rommel and his Chief Quartermaster gave different figures) a fortnight later; further, that in mid-November there had been constant complaints from Panzer Army about shortages of anti-tank guns and ammunition, backed up by a long appreciation of the performance of German anti-tank guns against Sherman tanks, which were said to fight at such long ranges that no German weapon could engage them effectively. All this Montgomery knew before the end of November.[37] What more encouragement did he need to persuade him that he could safely take a few risks in order to attempt encirclement and annihilation, in spite of his own supply problems and the defensive strength of the Agheila position?

Here, then, is a remarkable case of intelligence *not* affecting strategy. Suppose Montgomery to have done as Ultra implicitly suggested and wiped out Panzer Army at Agheila in late November instead of letting it escape in mid-December. He could then have gone straight on to Tripoli practically unopposed. He would probably have been too late to help the TORCH expedition into Tunis at once (Eisenhower called a halt at Christmas) but 8 Army's pressure on von Arnim's flank would certainly have forced him to surrender earlier than May 1943. Would there then have been an earlier invasion of Italy? The Chiefs of Staff had been considering the possibility in October. Would this have brought the Italian surrender forward? What would have been the effect on Mediterranean strategy? On OVERLORD? On the Russians? Speculation must stop before we make the same mistake as John Grigg and suppose that a 1943 OVERLORD could have succeeded.[38] Sobriety will return if we remember that 8 Army only deserved its reputation as a sharp instrument of war *after* the experience it gained in fighting its way to Tripoli, that the Americans learned a lot, and very fast indeed, from Kasserine in February 1943, and that there would have been 200,000 more Germans in arms on D-Day if the early capture of Tunis had prevented Hitler from stupidly reinforcing it. Nevertheless, the potential strategic consequences of the disregard of intelligence in November and December 1942 may have been very great indeed, for it is arguable that a quicker capture of Tunis might have altered the course of the war, and certain that Montgomery knew how anxiously London and Washington were awaiting final victory in Africa because without it they could not proceed with plans for the invasion of Europe.

If this was perhaps an intelligence opportunity missed, another and greater was being thankfully taken at the same time. The renewed breaking of the Atlantic U-Boat key in December 1942,[39] in combination with better radar, long-range aircraft, escort carriers and Support Groups, had by the following May ended the risk that Great Britain might be isolated and starved into submission, because it compelled Dönitz to suspend attacks on convoys from the US and Canada. This is now so well known that it needs no further emphasis from me; its strategic consequences can scarcely be measured.

The Italian campaign offers plenty of examples of the increasingly fruitful partnership between Intelligence and Operations and of the application of Intelligence to strategy. When in November 1943 Hitler accepted Kesselring's advice to contest every yard of Italy, rather than Rommel's to retire to a mountain line in the north, he played into the hands of the Allies, who had committed themselves to a Mediterranean strategy provisionally by HUSKY in July and definitely by AVALANCHE in September. Every man, tank and gun he sent to Italy meant one less to defend *Festung Europa* against attack from east or west. *Mutatis mutandis*, the same was of course true in reverse. Each side wanted to hold as many as possible of the other's divisions in Italy with the minimum expenditure of its own effort. 'Who is containing whom?' became the question both strove to answer. Allied Intelligence, resting on a firm Ultra foundation, was able to keep an almost daily check on the movements of German troops and equipment into and out of Italy and knew that for almost the whole of the next eighteen months it had the better of the bargain. How far that knowledge was responsible for converting the American command from its earlier scepticism to a more whole-hearted support of the Italian campaign does not appear, but regular confirmation that the agreed strategy was having the desired effect can only have carried considerable weight. The fact that Allied casualties in Italy were only three-fifths of German reflects the success of that strategy.[40]

By December, stalemate had developed along the Winter Line and the Anzio operation was laid on in the hope of breaking the deadlock. Whether or not the landing force could or should have seized the Alban Hills and pushed on to Rome at once will always be a matter of controversy. Ultra does not settle the controversy, but a study of the signals makes it clear that blame – if blame there be – was not confined to Lucas, the corps commander, but was shared by his superiors, who knew at all relevant times that far greater surprise had been secured than at Salerno and that for a few hours the road to Rome was quite undefended. If an opportunity was missed, it was not missed only by the man on the spot.[41]

FISCHFANG, Kesselring's last desperate effort to overrun the Anzio bridgehead, almost succeeded in February 1944. That it failed can in part be attributed to Allied foreknowledge of his battle plan and of the strength of his attack forces.[42] The failure certainly marked a turning-point in the Italian campaign and, in the opinion of Siegfried Westphal, Kesselring's Chief of Staff, also a turning-point in the war itself, because it revealed an irreversible decline in the standard of training of the German infantry[43] (he should have excepted the parachute divisions and the SS Panzergrenadiers). Within a few days of the failure of FISCH-FANG, Kesselring composed a lengthy appreciation of the situation in Italy,[44] and this too was read by Ultra intelligence. It showed that he intended to press on with the construction of a fortified line south of Rome and that he hoped, in spite of the dangers threatening Germany from east and west, that he might be sent new divisions to defend it. This is one of the rare occasions when we do not have to surmise the strategic consequences of a piece of intelligence but have direct evidence of it. Alan Brooke, the British CIGS, noted the value of the Ultra signal and used it to strengthen his argument that the active prosecution of the war in Italy was the best way to divert German troops away from Russia and the west. Three months later he used the decrypting of Hitler's order for new defences north of Rome in the same way, calling it 'the most marvellous information' because it showed conclusively that, as he had always maintained, the Germans were not going to retreat in Italy except under compulsion and were therefore willing victims of the strategy of using pressure in Italy to relieve OVERLORD and the Russian front.[45] It followed, of course, that the pressure had to be maintained, and that it would be better to retain in Italy and use for this purpose the divisions already earmarked for ANVIL. But by this time it was far too late for one piece of intelligence to outweigh the massive political and even emotional commitments to the Riviera operation which had accumulated meanwhile. ANVIL went ahead on 15 August, but within 24 hours Ultra showed[46] that Hitler had no intention of defending southern France seriously and that the mere threat of ANVIL would have had as much strategic effect in the west as the landing itself, while the troops used for it could instead have exerted far more formidable pressure in Italy.

Until the late summer of 1944 , Ultra – which had by now become the Allies' major source of intelligence, far outweighing any other in importance – played an equally prominent part in the west. We cannot properly count the success of the FORTITUDE deception plan to its credit, but we certainly should count the continuous revelation of that success and the proof that the German delusion of a future landing in the Pas de Calais was lasting unexpectedly long.[47] No other source could have shown so convincingly that the bait had been swallowed and the enemy completely fooled; the certainty that even in late July the defence was still being disposed to meet a direct attack on Paris as well as to rope off the bridgehead lay (in company with a number of others things !) behind Montgomery's confidence in persisting with the pressure round Caen in order to keep the western end of the German line weaker than the eastern.

There are several occasions in the first weeks after D-Day when a strategic, as opposed to a merely tactical, influence of intelligence can be sensed if not proven. The destruction from the air of the headquarters of *Panzergruppe* West on 10 June was inspired by Ultra's pinpoint location. The resultant paralysis of the counter-attack command. coming on top of Hitler's delay in releasing the Panzer divisions, had strategic consequences which must be purely speculative but were potentially vast. Again, there can be little doubt that the advance warning of the arrival of 1 SS Panzer Division from Belgium and of II SS Panzer Corps from Russia contributed to the success of EPSOM at the end of June.[48]

Between these two events came the Villers-Bocage operation, and it is instructive to compare three recent accounts, especially what they have to say about 2 Panzer Division, for this is another occasion on which intelligence might perhaps have had a far-reaching effect on strategy. Although in his second volume Nigel Hamilton has become quite critical of his hero, Montgomery, he passes over Villers-Bocage lightly, remarking only that 2 Panzer turned 7 Armoured Division back 'with consequences which were to affect the whole fabric of the Normandy operation'.[49] Max Hastings does little but record the five-minute action in which five Tiger tanks destroyed 7 Armoured's spearhead, and scarcely mentions 2 Panzer at all.[50] Carlo d'Este, fiercely critical of Montgomery and of 7 Armoured's failure to press home the advantage it had gained despite the Tigers, remorselessly insists that the failure to exploit the momentary gap in the German line was 'one of the costliest Allied mistakes in the liberation of France ... the one great opportunity to break open and exploit Rommel's still unsettled defences round Caen',[51] and stresses the part played by 2 Panzer in holding on to what the Tiger tanks had suddenly gained. None of them, however, takes the point I had already made myself – that twice (once in a letter to Brooke at the time, and again in *From Normandy to the Baltic*), Montgomery ascribed the failure of the Villers-Bocage operation to the fact that 2 Panzer 'suddenly appeared' on the night of 13–14 June.[52] This was disingenuous. Ultra had told him 24 full hours earlier that 2 Panzer was on its way to the danger area. Tactics and strategy merge mistily on occasions like this, and the implied criticism must not be pushed too far; there were certainly many urgent considerations apart from intelligence in the minds of Erskine and Bucknall (respectively divisional and corps commander) – Ultra not among them, of course, for Ultra was not distributed below Army HQ – as well as in the minds of Dempsey at 2nd Army and Montgomery, both of whom did receive it. Apart from the airy speculation that if the German line had indeed been broken then, the advance to the Seine and beyond might have started in July not September (with unpredictable consequences) the main interest of the affair is as an illustration of the difficulty of assessing the impact, both actual and ideal/potential, of an important piece of intelligence on the course of the campaign.

The last example of the strategic effect of intelligence in the west is also the best and the best-known: the story of Bradley's foreknowledge in late July first that the German divisions ranged against COBRA were so weak and exhausted that a breakthrough was likely at last and, a few days later, that Hitler planned a harebrained attack westwards toward Avranches, thus enabling Bradley to turn the COBRA breakthrough into an encirclement and eventually into the Falaise pocket with its gigantic toll of destruction.[53] Intelligence about the enemy cannot, of course, settle the debate whether all this was simply the accelerated fulfilment of Montgomery's original plan or whether it was an inspired bit of improvisation, adapting tactics to sudden circumstances

(Hamilton and d'Este contradict each other, each attesting his account with persuasive contemporary evidence!). But intelligence did, at all stages between 20 July and mid-August, enable the maximum advantage to be taken of German errors, thus helping to turn victory into rout. During the next few days, in consequence, the outline of a new strategy showed itself, bringing with it just a chance that the war might end in 1944. But the chance – if indeed it ever existed – was not taken, and about this time the story of the relationship between intelligence and operations bifurcates, ushering in my third period.

In the west, unhappily the relationship suddenly disintegrated, and by a double misfortune this happened just at the moment when, after the swift advance from the Seine to the West Wall, serious dissension entered the Allied High Command for the first and only time. The reason is still far from plain. Call it euphoria (a cover-all term of conveniently vague meaning), call it exhaustion after a long war, call it the reaction which always comes when a period of extreme tension has ended happily, or call it a mixture of all three; none satisfactorily explains why at all levels a hasty conviction that the rout of Army Group B spelled the collapse of Germany should have suddenly replaced the cooler and more cautious analyses of the past. Generals ceased to listen as before – both Montgomery and Eisenhower overlooked the necessity to control the Scheldt estuary if the capture of Antwerp was to be of any value, although both Hitler and Admiral Ramsay pointed out their mistake. Arnhem was a bridge too far perhaps only because the tanks half-hidden under trees there were dismissed as figments of a panicky imagination instead of being linked with Ultra reports of II SS Corps. Intelligence officers persistently overlooked signs of the coming Ardennes offensive.[54] All this represents a sad conclusion to two full years of progressively more profitable cooperation between intelligence and operations; casualties resulted which could have been avoided, and the war was prolonged though its outcome was not affected.

Perhaps because it was so much weaker, after giving blood transfusions to the west for both OVERLORD and ANVIL, in relation to its task than 21 Army Group in Normandy, the Allied Command in Italy seems completely to have escaped infection with the bug of euphoria. It could not be tempted to believe, like so many in the west, that all was over bar the shouting: the evidence to the contrary was a bitter daily experience. Geography and past events had by now settled the strategy of the Italian campaign for good, and no amount of intelligence could have altered it appreciably. But Ultra continued to show that the agreed strategy – that initiated for DIADEM in May by Harding, Alexander's Chief of Staff, who planned to use the Liri valley as a killing ground – was still having the desired effect of attracting divisions from other theatres to replace those weakened by constant fighting. At a lower but extremely valuable level it was an encouragement to Alexander and his staff to know from Ultra that the hurried move of 8 Army back across the Apennines to the Adriatic flank for OLIVE in August had not been detected by the enemy, or that von Vietinghoff, like his predecessor as OB Sudwest, Kesselring, could be tricked by Allied deception measures into moving 29 and 90 Panzer Grenadier Divisions away from the projected route of the Allies' final advance[55] (the last was particularly welcome in country as difficult to fight over as river-strewn Lombardy was proving to be). When von Vietinghoff explained on 14 April 1945, in one of the longest and most revealing memoranda ever intercepted,[56] that the exhaustion of his forces would compel him to abandon Hitler's preferred 'Stand Fast' strategy and retire to the Ticino, it was already too late to save his armies. They had been ground almost to powder by the Kesselring/Hitler policy of peninsular defence.

Alexander and Airey had always been more sceptical about the rumoured last Nazi bastion in the Alps than Eisenhower and Strong[57] (who were determined not to be caught napping a second time, as they had been in the Ardennes), although the Ultra evidence for it was circumstantial and full of persuasive implications, and although it would have affected them much more closely because it would have threatened their left flank if the plan to forestall the Russians in Vienna had ever been put into effect. One of the reasons why the bastion did not exist was that Alexander's (by this time Mark Clark's) mixed force had destroyed its only possible garrison.

***

Forty years on. it is hard to understand how sensible and experienced men could ever have believed that area bombing could win the war by itself, or have supposed that London was the only city which could 'take it'. Unfortunately, Ultra was unable to offer much guidance on this supremely important strategic subject. Until late in 1944, only a few bomb-damage reports were sent by radio; the rest therefore remained inaccessible to Ultra, along with almost everything bearing on the state of morale in the Reich. Such scraps as did come to hand could in most cases be read, by the many minds already predisposed to treat bombing theory as an article of faith, as confirmation (so far as they went) that the theory was sound. The Ultra evidence for STRANGLE, the interdiction policy in Italy in the summer of 1944, is a case in point. It prominently reported bomb-damage to railway tracks and the cutting of main supply routes, but it was also reassuringly confident that communications could be quickly restored – as, in fact, they usually were. Thus, both positively (as here) and negatively (by its absence, i.e. where there was no Ultra because the relevant reports had gone by telephone or teleprinter) Ultra could still be misleading if taken unreflectingly and at face value alone – as the Paulus report had shown long ago. Ultra always told the truth, but not always the whole truth. This was particularly regrettable in the case of air raid damage assessment and estimates of the effectiveness of repair and recovery measures. Had Ultra had more to say on the matter, it might have proved the only solvent powerful enough to break down the stubborn preconceptions of the 'bomber barons'; many lives and much effort would then have been spared to serve the Allied cause in more profitable ways, and there might have been a welcome change in strategy before Dresden. No other source could provide convincing evidence. The fact that Ultra could not do so either is in retrospect both a sufficient explanation why bombing seemed at the time a satisfactory means of cutting communications and destroying morale, and also at least some help towards understanding what would otherwise seem a deplorable strategic aberration.[58]

***

Are there conclusions to be drawn and lessons to be learned? Two or three stand out prominently. They are not pleasant, and they suggest that in some ways 1939–45 is already almost as remote as the Peninsular War.

In 1940 Great Britain was as unprepared in intelligence matters as it was to meet the *Wehrmacht* in the field, save for the few who created Ultra and organised its dissemination. The Anglo-American alliance eventually quite outstripped the enemy in intelligence, though perhaps never on the battlefield when the meeting was on equal terms. But it was two or three years before intelligence was properly understood, and even later on it was by no means always properly applied to operations. Such slowness to learn can never be safely repeated; defeat would come too soon – as, indeed, it might well have done in World War II had not

Hitler so often blighted his own prospects. Speed would have to increase in another respect too. Electronics, codes and computers have made secret communications enormously faster and more complex than they were forty years ago. Bletchley was justifiably pleased when it could occasionally get out a signal to commands abroad in a couple of hours from German time of origin. This would not do now – an ICBM is much quicker from ignition to impact, and the Warsaw Pact tanks are massed on the West German border. Since the V2 rockets of 1944 and the atom bombs of 1945, the development of missiles has meant that more lethal loads than were dreamed of then can now be delivered more quickly and over far greater distances than before. So much is platitude. But the effect of all this on the collection and use of intelligence has attracted far less attention, and it needs urgent thought and thorough examination. Between the beginning of this century and 1945, the role of intelligence in war increased, until from 1942 onwards intelligence exercised an influence it had never known before. It would seem that the evolution of new weapons may now have suddenly reversed this trend and restored the more primitive situation where brute force gives victory to the side that gets its blow in first, no matter how intellectually inventive the opposition.[59] Hitler very nearly benefited from this sort of situation in 1940; there may be no denying the benefit to a future aggressor unless entirely new intelligence procedures are devised in advance. The passion with which Gordon Welchman composed the second half of his *Hut Six Story* shows the conviction of one old Bletchley hand with wide knowledge of modern American intelligence that already in 1982 communications were too slow in an emergency.

But can satisfactory new intelligence procedures be devised? The contraction of the time-interval before the 'first strike' means that intelligence could in future only play a useful part if it were available before hostilities began, that is to say while peace still formally prevailed. This reopens in a new form the question discussed earlier – the difference between intelligence in war and in peace. The example of the Egyptians surprising the Israelis at the beginning of the Yom Kippur War in 1973 suggests that, even if the danger of complaisantly 'slanted' intelligence be overcome, the intending aggressor holds nearly all the cards and even the best intelligence can afford little protection against him.[60]

To consider the transmission of single urgent operational items is also to explore the frontier between tactics and strategy and to inquire for which intelligence was and is the more vital. There may be an inter-service distinction to be drawn here. An order for the *Bismarck* to sail or for a U-Boat pack to shift into the path of an Atlantic convoy was much more revealing of strategy than the move of even several Panzer divisions (advance warning of Alam Halfa gave away no strategy, the assembly of five Panzer divisions for the Mortain offensive did so only marginally and then only because of the extraordinary circumstances). Strategic inference must usually depend on the accumulation and collation of many items over a period of time. If in the future there will be too little time, then Intelligence will not be able to influence strategy at all.

British generals have often been justly accused of fighting the last war while they learn how to fight the one in which they are engaged. In some respects past experience may nevertheless be relevant to present need. When preparing his book *Overlord,* Max Hastings interviewed an officer who, having fought in Normandy, subsequently became a war correspondent and was sent to Vietnam. There he saw American infantrymen repeating the mistakes he himself had learned to avoid in 1944.[61] Has the British army been any better at passing on the fruits of experience? It would appear that things are still worse in the intelligence field. The spectacle, during the Falklands war, of war correspondents, the serving officers who briefed them, and an MP all gratuitously giving away valuable information to the enemy, was a bitter shock to those who learned by experience how and why not to do these things 40 years ago. As already noted, however, prevailing currents of opinion are flowing so strongly in the opposite direction that no change in the attitude of civilians can be expected. But has the continuity of intelligence training in the British armed forces been broken once more, as it was between 1919 and 1939? If so, the state of unpreparedness is alarming and calls for instant remedy. Otherwise, next time – but let us hope that there will be no next time – the end will come so fast that the generals will not even be able to fight the last war!

NOTES

1. The battle of Alam Halfa (31 August 1942) is an illustration of this, though somewhat extreme. Montgomery made troop dispositions which intelligence subsequently proved to be ideal – but he made them 48 hours before he received the intelligence. See p. 80 above.
2. For instance, Roy Godson (ed.), *Intelligence Requirements for the 1980s: Elements of Intelligence* (1979).
3. Some of them present or former members of the American intelligence staff, it should be noted. See the list in *Elements,* 89–91.

4. *Elements,* 23.
5. Major-General Strong's lame attempt *(Intelligence at the Top,* pp. 162–4) to show that he had warned Eisenhower (whose Chief Intelligence Officer he was) of the possibility of a German attack in the Ardennes in December 1944 is an oblique confirmation of this.
6. See for instance Ehrman: *Grand Strategy,* v. 15–19.
7. See p. 73 above.
8. As in *Elements,* 23 and above.
9. Security is specifically mentioned only on pp. 39–40 of *Elements,* and is not included in the definition. Perhaps readers were intended to take it for granted; but its supreme importance calls for far greater emphasis than this.
10. M. R. D. Foot, *SOE,* 130–4.
11. Conversely, it should not be forgotten that Enigma could probably never have been broken had the Germans observed their own security rules. See Gordon Welchman, *The Hut 6 Story, passim.*
12. Christopher Andrew in *The Missing Dimension,* pp. 46–7.
13. For example: no attack on an Axis supply ship crossing the Mediterranean was permitted unless and until the Ultra signal announcing its sailing and route had been confirmed by air reconnaissance. A sprinkling of rebukes for real or apparent breaches of this rule in the Ultra files shows that the rule was strictly enforced.
14. And even of those who did not officially know them: the newspaper proprietor, Lord Camrose, discovered the Ultra secret in 1941, but did not reveal it. See Martin Gilbert, *Winston S. Churchill,* vi, 1200–1.
15. Ultra discovered the German plan of attack on Crete in May 1941 well in advance and in considerable detail. Full advantage could not be taken of this foreknowledge because the range of aircraft in 1941 was too short to permit fighter cover for the island from even the nearest Egyptian bases and because neither troops nor tanks nor anti-aircraft guns could be spared to reinforce it.
16. *Elements,* 25–6.
17. According to reports in the British and American press, February 1985.
18. See p. 85 above.
19. *The Times,* 8 February 1985.
20. F. H. Hinsley, etc., *British Intelligence in the Second World War* (henceforth cited as *BI),* ii, 338–9, 382–3; D. Kahn, *The Codebreakers,* pp. 473–6.
21. P. H. Vigor, *Soviet Blitzkrieg Theory,* p. 15.
22. J. Rohwer/E. Jaeckel, *Die Funkaufklaerung und ihre Rolle im zweiten Weltkrieg,* p. 335.
23. Brian Gardner, *Allenby,* pp. 129, 154.
24. P. Beesly, *Room 40,* p. 162. Information contained in a decrypt which showed the course of the German fleet as it retired, battered, to its home port was never passed to Jellicoe, the British admiral.
25. *BI,* i, 176–82.
26. *BI,* i, 315–28, R. V. Jones, *Most Secret War,* pp. 92–106, 120–78.
27. OL 302. Successive series of Ultra signals sent to commands in the field and quoted here were prefixed OL, MK, MKA, QT, VL, KV, XL, BT, KO. All are in the Public Record Office, Kew, in File DEFE 3.
28. OL 211, *BI,* i, 396–7, Halder, *Kriegstagebuch,* ii, 377–8, 388.

29. OLs 1835 (Duisburg), 819, 976, 982, 1004, 1078, 1105, 1204, 1348, 1568, 1669, 1700, 1805, 1904. This and all other references to intelligence in the Mediterranean will be fully discussed in my forthcoming book, *Ultra and Mediterranean Strategy.*

30. Martin Gilbert, *Winston S. Churchill,* vi, 1130.

31. MKs 801, 1551, 1555, 1582, 1605, 1639 all contained indirect hints which were overlooked in Cairo. The convoys referred to in the last few signals in fact carried the 54 tanks which won Rommel his victory.

32. PRO WO 208/3575, p. 3.

33. See Correlli Barnett, *The Desert Generals* (2nd edn) and Nigel Hamilton, *Monty, The Making of a General.*

34. MKAs 2094, 2095, 2096.

35. MKAs 2282, 2623, 2624, QTs 585, 604, 607, 733, 758.

36. *From Alamein to the Sangro,* p. 30.

37. QTs 5794, 6839, 7012 are dated 9, 24 and 26 November respectively.

38. John Grigg, *1943, the Victory that Never Was.*

39. *BI,* ii, 549–72, P. Beesly, *Very Special Intelligence,* pp. 154–85.

40. E. F. Fisher, *Cassino to the Alps*, p. 545.

41. VLs 3552, 3987, 4302, 4331, 4464, 4476, 4506, 5383.

42. VLs 5398, 5449, 5594, 6352.

43. C. J. C. Molony, *The Mediterranean and Middle East,* v, 762; *Oberkommando der Wehrmacht, Kriegstagebuch,* ed. Schramm, iv, 167, S. Westphal, *Erinnerungen,* pp. 251–3, A. Kesselring, *Memoirs*, p. 198.

44. VL 8072.

45. KV 9843, A. Bryant. *Triumph in the West,* p. 224, D. Fraser, *Alanbrooke,* pp. 430–1, J. Ehrman, *Grand Strategy,* v, 352–8.

46. XLs 6753, 6919.

47. R. F. Bennett, *Ultra in the West,* pp. 51–3, 107.

48. Bennett, pp. 74, 83–7.

49. N. Hamilton, *Monty, Master of the Battlefield*, p. 654.

50. Max Hastings, *Overlord,* pp. 129–37, 143, 170.

51. Carlo d'Este, *Decision in Normandy,* p. 198.

52. Bennett, p. 80, Montgomery, *Normandy to the Baltic,* p. 221; KV 7707, despatched at 1701 hours on 12 June.

53. Bennett, pp. 103–5, 112–20.

54. Bennett, pp. 140–50.

55. Alexander, *Despatch (London Gazette,* 12 June 1950) 2959; BTs 8241, 9014, 9094, 9488, 9543, 9676, 9742, 9974.

56. KOs 496, 525.

57. Airey and Strong were the respective Chief Intelligence Officers.

58. For further discussion of Bomber Command and Intelligence, now see my *Behind the Battle*, pp. 133–67.

59. Intelligence provides no sufficient warning of the Russian attack in General Sir John Hackett's *The Third World War* (Sphere edn 1979, pp. 123–6, 134–5).

60. M. I. Handel, *Perception, Deception and Surprise: the Case of the Yom Kippur War.*

61. Hastings, p. 316.

5

Intelligence and Strategy: Some Observations on the War in the Mediterranean 1941–45

Can a correlation be established between the effectiveness of an army's performance and the quality of the intelligence supplied to its commander? It would seem obvious that there can (St. Thomas Aquinas might have begun like this, could he have been persuaded to extend his discussion of the just war[1] to include intelligence as well as deception), for otherwise an ignorant general is as good as a well informed one. But, following the method of the *Summa Theologica*, St. Thomas would at once have objected that such a correlation would degrade strategy into mere reaction to known enemy intentions and preclude the seizing of the initiative, which is absurd. The truth, as so often, lies somewhere in the middle. There is such a correlation, but it can never be very close. The most prominent of several reasons for this is the need to leave room in the theory for considerations of policy and resources, space and time. To say this is not blindly to accept Clausewitz's disparagement: 'Most Intelligence is false', so that 'for lack of objective knowledge one has to trust to talent or to luck'[2] – a view which was no doubt scarcely an exaggeration in his time but one which Sigint has substantially discredited today – but rather to emphasise anew his best-known dictum of all: 'War is the continuation of policy by other means'. The policy of a state, or the policy mutually agreed between a state and its allies, will specify objectives to be sought. The presence or absence of the means to achieve them will be the first qualification, the first guideline to action; intelligence about the enemy comes next, but it can seldom or never dictate the objective. The single greatest decision of the Second World War – at any rate apart from the dropping of the atom bombs on Japan – was the 'Germany first' decision taken by Allied agreement at

93

the Washington conference in December 1941, and that owed nothing to intelligence. The same holds good for TORCH, the invasion of North Africa, which was the British Gymnast plan of the previous year turned through 180° to meet the new circumstances of the American alliance, and for the later invasions of Italy and France. Not even the choice of particular landing beaches in Sicily, at Salerno or in Normandy derived from knowledge of enemy locations, which could and did change long after plans for HUSKY, AVALANCHE and OVERLORD were firmly settled. It might even be argued that the Baytown landing in the toe of Italy in September 1943 was conducted – though perhaps not planned – quite contrary to the available intelligence, for Ultra[3] had shown that all the major German troop formations had been withdrawn from the southern tip well before 8 Army's bombardment opened.[4]

There is another major obstacle to measuring the correlation between an army's effectiveness and the intelligence available to its commander. Clausewitz expressed it succinctly when he wrote that in battle 'the light of reason is refracted in a manner quite different from that which is normal in academic speculation'.[5] Writing in his study, perhaps long after the events he is describing, and possessing information which, however full, will almost always lack any record of the precise reason why a commander took a particular decision, the historian may miss the mark at which he aimed and fall unwitting victim to the hindsight he sought to avoid. The difference between the atmosphere of the study and the battlefield ensures that military history will sometimes err at critical moments and that any general principles it enunciates, including that of the relationship between Intelligence and action, must be regarded with caution. General principles distil only with reluctance from the mass of particulars in the Mediterranean theatre between 1942 and 1945 (with which alone this study is concerned); but hindsight, the perpetual foe of the historian, becomes an even greater menace than usual if it forbids all deductions from the past for the benefit of the future. In spite of the tremendous technological changes which the last 40 years have brought, the history of the Mediterranean theatre of war strongly suggests that there are still some lessons to be learned from it.

I

The story of British aid to Greece in the spring of 1941 strikingly demonstrates the primacy of policy over military intelligence. Chamberlain had pledged support for Greece in 1939; discussion about the form it should take accelerated in January 1941, when Ultra confirmed the existence of a Nazi threat to the Balkans, and became urgent with the formal Greek request for military assistance on 8 February. Meanwhile, in December and January O'Connor had driven the Italians out of Cyrenaica. If most of the troops which had gained this victory were now sent to Greece, would Cyrenaica be at once reconquered for the Axis by Rommel's embryonic Afrika Korps, which had landed at Tripoli on 14 February? The dilemma was serious and compromise impossible. In the circumstances of the time it was probably right to accept the risk of losing Cyrenaica for the sake of the moral gesture of aiding the threatened victim of aggression. But there is no evidence that the issue was ever considered in this seemingly obvious way. An extraordinary feature of the discussions which culminated in the landing of British troops in Greece on 7 March (they were driven out again at the end of April) was the complete disregard of military considerations, in particular the quite unfounded belief on the part of Wavell, the Commander-in-Chief, Middle East, that the flimsy remaining garrison would suffice to protect Cyrenaica. There was just enough intelligence (including a little Ultra; direct signalling to Cairo began in March) to alert him to the risks in both the Balkans and Cyrenaica, but he and Eden disregarded them in favour of the moral and political gesture even after Churchill had made it plain that his earlier ardour had cooled and that they were to decide in the light of the evidence they could assemble in Athens and Cairo. Military disaster on both fronts was far more the result of their bad judgement than of inadequate intelligence.

Almost immediately there followed an opposite but even more striking example of the correlation between Intelligence and Operations which particular circumstances can provoke. Because the assault on Crete was under the control of Fliegerkorps XI, which used one of the German Air Force Enigma keys (army Enigma was still baffling the cryptanalysts), Ultra revealed the whole German plan of operations two or three weeks before the first parachutists were dropped over Maleme airfield on 20 May. The reason why forewarned did not turn out to be forearmed was therefore not lack of intelligence. The garrison of Crete consisted of weary refugees from Greece. Wavell sent them no tanks (which could have wiped out the parachutists), their obsolete aircraft were either shot down or withdrawn from a combat they were bound to lose, and although more modern fighters were based in Egypt they lacked the range to operate over Crete. The battle was lost because the assailants could keep pouring in reinforcements to the airfield they managed to capture against stiff resistance but the defenders were unavoidably left to their own devices.

Crete is a peculiar case in other ways too. A few tanks and some modern aircraft might have given victory to the defence, and intelligence clearly indicated where they could best be used. But later experience was to show that the retention of Crete would have been a strategic misadventure, because the island would have claimed more men and equipment to defend it than could be spared from the greater task in Libya. The nearly victorious defence of Crete so shook the German command, which had made much of the novel airborne method of attack in 1940, that its parachute divisions became no more than élite infantry, and Malta – a far greater prize than Crete – was never assaulted from the air. Policy and intelligence both pointed to the wrong objective; sheer chance delivered it to the British command unsought.

Intelligence and strategy began to come together for the first time in the summer and autumn of 1941. Rommel and Auchinleck, the two ground commanders in Libya, were both anxious to strike first, but each was beset by almost insoluble problems of supply. Helped by Ultra and the unexpected diversion of a large part of the Luftwaffe to the Russian front, the RAF quickly regained an ascendancy it seemed to have lost for good over Greece and Crete. For the next few months, British naval and air power made the short Axis supply route across the Mediterranean so hazardous that it had few advantages over the far longer route round the Cape of Good Hope which the British were compelled to use. Because of this Rommel had to put off his offensive so long that Auchinleck managed to strike the first blow in mid-November although (to Churchill's fury) he had insisted on waiting until he had accumulated what he regarded as sufficient strength. Incompetence on the battlefield by his subordinates unfortunately let him down, and the early success of CRUSADER in December had turned into disillusion and defeat by February 1942. But when in the previous October the Admiralty took the risk of basing Force K (two six-inch gun cruisers and two destroyers) on Malta to prey on enemy shipping, the Axis loss rate (already onefifth of all cargoes loaded in Italy and Greece) rose to such heights that Hitler yielded to the arguments of Raeder (Commander-in-Chief of the German Navy) and Rommel, and reinforced the Mediterranean until a third of all operational U-boats were stationed there;[6] in the short term the pressure on Auchinleck was relieved and some respite even brought to the Battle of the Atlantic.

Despite these handicaps, in January 1942 Rommel recovered in a few days most of what it had taken CRUSADER six gruelling weeks to conquer, the U-Boats made the Mediterranean too dangerous for Force K, and Axis supply traffic flowed freely again. The tide was not to turn once more until the late summer. The autumn of 1941 had witnessed the first impact of intelligence on strategy in the Mediterranean theatre, but it had not affected the land campaign (Rommel's advance in January was largely attributable to the military intelligence staff's error in underestimating the number of his tanks) and it lasted only a few months. For the results which had been achieved then were made possible only by the Royal Navy's and the RAF's successful exploitation of the thousand or more Ultra signals conveying advance information about Axis shipping movements which were transmitted between June and October and by the knowledge, derived from the same source, that their efforts were causing signs of strain and even of panic to appear in the language used by the Axis supply staffs. Three out of four large liners were sunk on the only two crossings of the Mediterranean they made in August and September, for instance, and a cargo of petrol was sent to the bottom.[7] Ironically, this was just after Hitler had ordered special protection for convoys because of rising losses at sea, but it was not long before OKH was making a similar demand in respect of artillery shipments.[8] Again, all seven ships in the *Duisburg* convoy were sunk on 9 November,[9] to the Italians' consternation. Examples could be multiplied, but more valuable than any of them was the growing body of Sigint evidence about the broad logistical consequences of so many sinkings; it was possible, for instance, to calculate that the Luftwaffe's reserves of aircraft fuel in Libya had sunk from 4,000 tons in May 1941 to 3,000 in June, 1,400 in July and only 400 – a mere tenth of what they had been five months earlier – in September, and on the basis of known figures of daily consumption during the quiet summer months to make an informed estimate of the length of time petrol supplies would last when active operations began again.

As more Enigma keys (notably two used by the army, upon the inner workings of which the decrypts had till now been silent) were broken during the spring and summer of 1942, moreover, it gradually became possible to maintain regular statistics of the petrol, ammunition, tanks and rations Rommel could dispose of at the front, in stock at the main depot outside Tripoli (the only deep-water port between Alexandria and Tunis) several hundred miles to the rear, and at various intermediate points along the Via Balbia which connected them. This was an immense strategic advance; for the first time Ultra was really enabling us to 'look at the cards in the enemy's hand' and to estimate with some accuracy whether Rommel possessed the resources to carry through any large-scale operation he might propose (the absence of any way of doing this had caused several important decrypts to be misinterpreted the previous year) or whether, on the contrary, his operations could be disrupted and his plans stultified by intensifying the air and sea attacks on his supply line.

This new and happier state of affairs – which prevailed henceforth, with only minor fluctuations, throughout the war in the Mediterranean – was well illustrated during the two decisive battles of early autumn 1942. Since this part of the story is already well known in outline, and since the pattern of events repeats that sketched earlier, only a few of the outstanding details need to be recalled here.

Without petrol, aircraft would be grounded and tanks immobilised; oil tankers at sea were therefore the prime targets. An alarmist Panzer Army Africa appreciation of 18 August[10] revealed that at the current rate of consumption Rommel's petrol stocks would be exhausted by the 26th, the date Ultra showed that he had just set for the opening of his new offensive.[11] Thus the Commanders-in-Chief of the three services (Alexander, Harwood and Tedder) and the new commander of 8 Army, Montgomery, were just as well informed as the staff at OKW to which Rommel had addressed his plans and disclosed the meagreness of his resources, knew how thin was the thread by which Rommel's chances of success hung, and could calculate with some accuracy how many tankers it would be necessary to sink in order to bring his offensive to a standstill. Decrypts of the shipping programme for the next ten days and of the routes and sailing times of a number of individual vessels led to the sinking of at least ten tankers in the few days immediately before the Afrika Korps ran out of petrol under the Alam Halfa ridge on 1 September and was bombed so heavily that it had to retreat; it was even learned that the enforced halt was being attributed directly to the loss of two specified ships, the *San Andrea* and the *Abruzzi*.[12] The chaos into which the German supply system was falling became even more evident shortly before Alamein; by the third week in October Panzer Army could not even be described as living from hand to mouth for its petrol, so erratic and so subject to sudden delays had deliveries become. The devastating consequences of British knowledge of the complete tanker programme for 21–29 October (Alamein began on the 23rd)[13] were revealed almost at once in shortages[14] and confirmed after the war in Rommel's cry as three tankers went down in quick succession 'Now we are really up against it'.[15] The conclusion is plain: Montgomery and his fellow commanders went into battle confident that the enemy's resources were severely limited and that there could be no doubt which side could stand 'hard pounding' (in Wellington's famous phrase) the longer. Here at last the correlation between intelligence and operations was very close.

If Panzer Army Africa could be reduced so near to impotence by attacks on its supply routes why, it might be asked, were the attacks not stepped up enough to starve it to death altogether? It is difficult to give a wholly satisfactory answer. It is clear that Panzer Army was twice (in the autumns of 1941 and 1942) brought close to the point of extinction, yet each time it survived. One reason is that its commander's strongest suits were improvisation with slender means and boldness in taking risks; against the sluggish British command in 1941 and early 1942 his policy paid handsomely. Perhaps, too, some of the shortages were not as acute as they were made to appear. Ultra correctly reported what the German messages said, but it is a universal habit of quartermasters to exaggerate their difficulties in the hope of inducing their superiors to increase their next allocation to compensate; Rommel had occasion to rebuke his supply staffs for this practice only a few months later.[16] Security measures to protect the source are perhaps the most likely explanation. A few more tankers sunk – even the capitulation of Panzer Army Africa – would have been a poor exchange for the loss of Ultra; irresponsible use of it might easily have given rise to suspicions that Enigma had, against all the odds, been broken, and in consequence to its supersession by a new cipher which might have remained unreadable for the remainder of the war; the loss of Ultra's help, which was at last beginning to be properly appreciated, in the Battle of the Atlantic or in the future Second Front in Europe to which all looked forward, would have been catastrophic. There does not seem to be any contemporary record or any discoverable recollection of complaints that Rommel's supplies were getting through too easily, and a phrase in Lieutenant-General Cunningham's attack plan for CRUSADER ('It is understood that the enemy supply situation cannot be interfered with to a much greater degree than at present')[17] may mean that any increase in air or naval action in the Mediterranean was thought likely to endanger the security of Ultra.

II

The marked advance in the operational use of Ultra by the autumn of 1942 was preceded, and in part caused, by an equally marked improvement in the handling of intelligence at both the production and the consumption end of the signals link between Bletchley and Egypt. Prominent among the shortcomings of the British Army in 1939 was its almost complete disregard of the value of intelligence, apart from the merely tactical information derivable from patrolling a static front line, and the consequent almost complete lack of intelligence officers in its ranks. The gap was hastily filled on the outbreak of war by recruitment mainly from the academic professions, with an admixture of men who had business and managerial experience. In the long run and on the whole, this improvised policy was a success, perhaps mainly because most of the recruits were young and willing, in the spirit of those years, to learn a new trade quickly. The ultimate success of this improvised policy has led to the belief (first widely propagated by Donald Maclachlan in *Room 39*[18]) that amateurs make the best intelligence officers because they are not hidebound by inherited conventions and will rapidly grasp ideas which might remain hidden from men brought up in 'standard practice'. The argument is persuasive, but our experience suggests that it needs heavy qualification.

In spite of the undeniable similarities, the differences between the outlooks of the academic and of the intelligence officer proved at first an unforeseen handicap to efficiency. Both are of course accustomed to examining evidence with care. Yet one thinks in the long term, can always declare the evidence insufficient to base conclusions on, and will usually suffer no worse penalty for error than to have his theories rejected by his colleagues, while hours and even minutes matter to the wartime intelligence officer responsible for advising his general, for he must leave nothing, however scrappy, out of account if it might throw light on the enemy's plans; because lives may depend on his faithful presentation of the meaning of perhaps woefully incomplete information upon a matter of operational urgency. Looking back over our early signals in later life, I can see – what probably no one realised at the time – that to begin with we often failed to perceive all the implications of the texts in front of us. Untaught, we clearly did not at first grasp that (to invent a simple illustration) it was not enough to signal that the Afrika Korps was advancing on Tobruk at 1800 hours on a certain day if the German original entitled us additionally to state that according to Fliegerführer Afrika at 1800 hours it was advancing in that direction – for a Luftwaffe authority might not be correctly informed about army intentions (movement towards need not imply preparations for attack, but 'advancing on' seems to do so), and in any case Rommel might have changed his orders after Fliegerführer heard about them at six o'clock. Mercifully we learned fast – perhaps because we were amateurs – and the signals about Crete in May were better drafted than those about Rommel's movements in March, when the direct wireless link with Cairo was opened; but they still left something to be desired, and it was not until the summer of 1942 that all ambiguities were eliminated.

Our experience therefore tends to show that training is as important for the budding intelligence officer as for the infantryman or gunner, otherwise each generation must learn slowly and painfully from its own mistakes. This was very clearly demonstrated in the early stages of TORCH. Neither the British nor the Americans had prepared an intelligence organisation commensurate with the tasks ahead. American mistakes have received more publicity, because of Kasserine, but Anderson's 1 Army was in no better case, for its intelligence officers had not been given the chance to learn from their now far more experienced fellows in 8 Army. Not only does little or no attention seem to have been paid, during the first chaotic days of November and December 1942, to intelligence other than that which could be gained on the ground, but not even a rough sketch of the institutions required to collect, evaluate and disseminate anything like strategic intelligence appears to have existed, much less the personnel to man them.[19] When Sir David Hunt, then still a comparatively junior intelligence officer at GHQ Cairo, was sent over to Algiers in November 1942, he found that the (mainly British) Intelligence staff at AFHQ 'did not know what they ought to be doing and had learned a whole lot of wrong things they ought not to be doing'.[20]

The price for this unpreparedness was paid by American soldiers and a British intelligence officer. Kasserine – which was in reality no more than the last despairing throw by the losing side, intent on delaying its fate – did not disrupt Allied strategy and in historical perspective deserves recollection mainly for the lessons it taught, but it caused great dismay at the time. At different moments in February 1943 there were three different Axis plans of attack. The Ultra evidence about them was never conclusive and there were more gaps in it than usual; unhappily, one of the most teasing intelligence puzzles of the war confronted a very inexperienced intelligence staff. The result was a misreading of enemy intentions which prolonged beyond the danger-point a plausible but erroneous belief that the main attack would come through Fondouk rather than through the Faid pass; temporary disaster followed. Brigadier Mockler-Ferryman, Eisenhower's chief intelligence officer, has been accused of over-reliance on Ultra; his fault lay far more in forgetting (or, more probably, not possessing the experience to realise) that there were sometimes unexpected gaps in it and that an officer who had issued a given decrypted order might have changed his mind after issuing it, as Rommel in fact did on 18 February.[21]

Like Brigadier Shearer, who had miscounted Rommel's tanks because he disregarded Ultra clues and by so doing had facilitated the German reconquest of half Cyrenaica in January 1942, Mockler-Ferryman was dismissed for his mistake. Some sympathy may be felt for them both, for they were unfamiliar with the operational use of Ultra material, but the two cases underline the necessity for experience (or, when this is impossible, proper training) in the handling of a delicate source with peculiar characteristics. The refusal of Admiral Sir Dudley Pound to listen to the advice of officers who had long been accustomed to handling naval Ultra, to which Mr Beesly attributes Pound's unnecessary order for Convoy PQ 17 to scatter, offers a parallel; it also illustrates, more starkly than any single episode in the land campaigns, the supreme need to interpose the judgement of a proven intelligence officer between the raw material and a commander's operational orders. The qualities required for each can hardly be combined in a single man, for the previous experience, duties and responsibilities of the two are entirely different, but if in an emergency Operations takes decisions without previously weighing the opinion of Intelligence, disaster may be the result. This would no doubt have been the case in the western desert in 1941 if Auchinleck had not so stubbornly resisted when Churchill urged him on to premature attack on the basis of his own reading of isolated Ultra decrypts.

The momentary setback at Kasserine showed up defects in American battlefield command which were speedily corrected under Patton and Bradley. The shortcomings of Intelligence were rectified almost as quickly. Mockler-Ferryman's successor, Strong, was himself to make a comparable mistake over the German Ardennes offensive of December 1944, but during the next few months it became common for young American intelligence officers, destined to service Ultra in the field during OVERLORD, to be first introduced to their material by a period in Hut 3, where they worked alongside the rest of us, and then to be sent out on short attachments to Mediterranean commands where they saw Ultra in action; their 'Trip Reports'[22] are instructive, and their performance in Normandy showed how much they benefited from their period of acclimatisation.

By the time they went on their travels, changes in personnel and organisation in Hut 3 at Bletchley and in Cairo, which immeasurably improved the effectiveness of Ultra as an instrument of war, were already more than six months old. The transformation of what had been amateurs into professionals expert in an entirely novel technique had begun in the same months as the disaster at Tobruk and the ignominious retreat to Alamein in June and July 1942, and was bearing fruit by September. Tighter control and better drafting at home and a better understanding abroad of the potentialities of the source mercifully brought to an end a frustrating period during which good intelligence had seemed quite unable to stem the tide of defeat and the two halves of a common enterprise had seemed to be engaged in a dialogue of the deaf, perpetually doomed to misunderstand each other's needs and limitations. By the late summer of 1942 not only were the logistical studies already mentioned becoming a regular feature of the work but, even more important, the distant customer was beginning to comprehend the home supplier's problems and why he could not provide on demand everything the consumer wanted. The standing of Intelligence in the eyes of Operations was thus greatly enhanced shortly before the arrival on the scene of the first general really willing to listen to a well-prepared and well-presented intelligence briefing and – by way of an unlooked-for bonus – just before the decryption of the first message since Crete to give away the enemy's whole plan of attack in advance. The disclosure of Rommel's intentions in what became the battle of Alam Halfa had tremendous consequences not only for the reputation of Ultra but for the whole future conduct of ground operations in the West. It established Montgomery's reputation, in his own and the public's mind, as a general who won victories, and it showed hitherto often sceptical generals and air marshals what intelligence could do to help win battles.

When Montgomery took over command of 8 Army on 13 August he knew that Rommel was expected to renew his offensive in the near future, but he did not like the troop dispositions Auchinleck had made to meet it, particularly his failure to garrison the Alam Halfa ridge, the key to the whole defensive position, in strength. That same evening he asked Alexander for the newly-arrived 44 Division as a garrison, and was granted his request. Four days later a decrypt[23] revealed that

Rommel hoped to unhinge the British defences by capturing the ridge and so breaking through to the Delta. Such complete and immediate proof of the correctness of his judgement so confirmed Montgomery's confidence in his own supreme military insight that he came later on to believe that he could never err, but it raised 8 Army's morale and self-reliance tremendously to find that their new commander could outwit the hitherto invincible Rommel. The happy co-operation of Intelligence and Operations established in the desert in August and September prevailed (apart from a brief interruption during the early months in Tunisia and occasional lapses thereafter) for the remainder of the war in both the Mediterranean and the western theatres. Finally, it is not altogether fanciful to suggest still wider repercussions of Alam Halfa's confirmation of Montgomery's belief in his own infallibility: without it, would he have been able to insist so firmly on the revision of the assault plans for Sicily and Normandy, a revision which increased their scale enough to prevent what might otherwise well have been the collapse of both landings in a welter of blood on the assault beaches?

III

The decision to invade Sicily after the fall of Tunis was not made on intelligence grounds, and Ultra contributed relatively little to the conduct of operations there. In the empty desert, both sides had relied almost exclusively on radio communications, so that there was much traffic to intercept. The contrast as the war moved into populated areas where landlines existed or could be laid was first apparent when the volume of Enigma traffic dropped sharply as the Germans retreated into a narrow perimeter round Tunis and Bizerta, and it became progressively more marked in Sicily and Italy. In retrospect it is surprising that SIGINT gathered so much useful information on European soil, but in June and July 1943 it was only too obvious that the number and location of Axis troops in Sicily were known with far less precision than had been the rule in Africa. For the first time too, another novel phenomenon provided compensation, and this came in the end to be of even greater value. To confuse and distract the enemy from what seemed the natural assumption that Sicily would be the Allies' next target (in fact, Hitler had always thought the Balkans more likely, and he remained of this opinion for many months yet), the MINCEMEAT ('The Man Who Never Was') deception sought to divert attention towards Sardinia and Greece. Other sources were able to report that the Spanish authorities had recovered the body of 'Major Martin', as they were intended to do, and that they had shown his 'despatches' to the Germans, but only Ultra could confirm the success of the deception through decrypts which revealed, for instance, that OKW had accepted the false information 'Major Martin' carried as genuine within a few days of receiving it, and that 1 Panzer Division (then being re-equipped in Brittany after suffering heavily in Russia) was moving to the Peloponnese in May and June.[24] These were the first in a long series of signals showing the success of subsequent deception plans, culminating with FORTITUDE, which convinced the Germans that 'Army Group Patton' would land in the Pas de Calais in July 1944.[25]

In Italy deception plans frequently contributed to tactical successes; Ultra's assistance in revealing the enemy's delusions was never more welcome than when it confirmed that the secret transfer of 8 Army westwards across the Apennines for DIADEM in May 1944 and back east again for OLIVE in August had remained undetected. Positive demonstration was achieved in August, with signals showing that Kesselring was keeping two of his best divisions (16 SS and 26 Panzer) on the wrong side of the Apennines,[26] so weakening his defences at the real danger-point. Rather more negative evidence had to suffice in May, but the occasion provides fascinating proof of the way Intelligence and Operations could work together. The basis of the DIADEM plan was to bring 8 Army over to Cassino in order to ensure sufficient numerical superiority to effect the breakthrough which had hitherto eluded the Allies. If Kesselring discovered this, it would not be difficult for him to frustrate it in mountainous country which favoured the defence; it was therefore essential to find out whether or not he knew about it. It became clear from the early spring onwards that neither he nor OKH had the least idea what the Allies intended, so many possibilities did they air,[27] and even clearer that the depletion of Luftflotte 2 to strengthen the defences of France and Germany was depriving Kesselring of the chance to reconnoitre the Allies' lines adequately. Regular air activity reports failed to throw up any evidence that 8 Army's movements had been noticed and, more significantly, revealed that (as was to happen again and again) Kesselring was doing nothing to counter a blow he evidently did not expect, for he was taking divisions away from the threatened sector to meet amphibious operations which existed only in the deception planners' minds. Their air superiority enabled the Allies almost to blind the Germans, thus emphasising their advantage in the field of intelligence: they could observe the enemy's movements while denying him a sight of their own, and by reading his signals could discover what (if anything) his very occasional air reconnaissances had observed and what his own intentions were. A happier combination of Intelligence and Operations would be hard to imagine. It helped to make the surprise complete, and not for the first time emphasised the supreme value of Ultra in a period of preparation for the offensive.

Examples like these reinforce the argument of Professor Handel and others that surprise cannot be prevented,[28] but they add another dimension to it by indicating conditions in which the deceiver can discover whether his deceit has achieved its purpose, thus magnifying his advantage. By so doing they demonstrate that Sigint and techniques of intelligence-gathering have rendered invalid the theory (ultimately derived from Clausewitz's doctrine that defence is the stronger form of war and his belief that the 'right' method of defence – i.e. that in vogue in his own day – had made reconnaissance impossible) that intelligence is less necessary to the offence than to the defence.[29] Intelligence about the enemy, though of course its content was completely different, was just as important to Alexander's attack on the Gustav Line in 1944 as it was to Montgomery's defence at Alam Halfa in 1942.

After these further 'puffs' for Ultra, it would be only right to admit that the close co-operation between Intelligence and Operations broke down momentarily over the evacuation of Sicily. On 14 July 1943, only four days after the Husky landings, and a full month before the evacuation, Ultra reported the appointment of Oberst Baade of 15 Panzer Division to organise the all-round defence of the Straits of Messina in readiness for a future evacuation, should this become necessary, the delivery of extra flak for the purpose on Goering's personal order, and repeated instructions, which were faithfully carried out, that everything portable should be removed when the time came.[30] Standard accounts[31] rightly stress the strength of the Straits defences, and the most recent of them[32] insists that because of the heavy gunfire along both shores it was impracticable to attack sea traffic. Nevertheless, it is strange that almost to the end Alexander and Eisenhower believed that evacuation was not imminent[33] and did not take urgent measures against it, although Ultra reported on 1 August that a practice evacuation exercise would be held that night and later that fuel was being laid in against 'coming heavy demands on the ferry system';[34] moreover, a map had been captured which showed that evacuation would follow the loss of Adrano, which fell on 6 August, ten days before the last Axis troops left. The defence of *Festung Europa* had been deprived of nearly a quarter of a million men by the surrender on Cape Bon in May; another 50,000 could have been added had the wholesale evacuation of Sicily been prevented.

IV

Two episodes during the Italian campaign suggest further reflections on the relation between intelligence and strategy. The decision to invade the mainland, taken at the 'Trident' conference in Washington at the end of May 1943, depended for its execution and timing on an Italian surrender, which was at first envisaged as a sequel to the invasion, not as preceding it. In the event, the two coincided on 9 September. But while much thought, some of it unavoidably hurried, had been given to the landings, far less was directed towards trying to foresee what would follow them. It was vaguely hoped that German resistance would crumble soon after Italian and that a march of liberation would speedily carry the Allies far up the peninsula. This joint hope concealed a growing divergence between British and American forecasts of the future, which later on became very sharp. American opinion was persuaded that the Germans would quietly retire northwards in good order, but the British were convinced that they would stubbornly dispute every inch of the way; the American view credited Hitler with acting rationally in accordance with sound strategy, the British with continuing his emotional refusal to yield ground unless compelled.

In these circumstances it was of the utmost importance to discover the truth as soon as possible. If Ultra was to do this, it might have to gain access to intelligence at a higher level than had been usual in the past, for the tried and tested method of reconstituting high-level decisions from evidence of their implementation lower down might not serve in this case. The task was executed satisfactorily in the end, but it was complicated by a period of uncharacteristic indecision on Hitler's part; he changed his mind several times and did not finally resolve his doubts until November.

German misgivings that Italy might be intending to break the Axis took shape on the morrow of von Arnim's surrender in Tunisia with Hitler's instruction to Rommel to assemble a skeleton staff and prepare to occupy northern Italy if the Italians defected. Ultra identified a 'Planning staff Rommel' in Austria at once[35] but could not discover its functions until the first few days of August, when Army Group B, composed of three corps and seven or eight divisions, suddenly appeared under Rommel's command on the Austro-Italian frontier,[36] a more formidable force (it had almost 200 tanks, nearly half of them the new Panthers and Tigers) than had ever been at either his or Kesselring's disposal before. Army Group B's future task was defined as that of forming 'a self-contained strategic reserve in Upper Italy',[37] but as soon as it crossed the frontier on news of AVALANCHE and the Italian surrender the urgent need became that of determining whether it would remain as an army of occupation in Lombardy or move down to hold Rome and the south, with Rommel perhaps replacing Kesselring as theatre commander (unknown to the Allies, it was just this personal issue which Hitler was finding so difficult to resolve) – or, indeed, as eventually turned out to be the answer, whether the 'strategic reserve' was merely being placed in a convenient central position in which it might intimidate the Italians for the moment and then be dispersed to meet the emergency which had been building up on the Russian front since the failure of the Zitadelle offensive in June.

The first hints that a stand was to be made south of Rome came just after AVALANCHE,[38] but were heavily qualified by an Army Group B report that it had reconnoitred an 'Apennine position' – it was almost identical with the future Gothic Line – north of Florence.[39] In fact, Hitler had taken a provisional decision on 30 September, in order to gain time, to accept Kesselring's view that it was practicable to hold on south of Rome at least through the winter. The Army Group B report did not conflict with this because it carried no implication of the contrary – that Rommel had persuaded Hitler to economise forces by retiring to the mountainous north at once. (Rommel had in fact tried to persuade the Führer but failed.) Yet even the most obvious interpretation – that northern defences were being reconnoitred as a precautionary measure – left the timing obscure. This obscurity represented the truth – Hitler had already designated the Apennine position as the final line of defence in Italy, but had imposed no time-table for manning it – but it could only promote further disagreement between the Allies. Both the obscurity and the disagreement were, at this moment and for some time to come, the product less of any defect of intelligence than of Hitler's indecision.

If it was still impossible to predict what the Germans would do in the more distant future, the Ultra revelations forced an immediate re-appraisal of Allied short-term strategy. Alexander dated the birth of the Italian campaign from the discovery that there would be serious resistance south of Rome;[40] Churchill, who on 1 October had been planning to meet him in Rome at the end of the month, predicted only a week later that there would be bitter fighting before the city was captured.[41]

The implicit demand that Ultra should penetrate the secrets of the *Führerhauptquartier* to solve an immediate strategic dilemma had thus been satisfactorily met in the weeks before and after AVALANCHE, and new territories had been opened up to inspection as well. There had been practically no Enigma traffic from northern Italy until the arrival of Army Group B there, and none at all from Slovenia, which soon became its principal focus of interest; simply because Army Group B evidently found it impossible to communicate by land-line with its subordinate formations as they become scattered over a wide area to suppress 'guerrillas', therefore, Allied knowledge of resistance movements in northern Yugoslavia was greatly extended just as the Balkans were beginning to figure more prominently in, at any rate, the British scheme of things in the months after the parachuting of the first British mission to Tito at the end of May.

These developments emphasise another feature of wartime Sigint which is presumably equally characteristic of its successor today: its largely uncontrollable variability as a source of information. New keys, for new authorities and/or new areas, might come unexpectedly into use according to the exigencies of war or organisational fashions at the centre, and since in 1943 there were still too few of the 'bombes' which did the repetitive daily donkey-work of decryption to meet all requirements; from the intelligence officer's point of view there was always a degree of uncertainty and surprise about what each day's work might bring, in spite of the establishment of a system for deciding priorities. Considerable flexibility of mind was required of the Ultra intelligence staff from this time onwards, and in even greater measure among those whose duty it was to take strategic decisions on the basis of the information we provided. It seems reasonable to suppose that the same is true today.

This point can be illustrated from the Ultra intelligence of the summer of 1944. With the piercing of the Gustav Line at the end of May (it is perhaps worth pausing to note that, predictably, Ultra throws no light on Mark Clark's astonishing preference for capturing Rome instead of rounding up the greater part of the German armies in Italy), a general Allied advance began. It was known that fortifications were being constructed in the northern Apennines, but there had been nothing to indicate their state of readiness since April.[42] Alexander had already lost some of his best divisions to OVERLORD, and the debate whether he should be required to surrender more for the ANVIL landing in the south of France was now raging. On 13 June, ten days after Rome fell, he was ordered to give up seven more divisions to ANVIL (they included the French mountain troops which had performed such feats in DIADEM and would be required to form the spearhead of an assault on the Gothic Line). Believing that if he were allowed to retain intact the force which had gained stunning victories in May he could keep Kesselring on the run, get into the Lombard plain quickly and perhaps even penetrate as far as Vienna (or, if the Combined Chiefs of staff preferred, into southern France by the land route through the Italian Riviera) before the winter, Alexander appealed against what he regarded as a cruel and short-sighted decision.

On the same 13 June, following the return from a fact-finding mission of General Warlimont, the deputy chief of the OKW Operations Staff, Hitler issued a new directive[43] about the war in Italy. The directive was intercepted and decrypted. Here was another example of Ultra responding to the need to penetrate to a higher level than it had customarily managed to reach save in exceptional cases like Hitler's 'Stand fast' order which threw into chaos Rommel's effort to save his army from destruction at Alamein. Hitler was now addressing himself to the same question that was preoccupying the Allied command – the imminence of the threat to Lombardy – but in doing so he gave away an important new piece of information. 'Allied entry into the Lombard plain would have incalculable military and political consequences,' he admitted, yet so far little had been done over a large part of the chosen line to erect defensive works to protect it, and many months would be required to complete them. Therefore Kesselring was to contest every inch of the way back up the peninsula, and meanwhile the 'common misconception' that a fortified Apennine position already existed was to be 'scotched once and for all'. Alexander's apparently wild dream was here shown to have a firm foundation in reality because his enemy feared that he would do exactly what he in fact proposed to do, and the argument that General Marshall was at the moment deploying against his scheme – that it was unnecessary because the Germans were in any case about to retire voluntarily to the Alps with the minimum of resistance – was completely refuted. Had it been possible to decrypt Hitler's directive at once, instead of a fortnight later, the debates of the combined chiefs might have taken a different turn. By the time it became available on

27 June, unfortunately, the decision for ANVIL had for all practical purposes been taken, and the five more days before its formal promulgation were insufficient to reverse it, so deeply enmeshed had it become in national and political issues. Alexander lost so many more divisions that he was unable to force the Gothic Line until April 1945; had he not been deprived of them, he might well have advanced either up the Rhone Valley or to the Danube by the end of the year. As soon as the landings took place in August Hitler completely undermined the strategy upon which ANVIL was based by ordering Army Group G to retire at once to Dijon and beyond, so that not a single division was diverted from OVERLORD to defend the south.

Among much else, this episode exemplifies the grounds of possible conflict between intelligence and the politician. Churchill and Brooke, the British CIGS, who needed no further proof that the Germans would fight for every inch of Italian ground because they had already deduced it from Hitler's previous behaviour, remained convinced that the decision for ANVIL was wrong,[44] but by July 1944 the United States controlled so large a part of the Allies' resources that there was no gain-saying its leaders' wishes, even had Roosevelt not been unavoidably bound to consider how best to secure the votes which would give him a fourth term as President. It may well be, however, that had intelligence been available earlier in the debate Alexander might perhaps have been allowed to retain his army intact and that he might then have breached the Gothic Line many months sooner and have brought so much pressure to bear on the southern edge of the Reich that the Nazi empire might have collapsed in the autumn of 1944. With hindsight this appears a more promising strategic prospect than either Montgomery's 'pencil-like thrust' or Eisenhower's 'broad front' after the contemporary Falaise Gap battle in the west; in no other way, perhaps, could the war have been brought to an end in 1944.

V

The dispute over ANVIL and the advance through central Italy was the nearest the Ultra experience came to a topic which has been prominent in recent American literature and was much discussed at a conference at the Royal United Services Institution in December 1984: the risk of intelligence becoming debased and its sharp cutting edge blunted at the interface between the intelligence officer and his executive or political superior.

Various reasons are put forward to explain this risk. Because of the difference between the conditions of peace and war, the Ultra experience does not illuminate most of them at all brightly, but one at least rings familiar: the complaint that the advance of technology had so increased the volume of intercepted material that it swamps the absorptive capacity of the human mind and threatens to frustrate the whole purpose for which an intelligence service exists. The point that overload can paralyse thought and action was forcefully made 14 years ago in T.L. Hughes's article 'The Fate of Facts in the World of Men'[45] (the title alone sums up the central problem which every intelligence organisation must face). At Bletchley Park the threat of overload made itself felt in 1943 and 1944, when a proportion of incoming raw material had to be discarded, once it had been scrutinised for urgent items, without going through the rest of the normal processes, lest it choke the channels of communication with details of only marginal value. The solution adopted then, in what can only have been a microcosm of the present problem, was the obvious one of delegating the authority to discard to specialist departments, to rely on their judgement, and to hope that this delegation of authority would not lead to 'empire building', the creation of 'private armies', or the squirrel-like hoarding of precious information in obscure corners where it would be overlooked.

The trust and the hope were justified in our case; no one allowed his attention to be distracted from the single aim of providing speedy and accurate information which could help to win the war. A similar single-mindedness of purpose cannot be expected today, because the stimulus is lacking. The discipline of regular and objective reporting up the successive steps in the hierarchy, and the inculcation from above of the sense of responsibility which then came unbidden, must be the substitute for it. This is of course no more than to conclude that a standard practice cannot be radically improved;[46] but it is also to arrive more emphatically than ever at another familiar conclusion: that 'men not measures' are the crucial element in the business of intelligence, where one of the ground rules is 'You never know where you may find the vital clue' and where a single individual's alertness and insight may be the *sine qua non* of success.

As already implied, from the single-mindedness of purpose mentioned above it followed that we were immune from a disease which is said to be common today: that of shaping the evidence to suit the real or imagined predilections of superiors. On the other hand, it guaranteed no protection against a more subtle poison. No intellectual investigation can be successfully pursued without a working hypothesis, an approximate idea of the object to be attained; the danger then arises that the approximate idea imperceptibly becomes a fixed preconception, a pattern into which unconsciously all newly discovered evidence is forced, with the corollary that anything which will not fit is cast aside. It is agreed on all hands[47] that this is the single chief source of error in intelligence work, supreme above all others because it steals up on its victim unawares and leads him by easy stages further and further from the truth. We were enabled to escape this form of error because we were not required to draw operational deductions from our material, only to report it meticulously. Our customers in the field were sometimes less fortunate: Kasserine and the Ardennes are well-known examples.

What of the intelligence officer's superior, the general or the politician, and the other aspect of the danger of 'experts without authority and, authorities without expertise'?[48] Many mistakes were made during the first two or three years of the war by field commanders professionally distrustful of intelligence and not properly indoctrinated about Ultra. Some generals who rose to prominence later – Patton and Montgomery, for instance – are commonly credited with listening attentively to intelligence briefings (though it is hard to see the signs of this in some of Montgomery's actions), others with reluctance or worse. Past experience should here have guided the practice of the present, but it seems doubtful whether it has done so sufficiently, in England at least. Thorough courses of instruction are required in order to ensure that as far as humanly possible operational decisions will not be taken at variance with the latest intelligence.[49] It is entirely a matter of speculation whether anything could have altered Bomber Command's conviction that it could by itself paralyse German industry and destroy German morale, but in the spring and summer of 1944 there was enough evidence from Italy[50] to question its views seriously, and maximum use should be made of this kind of example.

This is not to make the mistake, noticed at the beginning, of converting all action into reaction or to risk becoming too intelligence-minded. Historians of intelligence have a special duty not to allow their vision to be distorted by their interests and to bear constantly in mind that 'the decisive factor is always the capacity to make use of intelligence'.[51] They should therefore be the first to point out that the early years of the Second World War saw examples of operational mistakes which could have been avoided by a better understanding of the value and use of intelligence, and to warn against the dangers which would follow a repetition.

NOTES

This paper was originally presented at the US Army War College Conference on 'Intelligence and Military Operations', Carlisle Barracks, Pennsylvania, 22–25 April 1986. Copyright US Army War College Foundation. The views expressed in this article are those of the author and do not reflect the official policy or position of the Department of Defense or the US Government.

1. *Summa Theologica,* Secunda Secundae, Quaestio XL articulus 3. – Art. 3 permits deception on the ground that Joshua used it to capture the city of Ai (Joshua viii, 1–22).
2. Carl von Clausewitz, *On War,* ed. and trans. Michael Howard and Peter Paret (Princeton, 1984), pp. 117, 140.
3. This paper is based mainly on the Ultra signals derived from the decryption at Bletchley Park of the German *Wehrmacht* Enigma cipher. I was intimately involved there with assessing Ultra Intelligence and drafting the resulting signals from early in 1941 until the end of the war.
4. JPs 2851, 3127, 3134, 3145, 3192. References in this form are to Ultra signals preserved in File DEFE 3 in the Public Record Office, Kew.
5. Clausewitz, p. 113.
6. I.S.O. Playfair, *The Mediterranean and Middle East,* ii, p. 281; iii, p.107. Stephen Roskill, *The War at Sea* (London 1956), i, p. 614.
7. OLs 936, 938, 954, 1125, 1149, 1192.
8. OLs 1227, 1322.
9. OL 1835.
10. MKA 2282.
11. MKAs 2094, 2095.
12. MKAs 2523, 2568, 2596, 2614, 2647, QTs60, 136, 245, 256, 310, 331, 585, 604, 607, 658, 733, 758.
13. QTs 3712, 3785.
14. QTs 3868, 3915, 3973, 4077, 4119.
15. B.H. Liddell Hart (ed.), *The Rommel Papers* (New York, 1958), p. 313.
16. QT 7058.
17. General Sir Claude Auchinleck, *Despatch,* p. 374, in *Supplement to the London Gazette,* 15 January 1948.
18. Donald Maclachlan, *Room 39* (London, 1968).
19. F.H. Hinsley and others, *British Intelligence in the Second World War,* Vol. II (London, 1981), pp. 499–500, 740–3.
20. Sir David Hunt, *A Don at War* (London, 1966), pp. 147–51.
21. Hinsley, Vol. ii, pp. 761–3, makes a half-hearted attempt to exonerate Mockler-Ferryman which does not accord with my reading of the evidence.
22. NSA. SRH-031.
23. MKAs 2094, 2095.
24. MLs 1955, 2400, 2513, 2733, 4439.
25. The Ultra evidence about this is sketched in my *Ultra in the West,* p. 53.
26. XLs 6013, 6257, 8575, 8610, 9527.
27. KVs 192, 773, 930.
28. M.I. Handel, *Perception, Deception and Surprise* (Jerusalem, 1976) and

'Intelligence and The Problem of Strategic Surprise' in *Journal of Strategic Studies,* Vol. 7, No. 3 (1984), pp. 229–81; Walter Laqueur, *World of Secrets* (London, 1985), pp. 256–71.

29. Michael Handel, *Military Deception in Peace and War* (Jerusalem Papers on Peace Problems 38), p. 35; Clausewitz, pp. 309, 361.
30. MLs 7518, 7543, 7562, 7638, 7658, 7709, 8301, JPs 1024, 1027, 1111, 1370.
31. E.g. Playfair, op. cit., v, p. 165, A.N. Garland and H.M. Smyth, *Sicily and the Surrender of Italy* (Washington, 1965), p. 370.
32. John Terraine, *The Right of the Line* (London, 1985), p. 579.
33. Playfair, op. cit., v, p. 174, Garland and Smyth, op. cit., p. 412, W.G.F. Jackson, *Alexander of Tunis as Military Commander* (London, 1971), p. 225.
34. JP 357.
35. C 132, ML 2394.
36. JPs 37, 1383, 1487, 1512, 2261, 2911, 2952, 3080.
37. JP 2760.
38. JPs 5651, 6048, 6758.
39. JP 6915.
40. Alexander, *Memoirs,* ed. John North (London, 1962), p. 117.
41. W.S. Churchill, *The Second World War* (London, 1951), v, pp. 135, 194.
42. KV 1578, 4321, 5245.
43. KV 9843.
44. John Ehrman, *Grand Strategy* (London, 1956), v, p. 356, Playfair, op. cit., vi/1, pp. 313–35.
45. Foreign Policy Association, Headline Series No. 233, December 1976; compare Laqueur, p. 315.
46. Laqueur (p. 341) concedes the 'prosaic' nature of any likely improvements in intelligence procedure.
47. E.g. Hughes, p. 10, R.K. Betts, 'Analysis, War and Decision. Why Intelligence Failures are Inevitable', in *World Politics,* Vol. 31, No. 1 (October 1978).
48. Hughes, p. 13.
49. But it is not very reassuring to learn from Laqueur, p. 321, note 15, that A. Cave Brown, *Bodyguard of Lies* (New York, 1976) is a set book in some American courses. General Sir David Fraser, *Alanbrooke* (London, 1982), *And we shall Shock them* (London, 1983), repeatedly stresses the lessons of the past.
50. Ultra reports of the effects of STRANGLE, the attempt to cut the road and rail communications of Kesselring's armies in the summer of 1944 by bombing them, though not conclusive, were enough to cast doubts on the effectiveness of the policy. See also my article 'Intelligence and Strategy in World War II' in K.G. Robertson (ed.), *British and American Approaches to Intelligence* (London, 1987), and the evidence assembled in my *Ultra and Mediterranean Strategy* (London, 1989).
51. Laqueur, p. 339.

6

Knight's Move at Drvar: Ultra and the Attempt on Tito's Life, 25 May 1944*

When its Sixth Offensive (as Tito and the Partisans called it) faltered during the winter of 1943–44, the German High Command began to realise that it was losing the initiative in Jugoslavia. Tito, his staff and large bodies of Partisans had repeatedly escaped from every trap that had been laid, and all efforts to destroy them had come to nothing. Increasing Anglo-American pressure in Italy (the assault on Cassino and the Gustav Line began on 11 May; Rome fell on 4 June) and the Russian advances further north were making it necessary to withdraw divisions from the Balkans: two had gone to Italy in the early spring and four more had been sent to occupy Hungary in March. Since further attempts to annihilate the Partisans by large-scale attacks were clearly out of the question, an alternative plan was devised: a bold stroke at its centre might paralyse the Partisan leadership, thus restoring the initiative to the Germans, and might even kill or capture Tito and his staff as well.

So runs the account in the OKW (Oberkommando der Wehrmacht) War Diary. It is an extraordinary admission of failure by an occupying power which had at first seemed to hold all the best cards in its hand and to be handicapped only by the natural obstacles presented by the mountainous nature of the country and by the necessity of protect-

*The substance of this paper was delivered at the Anglo-Jugoslav Colloquium held by the British National Committee for the History of the Second World War at the Imperial War Museum in London in December 1982. I am grateful for permission to publish a slightly enlarged version of it now. Up to that time nothing had been published about Ultra and the attempt on Tito's life.

Mr Hilary King (formerly Signals Officer with Brigadier Maclean's Mission to Tito; he was at Drvar on 25 May 1944) and Dr Rade Bogdanovic read related papers at the same Colloquium; I have borrowed a few details from each.

116

ing the long-drawn-out line of communications from Austria, through Zagreb and Belgrade, to Greece, the Aegean islands and Crete.

Popular resistance to the occupation of the country by Germans and Italians had emerged on the morrow of the defeat of Prince Paul's government in March 1941. By the beginning of 1944, the royalist Mihailović had long abandoned active opposition in favour of waiting passively in the Serbian mountains until the Allies should drive out the invader, and had himself been abandoned by the British who had at first given him some assistance. The communist Tito, who had once said, 'The sun will not rise in the west', had received little support from the hard-pressed Russians, but by skilful guerrilla warfare and continual movement had made his Partisans so serious a thorn in the enemy's flesh that the British had made contact with him in May 1943 and discontinued aid to Mihailović, transferring all their support to Tito by the end of the year.

The Fourth and Fifth Offensives (WEISS and SCHWARZ in German nomenclature) bore hard on the Partisans during the first six months of 1943, but Tito's fortunes took a permanent turn for the better in the autumn. Speedy action enabled him to take advantage of the Italian surrender in September, to extend the territory under his control and to double the size of his forces to about 200,000 men, arming them with captured Italian weapons. In late November he held a National Congress at Jajce in the area of north-western Jugoslavia which he had liberated, and proclaimed himself Marshal and Prime Minister. He set up his headquarters at Drvar in the Dinaric Alps nearby, abandoning for the moment his hitherto successful tactic of constant move-ment. 'Tito is our most dangerous enemy,'[1] admitted Field Marshal Maximilian von Weichs a few weeks later. As Oberbefehlshaber Südost (OB SE) since the end of August, he was finding his duties as Supreme Commander in the Balkans beyond his power to fulfil, and was fearful of losing control of the 750-mile long railway upon which his troops depended for present sustenance and future retreat. His predicament became still more awkward early in 1944, when first two of his divisions were sent to help Kesselring in Italy and then four more were called away to occupy Hungary in March, in order to stem the Russian advance. During these same months he mounted a series of 'special operations' (which together made up the Sixth Offensive) with the object of wiping out the Partisans in particular areas, but each time guerrilla activity flared up again with renewed vigour once the storm-wave had passed.

It was in this atmosphere of tension and stress that von Weichs prepared another 'special operation', bold in conception but planned and executed with the haste that spells despair (it was carried out less than three weeks after his first operation order). If Tito had indeed settled for the moment at Drvar instead of being continually on the move, then there was a chance that a rapier stroke might do, at the last moment, what blunter weapons had failed to accomplish – paralyse his organisation and perhaps seize him into the bargain. The combined air and ground operation was given the cover-name RÖSSELSPRUNG (Knight's Move). Ample aircraft, ground forces and paratroops were assembled (the expedition numbered some 16,000 men), but the preliminary intelligence work was inadequate. Unlike Skorzeny when he rescued Mussolini from the Gran Sasso a few months earlier, the leaders of the raiding party did not know exactly where Tito was; as will be seen, Ultra preserves traces of their uncertainty.

Success appears to have made Tito and his staff over-confident. A settled life in a mountain hide-out after years of wandering evidently induced a carefree disregard for security precautions. They received more than one warning that an airborne operation against Drvar might be in the wind (members of the British Mission were so convinced that prolonged German air reconnaissance of the valley below Drvar presaged heavy bombing that they moved their radio equipment a mile or two away on 23 May), but they made no plans to meet it.[2] The attack came at dawn on 25 May and gained complete surprise.

When it became known, 12 years ago, that decrypts of Enigma messages had given the Allies information about the fighting in Jugoslavia, the question was asked: did the Allies have advance knowledge of the raid on Drvar but forbear to warn Tito? An examination of the Ultra signals sent at the time to Allied headquarters in the Mediterranean, copies of which are open to inspection in the Public Record Office, makes it possible to answer this question with an emphatic negative.

According to the OKW War Diary, von Weichs issued his orders for Rösselsprung on 6 May. Panzer Army 2 was to carry out the operation with troops drawn from V SS Corps and XV Mountain Corps, plus Croat auxiliaries; Panzer Abteilung 202, a battalion of Regiment Brandenburg and Grenadier Regiment 92 would be lent from OB SE reserve, while OKW would provide a reconnaissance Abteilung and an SS parachute battalion.[3] When Himmler's initial objections to lending the SS had been overcome, OKW set out guide-lines for the conduct of the operation on 13 May, particularly stressing the need for the strictest secrecy in order to gain surprise at the outset and prevent the escape of large bodies of Partisans later on, as had happened so often in the past. Hitler gave his approval to OB SE's final plans on 21 May, and the operation took place four days later. The change in Tito's attitude – he had toyed with the idea of giving up mobile warfare altogether and fortifying the Drvar area as a permanent stronghold – and the extra difficulties it created seems to have been recognised: the Air Liaison Officer (Flivo) of XV Mountain Corps appreciated on 27 April that 'the guerrillas are determined to hold Drvar with all forces'.[4]

The first mention of RÖSSELSPRUNG in Ultra occurred on the evening of 22 May, the day after Hitler's approval of von Weichs' plan and only two days before the assault. There was nothing in the bald wording of the decrypted German message to explain what RÖSSELSPRUNG meant or to link it with Tito, and indeed a scrutiny of all the Mediterranean Ultra signals in May shows that there was nothing to suggest that RÖSSELSPRUNG meant an attack on Tito's headquarters until 27 and 28 May, long after the Drvar raid. The same scrutiny also shows that although Ultra did not reveal what RÖSSELSPRUNG was, every subsequent message which seemed to hold even the slightest possibility of being connected with it was signalled with high priority. If, therefore, any of our customers had been in possession of non-Ultra intelligence which penetrated the disguise, they had ample time in which to draw appropriate conclusions from a comparison of it with relevant Ultra signals. In fact, no such information appears to have been available.

The Ultra signal in question conveyed the information that shortly before midday on 22 May, orders had been issued (evidently by German Air Force Command Southeast [GAFSE]) to Fliegerführer (Air Commander) Croatia in the following terms: 'Tasks for 23rd as for 21st: First priority – Preparation for "ELDERLY" (Comment, German RÖSSELSPRUNG)'.[5]

Two things must be noted at once. Firstly, for security reasons, it was standard practice in Hut 3[6] to replace all German cover-names with the next English word from an arbitrary list prepared long in advance, and to refer in subsequent signals to the English name only; but on the first occasion to transmit both English and German in case local evidence at the recipients' end – perhaps gained from captured documents or through the interrogation of prisoners – might throw light on what lay hidden beneath the cover-name.

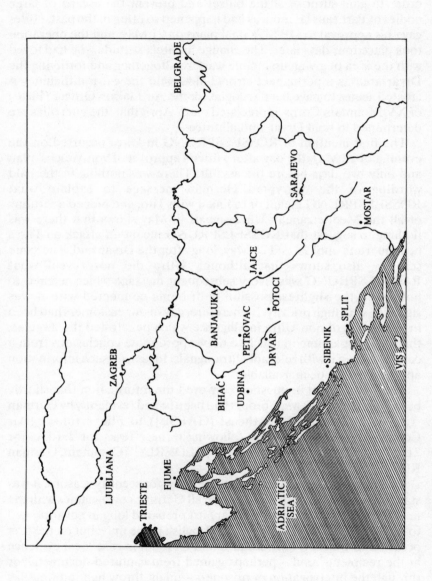

Dozens of operations with cover-names appear in Ultra dealing with Jugoslavia, most of them operations to capture, relieve or supply the Dalmatian islands or attempts to flush out and mop up the Partisans occupying a particular area. By May 1944, Hut 3's customers were thoroughly familiar with the way we handled cover-names, therefore, and knew that if we had any evidence pointing to the nature of an operation thus disguised, it would be appended to the signal in the form of a comment. The absence of any such comment on this occasion shows that Hut 3 had no clue at all to the meaning of RÖSSELSPRUNG and this would have been understood by every recipient.

Secondly, this signal was despatched to the Algiers, Caserta and Cairo headquarters at 7.30 in the evening of the same day as it was transmitted in German to Fliegerführer Croatia, i.e. only a little more than eight hours after the German transmission. It was given high priority even though its implications were obscure, in case one of the recipients might be able to understand and act upon it. It may be presumed to have been received during the night of 22/23 May, almost certainly before midnight on the 22nd.

In retrospect, it was clear that two messages already received and signalled might well be connected with RÖSSELSPRUNG.[7] Both had originated on 21 May, and both had already been signalled with medium priority earlier on the 22nd. The first was an order for the first Gruppe of Stukageschwader 2 to move from an airfield near Galatz in Rumania to Zagreb-Pleso by 23 May, 'for temporary employment from 25 May'.[8] In the second, Airfield Regional Control (ARC) Zagreb ordered bomb-craters on Bihac runway (Bihac is some 25 miles north-west of Drvar) to be filled in, so as to ensure the safety of aircraft using it, and for accommodation to be prepared for a hundred men.[9] On the same day, the same ARC ordered Banjaluka (which is about the same distance from Drvar as Bihac, but in a north-easterly direction) to arrange accommodation for 200 men.[10] The similarity between the two 'accommodation' messages was plain, and since by the time the second of them was decrypted the RÖSSELSPRUNG message had already been signalled, a comment suggesting that there might be some connection between all three was added to the signal about it.

It would be well to pause at this stage and reflect on two points. First, there was no clue to explain why 300 men (were they Luftwaffe ground-crews, paratroops or soldiers?) were suddenly being billetted on either side of Tito's headquarters and within striking distance of it. Indeed, it is very unlikely that the phenomenon would have been described in these words at the time, and still less likely that an attack on Drvar could have been deduced from this evidence. The moves would probably have seemed connected with one of the many anti-guerrilla sweeps which Ultra was constantly reporting, and it is beyond all question improbable that anyone could have seen them as part of a chain of evidence about a paratroop attack on Drvar, as hindsight enables us to do.

Second, all four of the messages so far recorded were clearly consequent upon OB SE's orders of 21 May, which Hut 3 had not seen.[11] This was in conformity with a fairly common pattern. Quite frequently, we had – if we could – to reconstruct the original orders for some big operation from consequential details which did not allude to them, although they derived from them, and to try to deduce German intentions by fitting small pieces of a jigsaw together to produce a plausible picture. Success might well depend on the chance that the pieces intercepted were central to the picture and not merely peripheral, and even then the result was not always convincing to the generals. Five months after RÖSSELSPRUNG, just this pattern of events preceded the German winter offensive in the Ardennes. Hut 3 never saw the operational orders for Wacht am Rhein, but in September it began assembling derivatives from them. During the following weeks there began to emerge a hazy but plausible picture which in fact corresponded quite closely to the later reality. No notice was taken of it, however, and the Germans gained complete surprise on 16 December.[12]

In the present case, of course, there were far fewer pieces to the jigsaw, and a far less plausible picture in consequence. By the evening of the 23rd, however, several messages to or from Fliegerführer Croatia and ARC Zagreb had added a little more detail to it, unfortunately without making its significance any plainer. ARC Zagreb had circularised the GAF stations under its control on 21 May, warning them 'for the last time' to send in proper daily ammunition returns and reports on new units arriving, and went on to say that duty refuelling crews were to be kept in a state of permanent readiness, 'especially in the next few days'.[13] A possible connection with the aircraft from Galatz was suggested in a comment to this signal. Next day, Jagdführer (O.C. Fighters) Balkans ordered the transfer of II/JG 51 (i.e. twenty or thirty Me 109 fighters) to Zagreb for a special operation; the Gruppe would probably be subordinated to Fliegerführer Croatia and would stay five days.[14] This time both RÖSSELSPRUNG and the Galatz aircraft were mentioned in a comment, and the signal was given high priority.

No message with the slightest possible bearing on the mysterious operation was intercepted during the 20 hours following the Banjaluka signal, and there was total silence on the subject of RÖSSELSPRUNG until GAF Command Southeast's orders to Fliegerführer Croatia for the 25th were signalled with extra high priority on the afternoon of the 24th, only five hours after they were issued.[15] The opening paragraph – 'Support of Elderly in accordance with special order' – made the first explicit reference since the original mention two days earlier to what we now know to have been the Drvar operation, but there was still not the slightest reason to connect ELDERLY/RÖSSELSPRUNG with Tito in any way. The second paragraph of GAFSE's orders repeated familiar routine instructions about reconnaissance of the Adriatic and added that Vis airfield was to be patrolled 'several times a day to ascertain whether the enemy is bringing up forces to support the guerrillas in Elderly'; two such reconnaissance reports were intercepted.[16] A little later, GAFSE told the Fliegerführer that a planned attack on Vis airfield in order to prevent aircraft using it 'at any rate for the first few days of the special undertaking' could not now be carried out, because of the demands of the Italian front,* and between these two we were able to signal earlier instructions for IV/JG 27 to cease current operations from its base at Steinamanger (Szombathely) in Hungary and move to Zagreb-Lucko by the evening of 23 May, 'to be at the disposal of GAFSE for temporary operations'.[17]

These were the last two signals sent before the attack on Drvar at dawn on 25 May. The best interpretation of all the evidence that could be offered at midnight on 24/25 May was that ELDERLY was an operation of an unknown kind somewhere in the general area of Zagreb, Bihac and Banjaluka (a triangle which does not, in fact, enclose Drvar), that it appeared to be under the control of the Luftwaffe, probably through Fliegerführer Croatia, that it was planned for 25 May or very soon thereafter, and that it was important enough to warrant the short-term transfer of three Gruppen of aircraft from the southern end of the Russian front. It was referred to as a 'special undertaking', but 'Sonder-unternehmen' was so common a word in the Wehrmacht's vocabulary, and one used so frequently to designate small as well as large-scale operations (often of an almost routine kind and of no outstanding significance), that no particular attention would have been paid to it. No reference had been made to infantry or parachutists in connection with it, and there had not been a single word about Tito or the location

---

*Where the Allied forces advancing through the Gustav line joined up with the Anzio bridgehead on the same day as the Drvar raid.

of his headquarters. This remained the sum of Ultra knowledge about RÖSSELSPRUNG throughout the 25th and 26th, and it clearly did not amount to much.[18] It would be very easy to point to a number of 'special undertakings' among the thousands of Ultra signals concerning Jugoslavia, about which as much and as little was known for a few days and which then lapsed into total obscurity.[19]

Far too late to be of more than historical interest, the mystery of the Knight's Move was solved during the night of 27/28 May, two days after the fighting round Drvar had ended with Tito's hairbreadth escape. The solution came in two late decodes of 24 May.[20] The first reported the arrival of the officer commanding an SS parachute battalion in Zagreb, and went on to enumerate Luftwaffe and army units belonging to Fliegerführer Croatia's signals net; they included a transport Gruppe, the SS Para Battalion, I/SG 2 and II/JG 51, the last two being described as 'new participants'. The second was much more informative. It revealed that a Major Benesch (whom we already knew to be an officer in the Brandenburg Division, which specialised in 'dirty tricks') was in possession of a report of the same day, 24 May, to the effect that Tito was at his headquarters at Uvala, in a house two kilometres from Potoci railway station[21] protected by a guard of 500 men. Benesch proposed a bombing raid on the house by Fliegerführer Croatia for the 26th, together with ground strafing of the surrounding hills and of Uvala and Potoci, the whole to follow air-landings at Drvar and Petrovac on the 25th. Benesch added that he had discussed his proposals with a Major Blaich who, a comment suggested, might be the same as the Hauptmann Blaich who had commanded a special GAF detachment in Africa and had been employed on tasks of an Abwehr nature.

Hindsight enables us to identify all this with RÖSSELSPRUNG and the attempt on Tito's life. The comments to the two signals show, however, that the identification could not be made with any confidence in Hut 3 at the time when the signals were despatched. The comments were composed in an ignorance of Tito's narrow escape as complete as that which had prevailed earlier about the purpose of the operation cover-named RÖSSELSPRUNG; there was nothing to prove a connection between the new information and RÖSSELSPRUNG, and the cautious tone of the comments makes it clear that unaided reason was only half inclined to see one. The comment to the first spoke only of a 'possible' connection with ELDERLY, while that to the second was still more reticent and would not go beyond saying that the first 'may be relevant'. Even three days after the raid, that is to say, those who handled Ultra were far from sure that RÖSSELSPRUNG was what we know it was. German security had been tight enough to obscure the relationship between the various preparatory measures, and was evidently still able to baffle the first attempts to investigate them.

But why, it may be asked, were these two signals – the first to link parachutists, Tito and some of the existing RÖSSELSPRUNG evidence – not signalled until the night of 27/28 May? They derive from decrypts of the 24th, and three earlier signals show that a key of that date had been broken while it was still in current use. No certain answer can be given to this question after the lapse of forty years and in the absence of information about the particular key from which each signal was derived. But the most probable explanation is that the five signals in question were not all based on decrypts from the same key; at least three keys were in regular use in the Balkans at this time, and one may have been broken for the 24th earlier than the others.

It is clear, however, that even the explicit mention of parachutists and Tito's whereabouts, though it came on top of all the other RÖSSELSPRUNG information, was not enough to suggest an attempt to kill or capture Tito. Ultra alone was insufficient to prompt the right conclusion.

But it is extremely doubtful whether any warning could or would have been issued on the basis of Ultra evidence, even if it had been possible to reach the right conclusion and to do so in time. Signals were currently being sent to Allied headquarters in Italy and to Cairo, which was still the chief centre for Balkan intelligence. (Operational responsibility for Balkan affairs was soon to be exercised from Balkan Air Force headquarters at Bari in Italy, which was added to the Ultra distribution list in June; but this was after the raid on Drvar.) This was all; at no time were Ultra signals sent to recipients on Jugoslav territory. No command lower than an army (and its naval and air equivalents) command was allowed to receive Ultra, and the Allied missions to Tito were not on that level. The reason was to minimise the risk of those with knowledge of Ultra being in jeopardy – as members of the missions plainly were – of capture and interrogation, lest Nazi brutality extort the secret of Bletchley's defeat of the Enigma machine from them. 'Better lose a battle than win it at the price of losing a source capable of winning the war' was the fixed rule; in conformity with it, no Ultra was sent to Arnhem five months later, for instance. A heavily disguised signal based on Ultra might, of course, have been sent to Brigadier Maclean's mission from Allied headquarters, had the evidence warranted it; but there was plainly no justification for this in time for the warning to have been of any use.[22]

Fortunately, the absence of a warning made very little difference in the end. Scrambling hastily down a mountainside, Tito narrowly evaded capture. Drvar was briefly occupied, and his staff temporarily dispersed; but the Partisans' harrying of the German retreat continued with scarcely a pause. Within a few days of his escape, Tito was flown first to Italy and then to the island of Vis, where the Allies already had a naval and air base and where he resumed control of Partisan operations. Closer contact strengthened his relations with the Allies, and his meeting with General Alexander in August was notably friendly. Later Soviet claims, made at the time of Tito's breach with Stalin in 1948, that the raid almost destroyed the Partisans, are quite untrue. Tito's sudden flight to Moscow in September was more the consequence of his life-long communism and the arrival of the Red Army on Jugoslav soil than of a new aversion to the West.

The long-term significance of the Drvar raid was simply that it failed. Had Tito been killed in May 1944, the history of the following years might have been very different. No single leader could have replaced him (the Russians could not even find a candidate in 1948), for his heroic fight had left his personal popularity without a rival. Without him, Jugoslavia would probably have disintegrated. The fragments would then have fallen victim to the Russian pressure which Tito was able to withstand in 1948, the eastern bloc would have been enlarged, and the Iron Curtain have been advanced to the shores of the Adriatic. But Intelligence can claim no part in preventing this.

NOTES

1. *Kriegstagebuch des Oberkommandos der Wehrmacht* (OKW/KTB) ed. W. Hubatsch, iii, 1252–55.
2. This was confirmed at the Anglo-Jugoslav Colloquium by British and Jugoslav officers who had been in or near Drvar at the time.
3. OKW/KTB, iv, 661–65.
4. KV 3013. References in this form are to Ultra signals. If, as seems likely, the German was 'mit allen Kräften', then a better translation might be 'with all their might'.

5. KV 4845.
6. Hut 3 was the department at Bletchley Park where Army and Air Enigma decrypts were serviced. My own membership of it permits the occasional use of 'we' and 'our' in the text. For the sake of clarity, the word 'message' is always used here to mean a German communication, 'signal' an Allied communication.
7. Two other, still earlier, messages were also probably connected, although this does not seem to have been noticed at the time and although there is no Ultra evidence to prove a connection:
   (i) The announcement on 8 May of a conference about a large-scale operation to be held at the HQ of Panzer Army 2 on 12 May; staff officers of V SS Mountain Corps and GAFSE were to be present (KV 4483).
   (ii) Part of the second Gruppe of Air Landing Geschwader 1 (II/LLG 1) was to move from Sarajevo-Butmir to Zagreb-Zirkle on 19 May. As a result, the aircraft were based west of Drvar instead of east, but no nearer to it (KV 4613).
8. KV 4788, signalled at dawn on 22 May.
9. KV 4842, signalled on the evening of 22 May.
10. KV 4948, signalled on the evening of 23 May.
11. It will be noticed that the messages were exclusively concerned with Luftwaffe preparations for the Drvar attack. The OKW War Diary makes no mention of an air component of the operation, but only of ground troops. Army units scarcely appear in the Ultra signals, on the other hand: KV 4733, which records the move of GR 92 and part of a Panzer Abteilung to Udbina (some 40 miles west of Drvar) on 12 May, is an exception. The army keys for Jugoslavia were broken less often than the GAF keys, and this may explain the discrepancy. The report of GR 92's move does not mention RÖSSELSPRUNG, and, in view of the many other operations in progress in mid-May, could not possibly have attracted any particular attention.
12. See my *Ultra in the West*, pp. 185–90.
13. KV 4886, signalled early on 23 May.
14. KV 4912, signalled at midday on 23 May.
15. KV 5059, signalled during the afternoon of 24 May.
16. KVs 4081, 5145.
17. KVs 5074, 5076, both signalled early on the evening of 24 May.
18. The only exception to this general statement is a message of the 24th (KV 5157, which, however, could not be signalled until the afternoon of 25 May, 7–8 hours after the raid on Drvar) to the effect that aircraft would be ready to load an SS parachute battalion at an unspecified airfield in the Zagreb area early on the morning of the 25th; a comment tentatively suggesting a connection with RÖSSELSPRUNG.
19. The following are among the operations which were taking place during the weeks immediately preceding RÖSSELSPRUNG. It is very difficult to distinguish troop movements etc. associated with one from movements associated with another, for more than one might be going on at the same time in the same army or Luftwaffe command area. Note 7 illustrates this difficulty.
   REMNANT/FRÜHLINGSERWACHEN in Montenegro. KVs 720, 761, 2645.
   MESSMATE/ROLFE against some of the Dalmatian islands. KV 3034. This seems to have replaced the larger *WIGAN/FREISCHÜTZ*, which was planned

for mid-February, but postponed because of the occupation of Hungary. VLs 6271, 6397, 6507, 7917, etc. VL 7917 showed that it was to have included a night paratroop landing. See OKW/KTB iv. 657.

PONSONBY/MAIBAUM and its extension PANACEA/BEFRIEDIG-UNG, to drive a group of Partisans NE of Sarajevo across the river Drina. Fliegerführer Croatia, V SS and XV Mountain Corps were the participating authorities (just as in RÖSSELSPRUNG) and there was to be an air landing. KVs 1898, 2227, 2469, 2581, 4404. See also OKW/KTB iv, 651–52.

BALEFUL/MORGENSTERN SE of Sarajevo, just north of Mt Durmitor. KVs 4483, 4558.

MURGATROYD/WIEDERKAEUER resembled RÖSSELSPRUNG more closely than any of the others, but was mentioned only once, in KV 3013. On 27 April, Flivo XV Mountain Corps reported that it would continue next day with a thrust southwards along a valley parallel to that in which Drvar stands towards the village of Trubar, which is less than ten miles from Drvar. 'German forces: assault battalion, reconnaissance Abteilung, two anti-tank platoons, 3 light and 3 heavy tanks, two Cetnik companies. Appreciated that guerrillas are determined to hold Drvar with all forces.' Did not so close a hostile approach cause some alarm in the Partisan high command?

20. KVs 5457, 5479, signalled on 27 and 28 May respectively.
21. This was wrong. Tito had an emergency headquarters at Potoci, but was himself at Drvar. Potoci station is some 15 miles east of Drvar.
22. It will be evident that the above account differs in one particular respect from that in F.H. Hinsley and others, *British Intelligence in the Second World War,* iii/l, 165, and Martin Gilbert, *Winston S. Churchill,* vii, 779, which derives from it. Both were published after this paper was delivered. Both state that Ultra information received prior to the raid authorised the issue of a warning, though in fact none was issued.

As the above account shows, this conclusion is mistaken. Only hindsight can connect Ultra decrypted before the raid with Tito or a raid on his headquarters. No warning could therefore have been issued on the basis of Ultra information, even had security regulations not prohibited it.

7

Ultra and the Gothic Line

The impact of Ultra intelligence upon the conduct of the Allied campaign in Italy and upon the battle for the Gothic Line in particular requires an examination of the nature and scope of Ultra intelligence itself as a preliminary. By 1944, it must at once be emphasised, Ultra was far and away the Allies' most important source of information about the enemy, quite outstripping in regularity, volume and reliability anything learned from agents, line-crossers or prisoners of war.

During the 1930s, the Germans bought up and progressively improved the commercial Enigma encoding machine. By passing an electric current through a set of three or four wheels, each with 26 terminals (one for each letter of the alphabet), which rotated with every depression of a key on the machine's typewriter-like keyboard, and by other complicating devices, the Enigma machine ensured that there would always be something like 150 million million million possible but unpredictably different code versions of a single text – i.e. that for practical purposes the code was unbreakable. Nevertheless, the Poles had managed to read some messages before the war, and in 1939 they passed on their methods and their results to the British and French, who proceeded to develop them further. Our first large-scale success came in mid-1940, and by the winter of 1940/41 one key (the Luftwaffe general purpose key) out of the many in use was being decrypted daily.

As this implies, there was not one Enigma but many. In a very simplified form, the variety of keys may be explained by supposing Enigma to be a parent with three children, army, navy and air force. Each child had many children, each with its own key, and each grandchild similarly. Take the Luftwaffe as an example. Besides the general code already referred to, each Luftflotte and each Fliegerkorps had its own key, and so did every Luftgau, the authority responsible for administration and supply. Similar subdivisions applied to the army and navy. Every one of these keys changed daily according to a pre-determined pattern, sometimes more than once a day. Thus many Enigma-breaking operations were necessary, and each had to be repeated every day. As the war progressed, more keys yielded to the code-breakers' assaults – by 1945 more than a hundred were being, or had been, broken regularly or intermittently – and the number of code-breaking operations required was enormous. Many keys could be read currently, but the army keys presented particular difficulty (because the operators adhered strictly to security regulations) and could sometimes be decrypted only with considerable delay.

Next, it is necessary to note one apparently obvious fact which can easily be overlooked. Any message sent by radio could be intercepted, and by the end of the war the majority could be decrypted. But that which was not transmitted over the air remained as inaccessible as a conversation between Hitler and Keitel in the *Führerhauptquartier*. In the desert, where there were no telephone lines, everything went over the air; in Italy, where land-lines existed in plenty and more could easily be laid, these were used instead for many purposes, and in consequence much remained hidden from Allied intelligence. This limitation had in general to be accepted, but if sabotage or a bomb cut a telephone or teleprinter line useful information might be intercepted until the line was repaired. Several long messages about the construction of defences, including the Gothic Line, were presumably to be attributed to one of these causes. Their length (over 2500 words in one case) and their content made them awkward to encode and transmit by radio: all were tables consisting of columns of figures, and since there were no figures on the Enigma keyboard each figure had to be spelled out as a word.

Since every decrypted Enigma message had been sent by one German to another in the course of duty, and sent in a code believed by its users to be unbreakable, there could be no doubt of its genuiness. But while this ruled out the uncertainty associated with agents' reports (the personal reliability and mental acuteness of the agent must be assessed before what he says can be acted upon) it introduced others. The German sender would naturally assume background knowledge on the part of his correspondent, and if the eavesdropper did not possess this he might find a message unintelligible. Again, it had always to be borne in mind that evidence is only reliable to the extent that the witness giving it is well informed. An air liaison officer, for instance, could be relied on to report accurately his division's present location and activity, but not necessarily to know what it intended to do next, for the army commander's orders might not yet have filtered down to his level; again, a bombing raid ordered by a Fliegerkorps might be countermanded by the parent Luftflotte in a message not intercepted. Unfortunately it was a general rule that the higher the authority and the farther his headquarters from the front, the more likely that his communications with Berlin and his orders to his subordinates would be transmitted by landline. It was not until the latter part of the war that Hitler and Keitel were frequent signatories of intercepted messages.

The decryption and translation of intercepted Enigma messages was carried out at Bletchley Park by two departments, one for the navy and the other for army and air together. From early in 1941 I served in the latter, sharing with three others a rota of duty as guardian of security and as head of the section responsible for deducing military intelligence from the translations and for signalling the gist of them to commands in the field. By 1944 we were sending between 100 and 150 signals a day to the two fronts in France and Italy (almost a hundred thousand signals in all had been sent by May 1945). Signals were sent to the headquarters of armies and the RAF/USAAF equivalents, but for security reasons no lower in the military hierarchy; it was held that nearer the fighting there was too much risk of an officer who was in the secret being captured, for the slightest suspicion by the Germans that Enigma was being decrypted might lead them to change their code and so deprive us of a valuable source of information. For similar reasons commanders were forbidden to use information derived from Enigma without confirmation from another source – for instance, foreknowledge of the route of a convoy carrying supplies from Italy to Libya could not be exploited until a reconnaissance aircraft had first been seen spotting the convoy.

Information derived from Enigma decrypts was known as Ultra, and it is this which forms the basis of what follows.

The success of the invasion of Sicily on 10 July 1943 encouraged the Allied Combined Chiefs of Staff to agree that they would proceed to invade Italy next, but it cautioned Hitler to consider the defence of the peninsula and to appoint Rommel to prepare it. On 17 July OKW told Kesselring, Oberbefehlshaber Süd, that the Führer would decide what reinforcements should be sent him and that Roatta, the Chief of the Italian General Staff, recommended three intermediate defence lines (one to run from Spezia to Pesaro) before a final position between Genoa and Rimini.[1] These two seem to be the first rough sketch of the later Gothic Line. None of this meant, however, that there was yet a firm German determination to defend Italy; German strategy was as undecided as Allied when the Salerno landing took place on 9 September. The dispute between the Americans, who wanted the whole Allied effort concentrated on a second front in the West, and the British, who favoured a Mediterranean strategy to assist both the Russians and a future western invasion by forcing the Germans to divert troops from both to protect Italy – this division of opinion was paralleled by Hitler's long hesitation between Rommel's advice to economise forces by withdrawing to a strong defensive position in the northern Apennines (on Hitler's instructions he reconnoitred one in the early autumn)[2] and Kesselring's to hinder the invaders as far south as possible. This hesitation lasted several months. Even at the end of October Hitler had still not made up his mind which policy to adopt and which man to appoint Commander-in-Chief in Italy (the decision 'bleibt noch in der Schwebe' (is still undecided) noted the OKW's war diarist on the 24th),[3] but on 6 November he took a sudden decision in favour of Kesselring (whose new title Oberbefehlshaber Südwest (OB SW) was at first intended to give him authority over all three services) and sent Rommel off to prepare the defence of northern France.[4] The fighting was now approaching Cassino and the Winter Line.

Preparations for OVERLORD were already beginning, and they made themselves felt in Italy with the withdrawal – the first of many – of 7 British Armoured Division and 82 US Airborne Division to England. The threat of invasion in the west soon affected German strategy too. At Christmas OB SW was ordered to surrender the Goering Panzer Division and 90 Panzergrenadier Division (the Goering Division did not in fact leave Italy until July, 90 PG never); in view of the situation in east and west, OKW continued, there must henceforth be only limited fighting in Italy, and this 'heisst bauen, bauen und immer wieder bauen' (build, build and keep on building).[5] This did not mean defence lines only across the peninsula, but anywhere likely to be under threat in the future. As an earlier widely-held belief that the purpose of the Allied invasion of Italy had simply been to secure free access to the Balkans began to recede, fears of seaborne assaults at almost any point on the long Italian coastline took their place, particularly after the Anzio landing on 22 January 1944. The multiplicity of orders issued because of these fears and in pursuance of OKW's injunction gave Ultra its first regular insights into what was being done over and above the already well-known defence lines south of Rome. The construction of defences on the west coast was referred to in December and January,[6] a defence authority for the northern Adriatic – GOC Lower Alps – was set up,[7] and a Kesselring order of 24 January[8] gave us our first glimpse of what was later called the Gothic Line: Armeegruppe von Zangen (a new command in north Italy) was to guard against landings north of a line roughly from Livorno to Ancona and 'to develop the Apennine position with the greatest energy'. (This was a most valuable intercept in other and more important respects too. It revealed Kesselring's reaction to the Anzio landing two days previously and went on to give a comprehensive review – the passage just quoted was only a small part of it – of the strategy he intended to adopt in consequence).

A week later GOC Lower Alps ordered the highest degree of readiness because of the risk of landings at any time at Ancona and in the Ravenna-Rimini-Pesaro area where 278 Division was stationed, and ordered the immediate development of the Apennine position, particularly at Pesaro[9] (the overlap of function with von Zangen was unexplained). This still gave no location for the Apennine position and no hint of what defence works were being constructed. The first precise details came in an immensely long report from Kesselring's chief Engineer dated 15 April.[10] It reviewed work completed and in progress on the Caesar Line south of Rome, on the Apennine position, and on both coasts, and implied that GOC Lower Alps's orders had been but slackly obeyed during the intervening six weeks.

Analysis of the report reveals some curious features. Defence against coastal landings was evidently being given pride of place, with a heavy emphasis on the west coast. Over 35,000 Italian civilians and 7,000 Organisation Todt personnel were employed between the French frontier and Rosignano (south of Livorno), a distance of over 300 kilometres; they had constructed or were constructing upwards of 8,000 field works (some of them in reinforced concrete), 200 'fortifications' (evidently more solid than field works) and 70 km of anti-tank ditches, had laid out nearly 200 km of wire and 85,000 mines, and had disposed a large part of all this to protect the coastal plain at the mouth of the Arno and to cover the approach to Florence from the sea. The east cost was being less heavily worked on (20,000 compared with over 40,000 men, for example), but preparations extended from the front line right round the head of the Adriatic as far as the Croatian frontier; half the workmen and all the 'fortifications' were north of Ravenna. In contrast with these two, the Apennine position was being taken comparatively lightly: in the 300 kilometres from Pesaro across to the coast north of Viareggio, just under 18,000 soldiers, civilians and Todt personnel were engaged on 3,000 field works (125 of them reinforced), one solitary 'fortification', 5 km of anti-tank ditches, 50 km of wire and fewer than 4,000 mines. Clearly, the protection of the coast, which could be assailed at any moment (the deception planners were constantly harping on this string in order to persuade Kesselring to disperse his forces) was more urgent than the preparation of a new defence line more than 200 km behind that front, but there was no note of urgency in the Chief Engineer's final paragraph of complaint that he needed more trained construction engineers and more mines, nor did he indicate where he wished to employ them.

Another conclusion, and from the Intelligence point of view an equally valuable one, can be drawn from these figures by observing the distribution of the work between the three unequal sectors into which the report divides the Gothic Line: from the west coast to Borgo a Mozzano (above the Serchio valley 15 km north of Lucca), thence to Monte Calvo, and from Monte Calvo to Pesaro. If Monte Calvo in Foglia is meant, as seems probable,[11] then it follows that there are two short sectors of under 50 km each, covering the two coast plains, and another, almost twice as long as the other two together, through the mountains between them. The proportionate attention devoted to the three sectors respectively is as follows (in round figures, reading from west to east): men – 5,000: 10,000: 3,000; field works built or building – 200: 25,000: 300; anti-tank ditches/wire – 0/0: 1.5 km/45 km: 4 km/8 km; mines – 0: 0: 4,000. If the figures for the central sector be divided by four so that all the figures are on the same per kilometre basis, the proportionate attention devoted to each sector becomes plain. Many more men per kilometre are working on the two coastal sectors than on the long mountain sector, which would obviously be more difficult for the enemy to penetrate even if no man-made obstacle were added to those provided by nature; field works are spread more evenly; the west coast has so far no ditches or mines, and the east is rather better off in these respects than the centre; the only mines being laid are all in the east.

Save that the request for more trained engineers to replace those withdrawn at the beginning of the year was repeated, there was no more urgency than before about a similar report issued a month later and signalled before the end of May.[12] This showed modest increases under most headings for work completed, but noticeably fewer starts. Unfortunately, the paragraphs dealing with the Gothic Line were incomplete, only the Monte Calvo–Pesaro section being available; this showed the labour force almost halved; field works nearly doubled, ditches unknown, only a few hundred metres more wire, and exactly the same number of mines as in April. The only conclusion possible is that very slow progress is being made everywhere, most noticeably in the eastern sector where three months later 8 Army's OLIVE offensive broke through the Gothic Line and reached the Romagna.

These two decrypted reports tell much the same story as the captured documents used as the basis of the account in the US Army official history,[13] but they present evidence for a somewhat earlier period than that cited there. The relevant British volume has not yet been published.[13a]

Unhappily, no more reports of this type came to hand (perhaps because no more bombs happened to cut teleprinter lines), but those already mentioned showed conclusively that as late as the middle of May – five days after the DIADEM offensive began to bite into the Gustav Line – the strategy of resisting south of Rome, which Kesselring had announced[14] as soon as he recognised at the end of February that he could not dislodge the American VI Corps from Anzio, was being pursued so wholeheartedly that the preparation of another line across the Apennines as strong as the Gustav was being seriously neglected. Signs that work was now to be accelerated began to multiply directly after the fall of Rome on 4 June. On the seventh, for instance, OKH asked OB SW how many more mines were needed for the Apennine position 'taking into consideration Hitler's demand for mining on a large scale', while Keitel called for the recruitment of more civilian labour and announced that efforts were being made to step up the production of mines.[15]

Unknown to Ultra but not unsuspected by the Allied command, the fall of Rome was prompting an urgent reappraisal of the German defensive situation. A gloomy forecast by Kesselring predicted that if the worst came to the worst he would not be able to hold out south of the Gothic Line for more than three weeks and might even have to abandon it altogether in order to prevent the total destruction of his forces.[16] Warlimont, the deputy head of the *Wehrmachtführungsstab*, was at once despatched on a fact-finding mission, and on his return Hitler issued a new directive on 13 June. This directive was intercepted on 17 June (radio transmission must for some reason have been delayed), and then it baffled the cryptographers for ten days before it could be decrypted and signalled on 27 June.[17] In it, Hitler ordered the Apennine position to be regarded as the final blocking position because 'Allied entry into the plain of Lombardy would have incalculable military and political consequences'. Yet nothing had so far been done in the way of defence works over large parts of the line (as has been shown, there was some exaggeration in this); therefore the common misconception that there was a fortified Apennine position* was 'to be scotched once and for all', and OB SW was to gain as much time as possible to enable its defences to be improved, 'a task which will require mighty labours for months to come'. (The slightly fuller version entered in the OKW War Diary says that seven months would be needed and instructed Kesselring to make a stand meanwhile on the line Piombino–Trasimene–Civitanova, where in fact he did manage to pause for a while at the end of June.)[18]

During the ten days' gestation period of Hitler's decision, Alexander had been reading the same evidence the other way round and concluding that because morale in his armies was 'irresistibly high' and the Gothic Line unready, an immediate advance could break the Line before Kesselring could occupy it. 'Neither the Apennines nor even the Alps should prove a serious obstacle', he telegraphed to Churchill on 7 June, and issued orders for hot pursuit as soon as Rome fell.[19] He expected to be in Bologna and across the river Po by August, and planned a thrust into Austria if all went well. One of his reasons for optimism was the conviction that DIADEM had seriously depleted Kesselring's forces. This conviction was based, at least in part, on Ultra signals he had recently received, which showed that three divisions in 14 Army had been very badly mauled, trained NCOs were lacking, tanks breaking down and anti-tank guns in very short supply,[20] and within 24 hours of his cable to Churchill it will have been greatly strengthened by OB SW's report[21] that he had suffered 38,000 casualties between 11 May and 2 June and had lost about 250 tanks. Alexander's reasons for urging that he should be allowed to pursue and destroy Kesselring's armies and to drive on into German-occupied central Europe were as soundly based on enemy intelligence as they were on detailed logistical planning,[22]

---

*The Apennine position was renamed 'Gothic Line' on 24 April 1944 (MME vi/1.57 n) but the older description also remained current; Ultra did not know of the change until 18 May (KV 4321). As the realisation grew that it might not be strong enough to keep the Allies out, 'Gothic Line' was replaced by 'Green Line' on 15 June (OKW/KTB iv. 519), but the Allies never adopted the new name. 'Green Line' appeared in Ultra almost at once (MVs 9645, 9843, for example), but at first caused some confusion in interpretation.

The second change was made lest the Allies derive propaganda advantage from capturing a defence position named after the Goths. Perhaps someone told Hitler that as Kesselring withdrew northwards from the Trasimene line his forces would pass through Gualdo Tadino, where the Ostrogoths were defeated in A.D. 552 by Justinian's Roman-Byzantine armies of reconquest under Narses, after which their sixty-year domination of Italy was soon brought to an end! (Procopius, *Gothic War* VIII, xxix 1–4, xxxv 31–8.)

but his chances of fulfilling his object were dashed by a directive from the Combined Chiefs of Staff issued, curiously enough, on the same day (13 June) as Hitler's directive to Kesselring but of course in ignorance of it: the advance was to stop at the Pisa-Rimini line (in effect, the same as the Gothic Line) and seven more divisions would be taken from Italy for ANVIL (the landing in the south of France which had been agreed in principle since the Quebec Conference of August 1943) and OVERLORD.[23]

Reluctant to see so great an opportunity disappear in front of his eyes, Alexander appealed against what he saw as a misguided decision, and during the next fortnight the divergence (apparent since the autumn) between British and American views of future Mediterranean strategy widened until the two became irreconcilable. If allowed to retain his present forces intact, Alexander claimed on 17 June, he could reach the Po valley by the end of July and capture the Ljubljana Gap – the natural route to Vienna – in another four weeks; to stop him, the Germans would have to being in ten or more divisions from France and the Balkans.[24] For the Americans, General Marshall dissented, arguing that the Germans might withdraw to the Alps instead of defending the Gothic Line, and that this would frustrate Alexander's plans;* a landing in the south of France was preferable, because it would hold some divisions away from OVERLORD and open the port of Marseilles to Eisenhower's supplies. The argument was still continuing with increasing heat, involving Churchill and Roosevelt, when Hitler's directive to Kesselring was decrypted on the evening of 27 June.

It is very seldom that the impact of Intelligence upon operations can be measured from contemporary writings, which are usually too sparse to prove the linkage conclusively, and the historian is therefore usually forced back against his will on the unprovable assumption that if subsequent action conforms with preceding information it is likely to have been influenced by it. Still less often does a single item make its mark on the record as indelibly as this decrypt, KV 9843. Brooke, the British CIGS, seized on it at once, concluding that 'there can be no further argument that the Germans are about to retire in front of us in Italy'.[25]

---

*The Americans had always taken the logical view that it would pay the Germans to free much-needed men, tanks and guns for more hard-pressed fronts by retreating to the northern Apennines, and that this would therefore be their strategy; the Allies need then pursue them no further. The British believed that Hitler's reaction to events was emotional not rational, and that since he had so often in the past refused to yield ground even if doing so would bring advantage he was likely to act in the same way again: that is to say, he would not permit Kesselring to retreat except under the compulsion of extreme pressure. By his 13 June decision, Hitler behaved as the British had predicted.

Next day he and the other British Chiefs of Staff quoted it in their latest attempt to persuade the US Chiefs to agree to cancel ANVIL and leave Alexander the means to accomplish his proposed end. The Americans refused to budge, Marshall taking the extraordinary view that 'if we had taken full note of all the secret information received, probably OVERLORD itself would never have been undertaken'[26] (in fact, of course, Ultra had been of considerable assistance in planning OVERLORD and had been still more useful since D-Day).[26a] The American view prevailed when the final decision in favour of ANVIL was taken on 2 July (Churchill had quoted KV 9843 in vain to Roosevelt on the first),[27] the British recognising the political wisdom of giving way, but without changing their minds about the military aspects of the controversy in the smallest degree.[28]

Hitler's directive, it will be remembered, was not decrypted until ten days after it was intercepted (delays like this were not uncommon with the intractable army keys). It is interesting to speculate whether, had it been possible to decrypt it at once, it would have had more effect on the heated debates of these weeks. Had Alexander been able to refute Marshall's arguments in his telegram of 19 June,[29] for instance, and to stress that Kesselring was under positive orders to hold the Gothic Line, instead of merely inferring 'it appears that the Germans will try and stand on the Pisa-Rimini line', it is just possible that a different decision might have been taken at Chiefs of Staff and government level. Much might then have been different. As things were, Alexander's depleted forces could not even reach Bologna and the River Po until April 1945, although 8 Army's OLIVE offensive had broken through the eastern sector of the Gothic Line six months earlier and 5 Army's in the centre shortly afterwards. Among the Americans, Mark Clark soon came to realise that it had been a mistake not to cancel ANVIL,[30] as Churchill had already told Roosevelt.[31] This truth was driven home directly the ANVIL landings took place. Hitler at once ordered the evacuation of southern France, and Ultra revealed this barely 24 hours later.[32] Thus ANVIL did not hold enemy forces away from Eisenhower's front even for a moment, whereas Alexander was still doing so and would, if permitted, have been able to hold a great many more.

In comparison with the spring, Ultra offered less guidance as the fighting approached the Gothic Line during the summer. A parenthesis in a message of 20 July[33] yielded one useful bit of information, however: OB SW reminded OKH that the defence of the Gothic Line would involve mountain warfare, asked for 'prompt and thorough training of the Army Group in this type of warfare (to which it is not accustomed)', and called for the attachment of suitably experienced staff officers to both Armies and the subordination of the Mittenwald Alpine School to himself. By confirming that the opposition possessed no comparable skills, this will no doubt have increased Alexander's regret at the loss of the French mountain troops which had breached the Gustav Line by scaling the Aurunci mountains in May. (The US 10 Mountain Division, which did sterling work in the final offensive, was not yet in Italy.)

More important, though less directly related to the Gothic Line until it was fully manned in August and September, was the constant flow of order of battle information. Those who used Ultra at the time all agree that order of battle news, which was provided day in, day out on all fronts from early in 1942 until the end of the war, was Ultra's single most valuable contribution to intelligence – Alexander's staff, says the latest volume in the British official history, 'followed formations and units with the piercing and almost affectionate scrutiny which a Victorian Great Lady devoted to a legion of grandchildren'[33a] – for it enabled Allied generals to know just what divisions were opposing them at any particular moment and whether reinforcements were reaching the front or not. At this juncture, it made it possible to observe that the recent movement of divisions into Italy from elsewhere (19 and 20 Luftwaffe Field Divisions from the west, 42 Jaeger from the Balkans, 16 SS from central Europe and 34 Infantry from the Ukraine) was slowing down, that new arrivals were cancelled out by departures in July and August,[34] and that if the Hermann Goering Panzer Division was at last leaving for the Russian front (its departure had been called for since the early spring), nevertheless 715 Division was being retained in Italy instead of moving to the west as planned.[35] This meant that there was little relative change in the tactical balance, that a weaker Allied force was still containing a stronger German, thereby holding troops away from other fronts and fulfilling the task laid upon it at its foundation, and that the retreat to the Gothic Line had not enabled OKW to economise forces to any marked degree. By the spring of 1945 Army Group C in Italy was in fact the strongest and most coherent fighting force left in the whole Wehrmacht.

Precision was lent to pure order of battle information by two standard types of return which were regularly intercepted. Several assessments of the fighting strengths of their divisions drawn up by Army commanders were decrypted during the autumn.[36] The fighting value of each division was assigned to one of four categories, and the returns showed that very few divisions except 26 Panzer, 29 Panzergrenadier and 90 Panzergrenadier ever escaped from the third category ('fully fit for the defensive') into the second ('capable of limited offensive operations') and that none of the others ever rose above it. The advancing Allies could therefore form a fairly accurate idea of the quality and capabilities of the troops preparing to hold the Gothic Line against them.

On the Adriatic sector, where 8 Army was to launch OLIVE on 25 August, tanks would count for more than in the mountains, and a knowledge of the enemy's tank strength was therefore desirable. Sets of statistics intercepted during the spring had revealed a substantial decline in numbers not only of tanks but of anti-tank and assault guns as a result of DIADEM,[37] and although there were fewer similar returns during the summer and early autumn, enough were decrypted to make it clear that new deliveries were scarcely making good natural wastage, that Kesselring began OLIVE with some 30 fewer Mark III and Mark IV tanks than he had possessed earlier (Panther and Tiger numbers were better maintained) and that anti-tank gun stocks were still falling.[38] This was welcome news to a commander conscious of the limitations which had been imposed on his own capacity to conduct an offensive, the more so since it was possible to deduce from the returns that a high proportion of the armour and artillery was concentrated in the hands of only two divisions, 26 Panzer and 29 Panzergrenadier, the movements of which from sector to threatened sector of the line were usually known with only a few hours' delay from the regular reports of their air liaison officers (Flivos).

Flivo and similar information proved particularly valuable as the launching of Alexander's two-fisted assault on the Gothic Line (in the east on 25 August, in the centre on 10 September) approached. The Adriatic coast blow had been planned partly because this was thought to be the least well-prepared sector (a belief which Ultra had encouraged and which photographic reconnaissance could confirm) and partly in the hope – disappointed in the event – that armoured exploitation could quickly reach the plain of Lombardy and outflank the whole German position. Negatively, Ultra helped the offensive by showing that there was no reason to think that the necessary preliminary move of 8 Army back east of the Apennines had been observed. (Luftflotte 2 was only managing twenty or thirty sorties a day for all purposes at this time,[39] petrol shortage was severely limiting aerial reconnaissance – there was only one photographic sortie a week over the Adriatic in August[40] – and

Goering, who had ordered fuel economy on pain of court-martial in July announced stringent restrictions on all air operations on 1 September.[41]) Indeed, so far from being reported on the Adriatic, 8 Army's headquarters was thought to have moved westwards to Siena on 8 August![42] (This was, of course, a week before the eastward move actually began.) Positively, Ultra helped by showing that Kesselring was so inclined to fear that ANVIL was to be launched against his own Ligurian flank (or perhaps presaged another landing there), rather than against 19 Army's front on the French Riviera, that he declared a state of emergency in the western half of Lombardy on 12 August[43] and was still gripped by the same fear as late as 6 September.[44] In consequence, he placed some of his best divisions west of the Apennines and held them there for several days after OLIVE began, evidently under the misapprehension that the main threat to the Gothic Line was to come in this sector. Thus 42 Jaeger and 16 SS Divisions were round Genoa and in the Serchio valley respectively on 29 August,[45] 90 PG was still near the French frontier on 3 September,[46] 29 PG was slow to move forward[47] and 26 Pz did not transfer to the Adriatic until 30 August.[48]

But here a note of warning must be sounded. Tactical information was never Ultra's strongest feature, because inevitably the whole process from intercept to signal, however rapidly it might be possible to conduct it, could seldom keep up with the speed of a quick-moving battle, where sudden shifts or reversals could come in minutes; the Y Service, decrypting lower-grade codes just behind the front line, could nearly always beat Ultra in this respect. The signal about 26 Pz was exceptionally late – it was not sent until 9 September – but the other four were all 24 hours old by the time they were decrypted and transmitted, so that even if sent with the highest priority the information they contained was probably out of date by the time it was received. For the same reason, although there were several useful reports that one division after another was manning the Gothic Line,[49] no satisfactory account of the battles for the Futa and Il Giogo passes can be derived from Ultra: intelligence received even four or five hours after the tactical movements it heralded would almost always have been overtaken by events and so have lost its operational value.

Although the rivers of the Romagna soon halted 8 Army and stiffening resistance stalled 5 Army a few miles short of Bologna, the rapid loss of the greater part of the Gothic Line was driving Kesselring to seek Hitler's permission to withdraw to the Po before September was out. His request was of course refused, for Hitler's faith in fixed defences was not to be shaken by the loss of one of them. In addition to a series of temporary local blocking lines on the east coast[50] in October and November, during the winter and spring repeated orders went out for the construction of elaborate fortifications along the lower Alps and in northern Jugoslavia.[51] When it also appeared[52] that a large headquarters complex was being prepared in the south Tirol, suspicions were aroused that this might be the intended nerve-centre of the rumoured Alpine bastion into which the most hardened Nazis would retreat. Strangely enough, these suspicions took far deeper root in Eisenhower's than in Alexander's entourage, but although at one time the evidence seemed very persuasive all fears proved in the end to be without foundation.

Any attempt to assess the operational value of Ultra in the planning and execution of the assault on the Gothic Line must concentrate on two aspects.

In the first place, it is clear that no other source could have provided so much accurate, detailed and reliable information. No agent or partisan could have purloined the constructional returns or Hitler's directive of 13 June and carried them safely across the front line, for instance, no could he have brought news of divisional moves anything like as quickly as Ultra. The difficulty is not in appraising the quality of the information but in discovering exactly how it was utilised. It is to be presumed that the Intelligence staff at Alexander's headquarters compared the constructional details with contemporary air photographs and that what they learned from the comparison stood them in good stead when they had to interpret subsequent photographs taken nearer the time of the assault, when Ultra had ceased to provide this information. But no positive record of this seems to have been preserved, and it must remain a strong presumption rather than a certainty (the regular Army Group Intelligence summaries were composed by men who had access to Ultra, but since they were circulated to a far wider audience any Ultra they incorporated was camouflaged beyond recognition).

There is no substantial doubt, then, that the attackers benefited from knowledge of the Gothic Line which they could not have acquired without Ultra, but the extent of their advantage cannot be precisely measured.

Secondly, the disproportion between the labour and materials employed on coastal fortifications and those employed on the Gothic Line, which has already been referred to, provided solid proof of the success of Allied deception measures, and this too could scarcely have been obtained in any other way. Kesselring's carefree boast (which was buttressed by Canaris' authority) in January 1944, just before Anzio, that he had no worries about his seaward flanks,[53] soon gave way to anxiety as the deception planners got to work. From small beginnings in Cairo in 1940/41 under a gifted director, deception had come to embrace the whole Mediterranean in a marvellous web of illusion, and by the winter of 1943/44 it was being copied in London to protect OVER-LORD. Its objects in the Mediterranean were twofold: to keep German forces away from the west, and to persuade Kesselring to disperse them on coast-watching rather than concentrate them on manning defence lines across the peninsula.[54]

The rumours of a landing in Dalmatia which were circulated under *Plan Zeppelin*[55] surfaced frequently in Ultra, interspersed with fears of another landing somewhere on the eastern coast of Italy or at the head of the Adriatic.[56] The construction reports already cited bear witness to the practical effectiveness of these rumours. The Allies never intended to land on the Adriatic coast of Italy; the labour and the concrete used in fortifying it would, if employed on the Gothic Line instead, have hastened its completion and made the assault more difficult. The success of this part of the deception plan appears the more remarkable when it is remembered that it had to be drastically recast at short notice in early August. Until then, Alexander had planned to mount the main assault in the centre, so the deception planners had been stressing the eastern end of the Gothic Line as the danger area. Suddenly the real and the notional changed places; truth had to become falsehood and vice versa – with only three weeks to go before OLIVE!

Similarly, the even greater expense of men and materials on the west coast, like Kesselring's retention of some of his best divisions there before OLIVE, demonstrated the effectiveness of *Plan Ferdinand*,[57] which aimed to distract attention from ANVIL by suggesting a landing in the region of Genoa. Thus an Abwehr report[58] that Italian partisans had been told to concentrate round Spezia (and at Ascoli Piceno on the opposite side of the Apennines too) to await landings showed that a deliberately trailed bait was being swallowed, as did the confident prediction of the Japanese ambassador in Madrid on 11 June that there would be landings south of Genoa and on the west coast of the Gulf of Lion 'in the next few days'.[59]

In these diversionary respects too, the Ultra contribution to the conquest of the Gothic Line was tremendous, but here it merges into the broader history of the Italian campaign as a whole.

NOTES

1. *Oberkommando der Wehrmacht, Kriegstagebüch* (OKW/KTB), ed. Schramm, iii. 799–800.
2. OKW/KTB iii. 1096, C.J.C. Molony: *The Mediterranean and Middle East* (MME) v. 319, 377n.
3. OKW/KTB iii. 1220.
4. OKW/KTB iii. 1465–6.
5. OKW/KTB iii. 1386.
6. VL 3809. Ultra signals sent to commands in the field were arranged in series with a two-letter prefix, the signals being numbered from 1 to 9999. The series which will be referred to in this paper are VL, KV, XL, HP and BT. All are in the Public Record Office, London.
7. VLs 3306, 4806.
8. VLs 5359, 5381.
9. VL 5503.
10. KV 1578; see also KV 3097.
11. However, there is a Monte Calvi between the Futa and the Il Giogo passes on the Florence–Bologna route, and this is marked Montecalvo on Map XI in the official American history volume – E.F. Fisher: *Cassino to the Alps*.
12. KVs 4321, 5245.
13. Fisher 299–302.
13a. Volume vi/2 of *The Mediterranean and Middle East* was published in 1987.
14. VL 8072.
15. KVs 7009, 7342.
16. OKW/KTB iv. 516–7.
17. KV 9843.
18. OKW/KTB iv. 519–523.
19. J. Ehrman: *Grand Strategy* (GS) v. 266–7.
20. KVs 5761, 5796, 5916.
21. KVs 6886, 7032.
22. Cf MME vi/1 320.
23. A. Bryant: *Triumph in the West* 211, 215, GS v. 346–7.
24. MME vi/1. 319–320.
25. Bryant 224, D. Fraser, *Alanbrooke* 430–1.
26. MME vi/1. 329.
26a. Ralph Bennett: *Ultra in the West* 48–65, 70–95.
27. MME vi/1 332.
28. GS v. 352–8.

29. MME vi/1. 323.
30. M. Clark: *Calculated Risk* 368.
31. GS v 356.
32. XLs 6753, 6919.
33. XL 3859.
33a. MME vi/1. 293.
34. XLs 4756, 7280, 7479, 7506, 7720.
35. KVs 6029, 6156, 6157, 6428, 6556, 6728, 7933, 9100, XLs 199, 1963, 2456, 2912, 3110, 3778.
36. HPs 1200, 1490, 1839, 1957, 2714, etc.
37. KVs 3190, 3791, XLs 30, 129, for instance.
38. XLs 5185, 5797, 6087, 6362, 6982.
39. E.g. XL 8587.
40. XLs 6882, 7908.
41. XLs 1438, 9806.
42. XL 6257.
43. XL 6013.
44. XL 9957.
45. XLs 8575, 8610.
46. XL 9122.
47. XL 8122.
48. XL 9857.
49. E.g. XLs 3998, 8374, 9754, 9875, 9993, HP 318.
50. E.g. HPs 4048, 4370, 4448, 8523.
51. E.g. HPs 8539, 8955, 9105, 9494, BTs 3776, 4356.
52. BTs 99, 890.
53. OKW/KTB iv. 122, 124–5.
54. The official British history of deception, M. Howard: *Strategic Deception*, which was not published until 1990, deals with the first but not the second.
55. Howard 147–155.
56. E.g. VL 3805 of 12 January, KV 4302 of 17 May.
57. Howard 155–9. A threat to Liguria was repeatedly mentioned or implied in May and June: KVs 3652, 3884, 6109, 6428, 6556, 6728, etc.
58. KV 4260.
59. KV 7751.

8

The 'Vienna Alternative', 1944:
Reality or Illusion?

However little regard may have been paid to intelligence in the planning of military operations in the past (and perhaps still in the present?), historians now commonly agree that during the second half of the Second World War plenty of reliable intelligence (mainly Ultra) was available to generals and their political masters and that it was highly esteemed and much used by most of them. This is of course not to pretend that it virtually directed operations – the primacy of policy was inviolate – but to insist that from the winter of 1942/3 onwards the planning and execution of policy took regular and serious account of intelligence about the enemy's situation and intentions. In the majority of cases no real conflict arose between the two: intelligence did not suggest that policy should be drastically changed, rather it assisted in solving problems which arose naturally out of the circumstances, and suggested no more than adjustments of policy.

But what of a case where intelligence and policy pointed in different directions? It is not usually profitable to investigate what did not happen, the might-have-beens of history – understanding what did happen is difficult enough – and the fashion for 'counter-factual history' ('How would America have developed if railways had not been invented?' and the like) has passed away unlamented. However, there is one case in 1944 which, if it does not fit the pattern of 'intelligence versus policy' with complete exactness, shows up the subordination of the one to the other in a particularly lurid light and offers an informative illustration of the now generally accepted dogma that political decisions are frequently made on the basis of preconceived ideas not rationally analysed information.

Few military operations which were never carried out can have had as much intelligence to recommend them as General Alexander's[1] proposal in June 1944 to strike from the head of the Adriatic towards Vienna,[2] yet there is no record that an evaluation of intelligence played a part in the discussions which followed: on the contrary, the rejection of his plan came about simply because of the preponderance of one party over the other in an inter-Allied debate about strategy. Because it was a 'non-event', historians have usually passed the Vienna proposal over with a bare mention. Only one study exclusively devoted to it has been printed, and this was based on research into the political rather than the military records.[3] Examination of the military intelligence bearing on the area (it has not previously been closely scrutinised) which would have been traversed shows that the prospects for an expedition were a good deal more promising than has been generally allowed.

The character of this intelligence calls for a word of preliminary comment. There was a very great deal of Ultra information about events in Yugoslavia throughout 1944,[4] and the amount of it tended to increase. At one time so much raw material was coming in every day that it threatened to swamp the intelligence staffs dealing with it; happily, the danger-point was never quite reached, and channels of communication were never choked by the glut about which many modern writers complain. This intelligence was derived from decrypts of army, navy and air force traffic in Enigma, most of it coming from army groups, armies, corps, divisions and even quite small units stationed all over occupied Yugoslavia. There was no need to fear that it contained deliberate disinformation; since the Germans had no suspicion that their traffic was being read, they took no steps to mislead eavesdroppers, though internal security called for some reticence about future operations. Signals conveying the essence of the intercepts were transmitted to Allied HQ and selected subordinates, but it must be remembered that at no time was a station authorised to receive Ultra set up on Yugoslav soil – a prudent security measure dictated by the absence of a sufficiently senior Allied command there and by fear that in such a disturbed country indoctrinated personnel might fall into enemy hands.

Phrase-making, one might say that the Vienna proposal began in illusion and ended in disillusion. During the autumn of 1943, well before Alexander put it forward seriously, it formed part of a deception plan to mislead the enemy about Allied intentions for 1944. Several months later it was strongly advocated as a genuine operation by a number of experienced professional soldiers, in spite of the manifest difficulty of carrying it out, not only as a means of defeating the Germans but also

THE ZENDA AREA AND THE 'ALPINE REDOUBT'

Source: Ralph Bennett, *Ultra in the West* (London, 1979)

as a way of influencing the post-war political settlement of Europe. (Such a reversal of roles was not unprecedented. In Italy, as earlier in the desert and Tunisia, topography so restricted the strategic and tactical options – and hence the convincing deceptions – that the one had sometimes to become the other at short notice. Operation OLIVE, 8 Army's attempt in August 1944 to breach the Gothic Line at its eastern end and reach the plain of Lombardy, went from one extreme to the other in three weeks). In essence, Alexander's plan was to isolate the large German armies of occupation in the Balkans by cutting their communications – principally the Zagreb–Belgrade–Athens railway – and to push on towards Vienna through the so-called 'Ljubljana Gap', a slight depression between the Carinthian and Dalmatian mountains. Because it never reached the operational planning stage, the scheme was not given a code-name at the time, and it has since been variously termed 'the Istrian Option', 'the Vienna Alternative', or referred to by a lengthy descriptive phrase. To repair the omission, and for simplicity of reference here, I shall call it Operation ZENDA,[5] in reminiscence of Anthony Hope's *Prisoner of Zenda,* near the borders of whose Ruritanian kingdom an expedition would have passed.

I

In the formal sense, the scheme was born in October 1943, when *Plan Jael*, the first draft of the OVERLORD cover-plan, put it about that as soon as they had secured bases in northern Italy the Allies would proceed to occupy Istria, cut German communications with south-east Europe, and use their Cairo-based forces (the size of which the Germans were induced by a series of deceptions to over-estimate very considerably) to invade Greece. Nine months later the 'notional' gave way to the real; as soon as he occupied Rome in June 1944 Alexander proposed to advance quickly to Lombardy and then to exploit either north-westwards into France or north-eastwards into Austria, preferably the latter. His proposal was not accepted by the Combined Chiefs of Staff and their political superiors; by the end of June fierce debates had ended in a decision to mount ANVIL, a seaborne invasion of the south of France, in mid-August, and this entailed the withdrawal of so many divisions from Italy that Alexander's weakened forces were unable to reach Lombardy until the spring of 1945. Several later attempts were made to revive the Austrian project, but all came to nothing.

In a very real sense, however, the origin of ZENDA was German, not

British or American. When he persuaded Hitler, in October 1943, that it would be practicable to hold a series of defence lines in Italy for an indefinite length of time and that there was no need to retire to the Alps at once in consequence of the Salerno landing (as Rommel urged), Kesselring[6] committed both sides to a long and punishing Italian campaign in which the balance of advantage was bound in the end to lie with the Allies if they played their cards right. Kesselring's advocacy made Germany a willing accomplice of the Allies in fulfilling the directive of the Washington conference in May 1943,[7] which had laid it upon Eisenhower as his first duty to attract as many Germans as possible towards the Mediterranean and away from the Russian front and the future Overlord area.

Every one of the defence lines to which Kesselring fell back in turn necessarily had both its feet in the sea, so that he always faced the risk that an amphibious operation might suddenly turn one or the other of his flanks. From January 1944, when he had made the vainglorious boast that the risk did not trouble him[8] – only to find the Anzio landing in his rear a fortnight later – he was always looking apprehensively over his shoulder in fear that the same thing might happen again. In his postwar *Memoirs*[9] he said that he would have carried out another Anzio-type operation had he been in Alexander's shoes. But as the Allied armies slowly fought their way up the Italian peninsula they exposed the Yugoslav shore of the Adriatic and threatened a landing on the flank of OB South-east as well. Kesselring's frequent efforts to improve its defences show that Istria, where his boundary marched with that of OB South-east, was one of his most sensitive spots. To protect himself from attack there was his constant anxiety, more particularly because the Zagreb–Belgrade–Athens railway, which runs not far inland at this point, was both the lifeline of the armies occupying Greece, Crete and the Aegean islands and also the route along which Yugoslav minerals, upon which Germany was dependent, were transported back to the Reich. The growing menace of Tito's Partisans endangered and sometimes interrupted it; ZENDA might cut it for good.

Long before this, however, and two years before ZENDA began life as a cover-plan, the idea of a Balkan operation at some future time had found a secure lodgement in Churchill's and a few other minds. Although caution seized him at the moment of decision, so that responsibility for the British expedition to Greece in 1941 rests with Eden and Wavell, Churchill had at first enthused over the prospects it opened up (perhaps in the hope that his Dardenelles plan of 1915 might at last prove to have been well grounded), seeing it as a first step towards a Balkan coalition based on Turkey to harass the Axis in what he was later mistakenly to call 'the soft underbelly of Europe'.[10] Wavell did not see things like this, but his successor as Commander-in-Chief Middle East, Auchinleck, borrowed a wide-angled strategic lens from his Indian experience which, though it made him over-sensitive to the threat that a German advance deep into the Caucasus might pose to his whole command, also convinced him that the road to eventual victory would lie from the head of the Adriatic into central Europe.[11] Thus even before the end of 1941 two future invasion routes were tentatively sketched out – north-west from the Aegean and north-east from the Adriatic. So long as disappointment and disaster remained the lot of British arms in 1941 and the first half of 1942 there was no possibility of making use of either. The Aegean form of the idea was the first to take on a semblance of life. Churchill's sketch of possible campaigns, prepared for the Washington conference of December 1941, spoke of liberating the captive peoples of Europe by landing 'armies strong enough to enable the conquered populations to revolt' in a long list of places which ended with 'Italy and possibly the Balkans'.[12] Although this was a morale-raising vision of hope, at the time it was scarcely more realistic than his exhortation to Dalton the previous year to 'set Europe ablaze' through the Special Operations Executive.

With the beginnings of change in the fortunes of war, the prospect of action in the Balkans became less remote as the growth of resistance movements in Yugoslavia and Greece suggested new allies and as the search for strategic advantage intensified. But what lends the concept of ZENDA its peculiar interest is that it was at almost exactly the same time that the flow of Ultra information about the Balkans – hitherto almost non-existent – began to increase until it eventually became a very large proportion of the total Mediterranean intake. Before long Ultra was offering so much information which invited intervention somewhere on the eastern Adriatic littoral that the question 'Why was no advantage taken of it?' almost asks itself. There are plenty of cases where less information led to more action.

Encouraged by Montgomery's feat of halting Rommel at Alam Halfa in September 1942, the new Commander-in-Chief Middle East, Alexander, could spare a little attention for events outside Egypt even before Alamein. He called for sabotage of the Belgrade–Athens railway, along which supplies and reinforcements were carried to Rommel, and a British-led party of Greeks blew up the Gorgopotamos viaduct at the end of November 1942. Together with the growing threat of Partisan resistance in Yugoslavia and the prospect that Turkey would join the Allies (Churchill's visit to Adana in January 1943 made this seem imminent), this led Hitler to issue his Directive 47 reorganising the Balkan command structure and its defensive stance against assault landings 'in the foreseeable future'.[13] Goering undertook to provide additional aircraft to repel landings, and OKW concluded that even without Turkey the Allies had enough troops in the Mediterranean to open the Aegean, though not enough to push on to the Danube, and sent Warlimont to Rome to warn Kesselring to look to his flank defences.[14]

The Casablanca conference in January decided that the conquest of Tunisia should be followed by an assault on Sicily in July (and thus, by almost unbreakable logic, by the invasion of Italy later on) but did not contemplate a landing in the Balkans. The northern and southern shores of the Mediterranean were in fact becoming a single theatre of operations, but strategic horizons had not widened enough to take account of this. Churchill's attention was forcibly drawn to the new developments in January; when he was in Cairo on his way to meet the Turks at Adana he was shown evidence that the Partisans deserved the support they had so far been denied because they were assisting the three major Allies by holding a large number of German troops away from other fronts. Churchill's temporarily dormant interest in the Balkans was immediately reawakened, and direct contact with the Partisans was established when the Deakin mission was parachuted to Tito in May. Before long Churchill was telling Alexander 'Great prizes lie in the Balkan direction'.[15] The political and the military approaches were evidently converging, but Grand Strategy still lagged behind: the Washington conference in May (Trident) laid no Balkan plans, American opposition to which built up steadily from this time onwards, while the British Chiefs of Staff were more concerned to hold their allies to the Italian campaign to which they had reluctantly agreed than to inveigle them into Balkan adventure – Churchill even forswore it when trying to secure Roosevelt's assent to ACCOLADE, his pet scheme of capturing the Dodecanese islands which came to an inglorious end in Cos and Leros during the autumn.

That same spring the MINCEMEAT deception had played on existing German fears to divert attention from the assault on Sicily by posing a 'notional' threat to the Peloponnese, and the success of the ruse was known through Ultra almost at once: OKW ordered still further measures for the defence of Greece and a Panzer division was sent right across Europe to reinforce the threatened area.[16] Churchill optimistically forecast that the Germans would soon have to withdraw almost to the northern borders of Yugoslavia, and Wilson (C-in-C Middle East since February) urged that Balkan opportunities were as inviting as Italian after the fall of Mussolini and the surrender of his successors.[17]

It was on every ground natural that the first steps of actual or contemplated Allied intervention in the Balkans should concentrate on Greece and the Aegean route into Europe. The increased flow of Ultra in the spring and summer of 1943 encouraged this by showing the enemy's heightened anxiety about landings on the Greek coast, their continuing grossly exaggerated estimate of Allied capabilities – only 30 or 40 per cent of Allied shipping was committed to the invasion of Sicily, according to the Balkan air command in late July, leaving the rest free for employment elsewhere – and the movements and locations of the existing occupation forces and new arrivals, which were now regularly reported.[18]

The centre of gravity began to shift northwards in the late summer and autumn. Anticipating that the Italians might defect, in August the Germans reorganised the structure of command in the Balkans again, moving its HQ from Athens to Belgrade. When Italy surrendered in September, they quickly ousted the Italian garrisons from Greece, but the Partisans won the race to replace the Italians along the Yugoslav coast, seizing enough Italian weapons to double the size of their army and enlarging the liberated area accordingly; by the end of the month Foreign Armies West reported that Tito was moving north into Slovenia and strengthening resistance there. Free elections were held in Slovenia in September, and a national assembly met.[19] Slovenia became the main preoccupation of Rommel's Army Group B when, very shortly after it moved into Lombardy under the ACHSE programme, it began to stretch out eastwards to occupy the strategically important Save valley. A newly-decrypted key carried Army Group B's daily reports, thus opening up to surveillance an area about which there had hitherto been very little information. The order of battle of the Army Group and its subordinate 1 SS Panzer Army (with HQ at Ljubljana) were soon well known, and the districts which it considered 'pacified' were accurately delineated.[20] For the moment, the gateway to the ZENDA area was well protected.

The Allies' slow progress in Italy and the Germans' aggressive defence of Greece and the Aegean (most recently demonstrated by the Cos/Leros affair) were turning attention away from the Aegean and towards the head of the Adriatic at the end of the year; the essential pillar of an Aegean operation was removed when all efforts failed to shift the Turks from their neutral stance. True, the Partisans were losing most of their September gains at the turn of the year, but nevertheless, aware that the Russians had recaptured Kiev and were still advancing and that OKW was in consequence obliged to draw upon Army Group B's once-menacing power – the only remaining strategic reserve of any size – to stem their onward rush,[21] Churchill and Eisenhower briefly discussed during November alternative strategies which might be followed once the Po valley had been occupied – to push either westwards to the French Riviera or eastwards through the Ljubljana Gap.[22] The transfer of the Army Group B staff to France, where Rommel was to supervise the Channel defences, and the gradual dispersal of its divisions, meant that the head of the Adriatic was weakly defended once more; as for the approach thither, 'The way to Venice was open' on the second day (24 November 1943) of Montgomery's attack across the river Sangro, declared Westphal, Kesselring's Chief of Staff, in his post-war *Memoirs*.[23]

Remarkably enough, in view of his previous hostility to Balkan entanglements, it was Roosevelt who, at the Teheran conference later the same month, put ZENDA firmly on the map by proposing 'to strike northeast from the head of the Adriatic ... with the design of reaching Vienna through the Ljubljana Gap'; Stalin preferred the Riviera alternative, but did not dismiss the other out of hand.[24] While it would be too much to call this the foundation charter of Operation ZENDA, since no military feasibility study had been undertaken, the idea was at least now being seriously considered at the highest political and strategic level. In mid-January 1944 Churchill speculated that ANVIL might force the Germans to withdraw behind the Alps and 'it would then be open to us to turn left into France, or to pursue the Germans towards Vienna, or to turn right towards the Balkans'.[25]

Throughout the winter of 1943–44, the period of Anzio and vain battering at Cassino and the Gustav Line, intelligence was far more plentiful about the Italian front than about the confused fighting in Yugoslavia and revealed little of strategic importance there. Allied co-operation with the Partisans, together with JAEL and other cover-plans designed to distract attention from the preparations for OVERLORD by creating uncertainty about the destination of vast notional reserves in the Mediterranean, fuelled local German fears of a landing on the Dalmatian coast[26] to expedite the supply of arms to Tito or to effect a junction with his Partisan brigades. OKW and OKH, on the other hand, were more inclined to doubt whether any large-scale operation was now intended, and gave warning that no new Flak could be provided and that the GAF commands in the Balkans must henceforth live from hand to mouth for spare parts.[27] Admiral Adriatic's protest against a rumour that the army would not defend Istria, the key to the defence of the Balkans,[28] seemed for a moment negated by evidence that 1 SS Panzer Army was still based at Trieste in late November and by OB South-west's establishment of a new headquarters to defend his Adriatic coastline in January 1944,[29] but that OB South-east was under pressure to surrender troops to more hard-pressed sectors became apparent through Ultra only a fortnight after an OKW decision in mid-December that because it was the least threatened command it should make the greatest sacrifices, the seasoned troops it lost being replaced by newly-raised formations.[30] This was conclusive, and its enforcement could be noted when 114 Jaeger Division was ordered out of northern Dalmatia to Cassino to release the Goering Division for service in the west (in fact the latter was retained in Italy for several more months and then went to the Russian front), and by other similar evidence, notably the move of four divisions in March to hold Hungary against the advancing Russians. What the German command most feared throughout the spring of 1944, wrote Westphal 30 years later, was a large-scale landing in Istria; sufficient troops to beat it off could not have been collected in time, and it could easily have carried the Allies on to Vienna and Budapest.[31] Cumulative signs of a gradual weakening of the western Jugoslav coastal defences could only encourage the Allies to consider intervention.

II

Exactly when Alexander conceived the Ljubljana–Vienna plan is not clear. He had opposed ANVIL from the start, but he could hardly have put the Vienna alternative forward in so well-rounded a form immediately after the capture of Rome on 4 June if he had not already considered it the ultimate objective of DIADEM, and had staff studies made during May (Harding, his Chief of Staff, Robertson, his Chief of Administration, and the US Air Force General Cannon were 'already at work on the details' at the beginning of June).[32] In proposing it, Alexander took an unaccustomed strategic initiative[33] in which he had the backing of Maitland Wilson, C-in-C Middle East; but permission to execute the plan depended on the Combined Chiefs of Staff (at whom Churchill's January speculations had been directed), and this meant overcoming the objections of the Americans and of Brooke, the British CIGS. Brooke forcefully pointed out that, even on Alexander's own optimistic forecast, the move towards Austria could not start until September, so that winter was bound to catch the expedition somewhere in the mountains (as it in fact caught the whole Allied force on the Gothic Line later on): to take on topography and the weather as well as the German army, he argued, would be asking for trouble.[34] Marshall, the US Chief of Staff, urged that nothing should be allowed to distract effort away from OVERLORD (which ANVIL was supposed to assist, by striking at the rear of the German position in France), and the Combined Chiefs of Staff decreed that Alexander should lose seven experienced divisions to ANVIL and halt when he had reached the latitude of Pisa and Rimini.[35]

The fierce inter-allied debates which raged in June and July were about rival strategies for western Europe, not mainly about the centre and south-east at all. The two were linked only by the fact that ANVIL would remove from Italy troops without which a quick advance into Lombardy would become problematical and the Ljubljana Gap unattainable. But the main defect of ANVIL in the eyes of its bitterest opponent, Brooke, was that the removal of these troops would so weaken Alexander that he would not be able to smash Kesselring before he could retreat to the protection of the Apennines north of Florence. In comparison with this, the military shortcomings of ZENDA (it was 'not based on any real study of the problem', he wrote somewhat unfairly) were relatively unimportant. It irritated him that Churchill and Alexander insisted on raising a new side-issue at a moment when crucial decisions were imminent. For although American insistence on ANVIL was based partly on an exaggerated forecast of the help it would give to OVERLORD and partly on a misreading of Hitler's likely policy in Italy (Marshall was convinced that he would soon order a retreat to the Alps, thus rendering it unnecessary for Alexander to mount a new offensive and in consequence freeing troops for ANVIL) which persisted even after Ultra had revealed the contrary at the end of June,[36] the introduction of ZENDA into the discussions lent extra force to their arguments because it gave them reason to suspect that, in spite of Churchill's frequent denials and Alexander's clearly stated wish to advance north-east towards Vienna, not south-east towards Belgrade and Athens, the British were indulging in Balkan fantasies ('Say, where is this Ljubljana? If it's in the Balkans we can't go there', said Marshall).[37] Eisenhower's remark that 'to contemplate wandering off overland via Trieste to Ljubljana is to indulge in conjecture to an unwarrantable degree' chimed exactly with Brooke's strictures on Alexander's 'dream of marching on Vienna'; Roosevelt, unmindful of his own Teheran suggestion of an Istrian landing and of the decrypt which ended all doubts about Hitler's intentions in Italy, explained that in a Presidential election year he would not survive even a slight setback to OVERLORD 'if it were known that fairly large forces had been diverted to the Balkans'.[38] Unintentionally, Alexander had increased American hostility to his retention of strong forces in Italy, the *sine qua non* of ZENDA, by seeming to want them for dark and suspicious British purposes; looking back on the controversy soon after the final decision for ANVIL, Brooke reflected that 'Alexander's talk of an advance on Vienna has killed all our arguments [against ANVIL] dead'.[39]

Whether, without it, the revelation of Hitler's intention to contest every inch of Italian ground would have persuaded Marshall and Eisenhower that a renewed Italian offensive in Italy to draw German divisions away from France would be a better investment than ANVIL is a matter of conjecture; the timing makes it just possible – Hitler's directive decrypted on 27 June, the final decision to mount ANVIL not until 2 July. Hindsight suggests an additional reflection. Sir David Hunt has persuasively argued, in an unpublished paper presented to the Anglo-Jugoslav Colloquium at the Imperial War Museum in December 1982, that Hitler's successive decisions to resist strongly in Italy, coupled with the defence of the Gothic Line, 'removed both the necessity and the possibility of an Allied campaign in Jugoslavia' because they showed that the Germans would co-operate in fulfilling the sole purpose for which the Allies were engaging in operations in Italy – to contain as many German troops as possible. Alexander, intent always on ensuring that his armies made a positive contribution to final victory and did not become merely a magnet to attract Germans away from other fronts, was slow to draw this conclusion, and continued to advocate a thrust into central Europe.

Military intelligence had as little influence on discussion of the Ljubljana expedition as on the ANVIL debates, although Ultra provided it in ample volume. Signs of German anxiety about coastal defence continued – in June a landing in the Venice area was considered imminent and Luftflotte 2 could not spare aircraft to tackle the heavy bomber streams which regularly flew over Istria on their way to attack central European targets[40] – but for the moment most of the new Ultra intelligence suggested rather that apprehension was being replaced by prudent measures to defend the northern Adriatic region. Preparation of a 'Lower Alps defensive position' *(Voralpenstellung)* had been ordered as long ago as September 1943;[41] an incomplete Ultra decrypt sketched in the section connecting Bergamo with a point north of Vicenza in mid-May,[42] and in September 1944 another made it possible to conjecture with some confidence that a continuation ran along the Alpine foothills to Tolmino, north of Trieste.[43] At the cost of leaving Istria undefended, this line could not easily be outflanked (this remedied a defect in the first proposal); it gave some protection to the approaches to Ljubljana and was supplemented in July by a Hitler order for the construction of defences to prevent the Allies from penetrating into the Udine basin.[44] In view of the very incomplete state of the far more urgently needed Gothic Line revealed by the Hitler order decrypted on 27 June,[45] it was reasonable to suppose that little progress had been made with the building of these fortifications, but there seems to be no sign that considerations of this kind played any part in the evolution of ZENDA.

Undaunted either at being overruled or by the prospect of losing seven of his best divisions and more than half his air-power, Alexander flew to London at once and attended a War Cabinet meeting on 7 July. There he repeated his arguments in favour of an advance through the Ljubljana Gap: it would either force the Germans to abandon the Balkans or compel them to withdraw at least 15 divisions from France or the Russian front to bar his way. Churchill, who had only reluctantly surrendered to American *force majeure* over ANVIL, gave his approval and undertook to ensure that, notwithstanding the loss he was being made to suffer, the maximum possible forces should be put at Alexander's disposal.[46] For the moment, the Allied armies were still making steady progress northwards. Though the much weakened 5 Army came to a halt after capturing Leghorn in mid-July, 8 Army continued its advance with Operation OLIVE towards the end of August. Not until the one beat vainly at the last fortifications of the Gothic Line and the other stalled on the river-barriers of the Romagna as winter approached were the disastrous consequences of ANVIL (by now renamed DRAGOON) for the Italian campaign – and hence for ZENDA – fully apparent. As Churchill was to write much later: 'A very little more, half of what had been taken from us, and we could have broken into the valley of the Po, with all the gleaming possibilities and prizes which lay open towards Vienna'.[47]

All through these months of strategic controversy a steady stream of Ultra made it clear that the combined pressure of the Red Army on their left flank (more severe after the defection of Romania and Bulgaria from the German cause in August and September) and the Partisans to their front, aggravated by the need to extricate Army Group E from Greece speedily (the evacuation of the islands was ordered in late August, most of Greece was clear, amid scenes of demoralisation,[48] by the end of September, and the last German troops left Athens in mid-October) were making the Germans more nervous than ever that an Allied landing in Istria might compel them to face in yet a third direction as well. 'June, July and the first half of August', wrote Percy-Ernst Schramm in his edition of the OKW War Diary, 'like the previous months, were overshadowed by uncertainty about what the enemy would do with his reserves in Italy and North Africa', and put together evidence of the defensive measures consequently taken in Istria.[49] The Normandy experience showed that the British and Americans liked landing in estuaries, mused 2 Panzer Army in July, and set up defence measures in northern Dalmatia accordingly. 'Ever-growing audacity' on the part of hostile light naval forces, according to the East Mediterranean naval headquarters, heralded the formation of a bridgehead on the mainland opposite the islands of Vis and Hvar: there was shipping enough to lift this and an Aegean expedition simultaneously. One of the many handicaps under which the defence of the Balkans laboured was set in sharp relief by an order from Goering in early August restricting the hitherto regular aerial reconnaissance of the Anglo-American-Partisan base on Vis (from which the first stage of an invasion might be launched) to once a week because of the mounting petrol shortage. By the beginning of September Admiral Adriatic (no doubt partly on the basis of the same intelligence which was now piling up in the Ultra files) expected a landing sooner rather than later, and at the end of the month Admiral Aegean feared an airborne descent on the Corinth Canal so much that he planned to destroy it. The success just gained by the OLIVE offensive during its first week, which suggested that 8 Army might soon make a big enough breach in the Gothic Line at its eastern end for it to begin rolling up the rest of the last German defensive position south of the Alps, justified Admiral Adriatic's fears and seemed about to make a thrust into Slovenia tactically more feasible by ensuring Allied control over the adjacent Istrian coastline. The establishment of a bridgehead in Istria would be the first move in a drive to link up with the Russians – an idea which OKW had already entertained in August – whose rapid advance was leaching German divisions away and thus preventing OB South-east from giving proper protection to his boundary with OB South-west; a month later 2 Panzer Army put it the other way round – the threat of a landing was keeping troops idle on coast-watching duty when they were urgently needed to stem the Russian advance. Either way, the inference was plain: too few men and weapons, and too many calls on them. By 2 October the situation had deteriorated so far that von Weichs, in the hot seat as OB South-east, could see no way to hold off the Russians along the Danube save by drawing on the occupation forces in central Yugoslavia, thus 'uncovering the divisions' "pacification zones"' and giving Tito's Partisans almost complete freedom of action. For once, Hitler sanctioned the withdrawal von Weichs consequently requested permission to execute.[50]

Details of coastal defences and of the low fighting quality of the divisions stationed at the head of the Adriatic, and the news that further fortifications were 'envisaged' on the northern edge of the Ljubljana Gap filled out the picture. A debilitated and demoralised force with a purely defensive outlook was holding the area it would be necessary to seize as a first step towards ZENDA, an area moreover through which ran the weakly-defended boundary between two commands – the classical condition for a successful offensive. An unbroken chain of evidence invited intervention.

In the aftermath of Alexander's July visit, his ideas gained renewed momentum in British circles. Full realisation that he had been irrevocably deprived of the means of realising them had not yet dawned at the end of July when the Chiefs of Staff urged Wilson to be ready to send four divisions to seize Austria should Germany suddenly collapse – an early hint of the over-optimism which was to prevail in the weeks following Falaise[51] – nor when Alexander and Tito met briefly at Alexander's camp on the shores of Lake Bolsena (9 August) and the two of them conferred more formally with Churchill at Caserta a few days later. Only six weeks after his hair's-breadth escape from death or capture when the Germans raided his headquarters at Drvar, Tito's attitude to his British rescuers was still friendly. The tripartite discussions were mainly concerned with political matters (King Peter, the Yugoslav government in exile, current Partisan–Četnik and post-war British–Yugoslav relations), but on Tito's initiative the two commanders touched on the military aspects of a British landing in Istria. Tito raised no objection to a future British presence there (he was to change his mind before long) and agreed to the establishment of British lines of communication through Trieste and Ljubljana towards Austria, provided that the British recognised the Partisan civil administration which, he claimed, was already in existence there.[52]

The precipitate German retreat across France after Mortain and Falaise in August induced in many minds what was soon to prove a quite unwarranted optimism in which a total German collapse seemed imminent; as early as the beginning of August even the usually cool and cautious Brooke felt that 'the Boche is beat on all fronts. It is only a matter now of how many months he can last',[53] and on the last day of the month Churchill, usually sceptical about a quick victory, went as far as to write, 'Even if the war comes to an end at an early date, I have told Alexander to be ready for a dash with armoured cars' towards Vienna. At the Quebec conference in mid-September the strategic disagreements of the summer melted away in the last days of euphoria before Arnhem brought a rude awakening. In this cheerful atmosphere an Istrian landing and subsequent exploitation north-eastwards were treated as realistic possibilities (as if foreseeing this, Hitler was at the same moment ordering the construction of a new line of fortifications blocking the route north-east from Ljubljana).[54] *En route* for Quebec Churchill had minuted the Chiefs of Staff: 'We know from former Bonifaces[55] the great anxiety the German Admiral of the Adriatic has always expressed about Istria. We know that at present it has barely a division' and had urged an amphibious landing there – an operation Brooke and Portal (Chief of Air Staff) had favoured a fortnight earlier.[56] At the conference itself he reverted to the 'right-handed movement on land' with the purpose of giving Germany 'a stab in the Adriatic armpit'. The Americans undertook to hold back the required number of landing-craft from the Pacific, and even Brooke spoke in favour of the plan.[57]

No sooner had the conference dispersed than Tito suddenly disappeared from his refuge on Vis. It was some time before it became known in the west that he had gone to Moscow, where he remained until he entered Belgrade with the Red Army in October. He had already begun to restrict the activities of the British liaison missions, and the renewed dose of Stalinism which he had presumably been given was not calculated to make him a more amenable ally at a time when the Soviets were allowing the Germans to crush the Warsaw rising.

The Quebec conference has been described as the moment when the Vienna project came nearest to realisation.[58] In the political terms in which Miss Barker was thinking when she wrote these words, there is truth in her description. But Alexander's proposal had been a military one – not that he was unaware of its political overtones, of course – and the means to carry it out had already been refused him; in the true military sense, therefore, ZENDA was dead long before the Quebec conference met. Moreover, the plan had been predicated on friendly relations with Tito (to give flank protection) and with the Russians (to avoid head-on collision), neither of which could any longer be guaranteed in the autumn of 1944, as Tito's flight to Moscow and the Soviet attitude to the Polish Home Army in Warsaw (which enjoyed British support through the Polish government-in-exile in London) indicated. The shadow of the post-war settlement and the future partition of Germany into occupation zones, together with the rivalry of two contrasting political systems which had been forced into unnatural alliance in June 1941, had been growing darker since the spring. In his famous conversation with Fitzroy Maclean in Cairo in December 1943 – 'Do you intend to make Jugoslavia your home after the war?' Churchill disavowed interest in Tito's Communism and only wanted to know whether he was killing more Germans than Mihailović.[59] There is no sign, save in a few Foreign Office minutes, that in advocating a landing in Istria and a drive towards Vienna the British had been in any way motivated by a distrust of Russian intentions before the spring of 1944, or by a desire to beat them to Vienna in order to confine Communist influence to the territories farther east. All through 1943 and the early months of 1944 Churchill had pressed for maximum aid to Tito, well aware that Tito would set up a Communist régime after the war, but in April 1944 his vain (and surely foredoomed) attempt to reconcile Tito with King Peter scarcely concealed the hope that he might thereby restrict Soviet influence in Yugoslavia.[60] In the following July he was grimly foreseeing that Stalin might prefer his Western allies to exhaust themselves in France so that 'eastern, middle and southern Europe should fall naturally into his control', and at his meeting with Tito in August he urged democracy on Yugoslavia and even wanted Tito to make a public declaration that he did not intend to impose Communism on the country after the war. It was the last flicker of the obsolete 'T.E. Lawrence complex'[61] and the delusion that Britain could still determine the fate of lesser nations as it had been accustomed to do in the nineteenth century. On the way to Quebec in September Churchill quoted Ultra indications of German nervousness about Istria as good auguries for a landing, but went straight on to reflect that a thrust to Vienna might prevent central and southern Europe from passing into the Soviet orbit 'with incalculable consequences for the future'. At the conference itself he referred to 'the dangerous spread of Russian influence in the Balkans'. Six months earlier he had spoken of 'rolling up Europe from the south-east and *joining hands* with the Russians' (my italics).[62] On the Vistula and in the Carpathians the Red Army was menacingly nearer the heart of Europe, and attitudes towards it changed accordingly.

III

Logically, then, September 1944 is the latest date which can possibly be reckoned the end of the 'non-operation' which I have frivolously called ZENDA. But history does not proceed logically, nor did the proponents of ZENDA give up as soon as the French and American divisions left the Italian front-line for ANVIL in July. A change came over their thinking, however, corresponding to the changed outlook of the politicians. Brooke foreshadowed it at Quebec; when he spoke kindly of the plan, he added the proviso that the Germans should first have withdrawn from Greece and Yugoslavia.[63] Notwithstanding that the port of Trieste and lines of communication northwards would still be needed if Britain was to share in a four-power occupation of Austria, this was to transform Alexander's original proposal completely, turning it from a military means of defeating Hitler into something primarily concerned with the political configuration of post-war Europe and substituting Stalin for Hitler as the opponent to be outwitted. (Stalin's suggestion at Moscow in October of a joint attack on Vienna was hardly to be taken more seriously than Churchill's famous 'percentage' note, on the same occasion, allotting Britain and Russia equal influence in Yugoslavia.) Alexander continued to hope for a chance to put his 'dream' into practice in one form or another during the spring of 1945, but by then he was almost alone in entertaining it. The German occupation of Budapest in February made it certain that he would not be able to reach Vienna before the Red Army, and the city itself fell in April, while the Allied armies in Italy were only just beginning their final offensive in Lombardy. As for Churchill, he wrote in December that 'Tito has turned very nasty' and in January 1945 that there was nothing he could do to prevent the Balkans, except for Greece, from being Bolshevised and that he had 'given up hope of a right-handed thrust into the armpit of the Adriatic'.[64]

The subsequent move of the British XIII Corps into Venezia Giulia and the delicate negotiations with the Partisans over Trieste had much to do with the post-war settlement of south-east Europe but nothing save geography in common with ZENDA in its original form.

The seizure of Istria, still more a march on Vienna, may have been out of the question for the last six months of the war or longer, but throughout that period Ultra continued to provide proof that the forces available to defend Istria and the surrounding countryside were very weak, and that the enemy commanders doubted their ability to put up much resistance to a seaborne landing. Alexander must be presumed to have based his continued advocacy of ZENDA partly on this evidence and the unmistakeable invitation which it gave him. Three German fronts (in Italy, Yugoslavia and Hungary) were being forced into convergence about the head of the Adriatic, and their convergence led to constant changes of boundary, giving opportunities to strike at weak spots.[65] The locations of the various units defending Istria were regularly reported, and their steadily diminishing strength revealed.[66] Intelligence on the whole area affected was more plentiful than ever in these weeks, so plentiful indeed that at times the pressure of incoming raw material proved almost too great for the staffs who had to deal with it, yet positive evidence of the part (if any) it played in planning operations is lacking. This is often the missing link in any attempt to recreate the genesis of military action, but it is particularly regrettable on this occasion, as throughout the whole history of ZENDA.

The groundless fears of a landing at the head of the Adriatic which had for so long dogged German intelligence and prevented Kesselring and von Weichs from disposing their forces to the best advantage continued to the end, and provided a fitting climax to the deception-planners' repeated and successful efforts to destabilise the defence. The Germans were deluded into believing that Istria was still the Allies' target. Von Vietinghoff inherited all Kesselring's preoccupations when he succeeded him as OB South-west in March and faced the prospect of the final Allied onslaught. He allowed one of his best counter-attack divisions, 29 Panzergrenadier, which he had been holding in strategic reserve, to be lured away by false fears farther and farther from the point at which it was soon to be needed. Commandos were scheduled by 8 Army to capture the 'spit' between Lake Commachio and the sea, but the cover-plan put their objective further north; 29 PG first moved from strategic reserve in central Lombardy to useless coast-watching on the far side of Venice and eventually (on expectations that a Partisan drive northwards from Croatia would be timed to coincide with the Allied offensive) right out of von Vietinghoff's command area altogether and into Slovenia before it was recalled – too late.[67] During the 18 months or more of their occupation the Germans had never discovered – though

Alexander's naval advisers had – that the sea round Venice was too shallow for a landing![68]

Was ZENDA at any time a practical possibility, or is David Eisenhower right to condemn it as 'visionary and unpractical' like MARKET GARDEN and SLEDGEHAMMER?[69] It was conceived as the culminating stage of DIADEM, but until the Gustav defences had been breached the distance which the momentum of the assault might carry the advance could not be estimated, and so the ZENDA stage was left as an outline. It presupposed the retention of Alexander's whole force, and when the seven divisions were removed it remained an outline because the second stage, the occupation of Lombardy, proved impossible within the planned time-frame. Field Marshal Lord Harding, who drew up the plan as Alexander's Chief of Staff, has gone on record[70] as believing that the whole three-stage plan could have been successfully completed had the assumptions which underlay it not been altered by higher authority; and he has more than once repeated to me his conviction that, if Alexander had been allowed to retain the French mountain division which had paved the way for DIADEM by driving the Germans from the Aurunci mountains guarding the Liri valley, he would have breached the still incomplete Gothic Line quickly enough to reach Lombardy by autumn.

In the new conditions created by the depletion of the Allied armies, ZENDA now looked impossible to realise, but it must not be forgotten that Alexander, a soldier of great experience with a reputation for ability to 'read the battle', evidently believed in it for many months more. If it were worthwhile speculating seriously about the chances of success, whether on the original or the altered terms, several points which have never been properly canvassed would have to be examined:

The Ultra evidence for the slenderness of the Istrian defences is also evidence that surprise would not have been gained. Would this have been a severe handicap?

In May and June, the Partisans could probably have been relied on to give flank protection on the right, but this was more doubtful by September and October, the earliest at which ZENDA could possibly have taken place.

The left flank was always much more problematical. Ultra gave a fairly complete picture of the Alpine fortifications being prepared to wall-in the shrinking Reich.[71] Without prejudice to belief or disbelief in the rumours which foreshadowed an 'Alpine Redoubt' into which the unrepentant Nazis would retreat, it had surely to be assumed that Kesselring (or von Vietinghoff) would withdraw Army Group C behind them, and that it might later sally forth to deliver a paralysing blow at the flank and rear of an advancing ZENDA force – the same situation as would have arisen if the Anzio landing had been followed by an immediate thrust for Rome.

At some point, whether in Vienna or elsewhere, the advance would have made contact with the Russians. How welcome would a western intrusion into the Soviet sphere have been? The head-on meeting of armed allies might easily have become the collision of near-enemies. At Torgau in April 1945 Russians and Americans met on friendly terms, but Bradley was so alarmed that Patton might really fulfil his promise to drive the British back into the sea that he had reined him in and prevented the closing of the Falaise pocket in August 1944.

NOTES

1. Alexander commanded the Allied Armies in Italy from the first landings in September 1943 and continued to direct strategy when he succeeded Wilson as Supreme Commander, Mediterranean, in December 1944.
2. Field Marshal Earl Alexander of Tunis, 'The Allied Armies in Italy from 3 September 1943 to 2 December 1944', in *London Gazette,* 12 June 1950, pp. 2953, 2955.
3. Elisabeth Barker, 'L'Opzione istriana: obietti politici e militari della Gran Bretagna in Adriatico (1943–1944)', in *Qualestoria N.S.*, Vol.X, No.1 (February 1982). D. Fraser, *Alanbrooke* (London: Collins, 1982) gives a good short military account.
4. See, for instance, note 50, below.
5. Conscious that I thereby disregard Alexander's own warning (*Memoirs*, ed. John North (London: Cassell, 1963), p. 137) against choosing code-names with a built-in clue to their meaning. But Zenda is at least more elegant than Armpit, the name used by Harold Macmillan and his circle in Algiers (Macmillan, *The Blast of War* (London: Macmillan, 1967), p. 505). Churchill liked to talk of striking a blow 'in the armpit of the Adriatic' (Arthur Bryant, *Triumph in the West* (London: Collins, 1956), p. 267).
6. Kesselring's position as *Oberbefehlshaber (OB) Suedwest* (Commander in Chief South-west) gave him an authority over Italy which roughly corresponded to that of an Allied Supreme Commander. OB South-east had similar authority over Yugoslavia, Albania and Greece.
7. Michael Howard, *Grand Strategy* (London: HMSO, 1972), iv, pp. 663, 669.

8. P. E. Schramm (ed.), *Kriegstagebuch des Oberkommandos der Wehrmacht* (OKW/KTB) (Frankfurt: Bernard & Graefe, 1961), iv, p. 122.
9. A. Kesselring, *Memoirs* (London: Kimber, 1974).
10. W.S. Churchill, *The Second World War* (London: Cassell, 1948), iii, p. 152.
11. Fraser, p. 273.
12. J.M.A. Gwyer, *Grand Strategy* (London: HMSO, 1964), iii, pp. 334–5.
13. OKW/KTB ii, 139; iii, 33. H. R. Trevor-Roper, *Hitler's War Directives* (London: Sidgwick & Jackson, 1964), pp. 137–41.
14. OKW/KTB iii, 46, 121, 168–175.
15. Churchill, iv, p. 736; v, pp. 121, 411.
16. PRO. DEFE/3 MLs 1955, 2400, 2513, 2733.
17. Churchill, v, pp. 53–4; PRO. CAB 66/40 WP (43) 353, quoted in Barker, 'L'Opzione', p. 6; Howard, iv, p. 491.
18. E.g. VM 8955, MLs 1983, 2779, 3133, 3755, 3775, 3970, 4600, 6507, 8974, etc.
19. JPs 6009, 6282, 8899, S. Clissold, *Whirlwind* (London, 1949), p. 174.
20. E.g. JPs 4214, 4421, 5952, 6473, 6807, 8278, 8353, 8715.
21. JPs 8658, 8868.
22. D.D. Eisenhower, *Crusade in Europe* (New York, 1948), p. 219.
23. S. Westphal, *Erinnerungen* (von Hase & Koehler, 1975), p. 235.
24. J. Ehrman, GS v, p. 175; Churchill, v, p. 312; W. Averell Harriman, *Special Envoy* (London: Hutchinson, 1976), p. 267; F. W. D. Deakin in P. Auty and R. Clogg (eds), *British Policy towards Wartime Resistance in Jugoslavia and Greece* (London: Macmillan, 1975), p. 111.
25. M. Gilbert, *Winston S. Churchill*, vii, p. 656.
26. The occupation of Durazzo as a port of entry for supplies to Tito was in fact briefly under consideration in November.
27. C. 221, VLs 578, 3053, 3771, 3805, 3855, 3925, 9662, 9724, KVs 192, 628, 773, OKW/KTB iii, 1322, iv, 478.
28. VL 900.
29. VL 3809.
30. OKW/KTB iii, 1361.
31. VLs 3361, 4340, 6921, 7044, 9625, KVs 4313, 4400; Westphal, *Erinnerungen*, pp. 257–8.
32. Macmillan, p. 502. See also Alexander's *Despatch*, p. 2935.
33. M. Nicolson, *Alex* (London: Weidenfeld & Nicolson, 1973), p. 258.
34. Bryant, p. 223.
35. Howard, v, pp. 268–9, 346–8.
36. KV 9843.
37. Macmillan, p. 503.
38. Gilbert, vii, p. 815; Bryant, p. 227; Churchill, vi, pp. 57, 664. Outraged by the apparent geographical misconception, Churchill italicised these words in his account of the affair. Infuriating as it no doubt was at the time, the misconception may have been purely verbal, and the point does not now seem of great importance. Nevertheless, it is curious that David Eisenhower, *Eisenhower at War 1943–5* (London: Collins 1987), p. 324, passes it over in silence, thus appearing to share the same misconception himself.
39. Bryant, p. 256.

40. KVs 8486, 9550.
41. OKW/KTB iii, 1137.
42. KV 4145.
43. HP 166.
44. XL 5638.
45. KV 9843.
46. PRO. CAB 65/47.
47. Churchill, vi, p. 96.
48. VL 9081.
49. OKW/KTB iv, 507–13, 539–43, 545, 547, 550.
50. This and the next paragraph are based on XLs 1438, 1732, 1791, 2548, 4031, 4192, 5079, 6013, 6882, 7807, 8244, 8887, 9081, 9505, HPs 166, 178, 193, 680, 1957, 2282, 2875, 3026, 3180, 3316, 3776. In addition some 30 or 40 summaries, many of them several hundred words long, detailing the activities of German units and the Partisan brigades they were endeavouring to destroy, were transmitted between June and September
51. Howard, v, p. 389.
52. PRO. WO 202/177B, Clissold, p. 194. The contemporary accounts of these meetings lack precision on the point, but it would appear that the discussions concerned a peaceful (presumably post-war) occupation rather than a military operation. None expressly considers the possibility of fighting, but most use the word 'operation'. In a letter to Churchill on 13 August Tito mentioned 'Allied forces which will operate in this area'. Brigadier Hollis of the War Cabinet Office wrote that the second Tito–Churchill meeting was 'pretty vague, and no concrete operation was talked of'. I derive this information from a paper presented to the Anglo-Jugoslav Colloquium at the Imperial War Museum in December 1982 by Sir William Deakin.
53. Bryant, p. 260; Gilbert, vii, p. 931.
54. Trevor-Roper, p. 195.
55. Boniface was an old cover-name for Ultra which Churchill continued to use. He was presumably referring to VLs 900 and 9505 among others.
56. Their reason was that the overland route was difficult and that a seaborne assault might be easier. The hold-up on the Gothic Line ruled out a landward advance in the immediate future, and by October Alexander was thinking of handing the Italian front over to 5 Army and putting 8 Army ashore at Split or in Istria (Gilbert, vii, p. 986). German fears concentrated on the seaborne threat from the start.
57. Howard, v, p. 510; Bryant, p. 273; Gilbert, vii, pp. 911, 948–9, 959.
58. Barker, 'L'Opzione', p. 30.
59. Fitzroy Maclean, *Eastern Approaches* (London: Cape, 1949), pp. 402–3.
60. Barker, 'L'Opzione', p. 17.
61. Gilbert, vii, p. 889; Barker in Auty and Clogg, p. 30.
62. Gilbert, vii, pp. 829, 949; Barker, 'L'Opzione', p. 29, quoting PRO. CAB 80/80, 10 September 1944; Howard, v, p. 555.
63. Howard, v, p. 570.
64. Gilbert, vii, pp. 1082, 1159.
65. HPs 4111, 6659, 8539, BTs 7340, 9922, KO 260, bearing dates between October 1944 and April 1945.

66. HPs 4048, 4370, 6748, 9340, 9668 (its commander reporting in December that 2 Panzer Army was 'too weak for the tasks confronting it'), BTs 1994, 2724, 2953, 3261, 3444, 4034, 4850 (a particularly detailed strength return in mid-February), 5513, 8786, 8954, 9035, 9422, 9793 (Jodl reporting Hitler's decision to transfer a division to the Russian front and to entrust the defence of the coast between the Tagliamento and the Isonzo to a single regimental group).
67. BTs 8241, 9014, 9044, 9293, 9676, 9742, 9974, KO 260.
68. Alexander, *Despatch*, p. 2959, note.
69. Eisenhower, *Eisenhower at War,* pp. 443–4.
70. E.g. Nicolson, *Alex,* p. 262.
71. In addition to signals already quoted, see BTs 99, 890, 2799, 3454, 3776.

9

FORTITUDE, Ultra and the 'Need to Know'

The Second World War began in force and violence – *Blitzkrieg* in Poland and France – and ended when massive industrialisation enabled Anglo-American and Russian armies to trample on the Germany which the heavy bombers of the RAF and USAAF had already laid waste. But between the two periods when might alone prevailed there was a long interval during which intelligence and deception were called in aid by the Allies to assist the defensive war on land. To deceive the enemy and lure him to waste his superior strength by vainly beating the air in pursuit of will o' the wisps is the natural recourse of the weaker party as it seeks to compensate for its lack of material power. Yet, as FORTITUDE showed, and contrary to what is often said, deception is not the province of the weaker party alone;[1] tricks learned for self-protection in adversity can later be used to sharpen a counter-offensive when the balance of power has changed.

Both the western and the eastern enemies of the Nazi war-machine made extensive use of deception during their years of weakness.[2] In doing so, the British in Egypt discovered an unexpected aptitude for deceit, reinventing from scratch tricks as old as war itself and refining them with a practical skill which as early as the winter of 1940/41 helped Wavell's tiny Western Desert Force to outwit Graziani's quarter of a million Italians and eject them from Cyrenaica in a campaign lasting only two months but covering 700 miles. There was to be no living up to this standard when Rommel intervened, but 'A' Force, created and directed by Colonel Dudley Clarke at Wavell's initiative, already had a long list of smaller successes to its credit before its deception plan made a major contribution to the victory of Alamein. These were still defensive (often confined to camouflage) and tactical, however. The plan which disguised the strike area of TORCH in November 1942 was the first to tackle a larger objective, and the cover-plan for the invasion of

Sicily next year the first which attempted widespread strategic deception; the several hundred thousand troops whose presence in the eastern Mediterranean Dudley Clarke simulated for the purpose were still distorting German strategy as late as the summer of 1944. In Italy deception constantly wrong-footed Kesselring about Allied intentions, helping Alexander to fulfil the directives which, in order to reduce pressure in the eastern and western theatres of war, bade him attract as many Germans to his front as possible but denied him the means to execute the task properly.

Drawing on experience gained during these years, 'A' Force's off-spring, the London Controlling Section (LCS), scored the greatest triumph of all when FORTITUDE hoodwinked Rundstedt and Rommel, Hitler and OKW into believing that the main assault in the summer of 1944 would be round Calais rather than in Normandy. The plan was operated by a tiny handful of men known collectively as Ops B, who worked during the critical months of spring and early summer 1944 in close accord with SHAEF and 21 Army Group.[3] Their *modus operandi* was through enemy agents who had been rounded up and 'turned' by the XX Committee to transmit misleading information to their *Abwehr* controllers in the Reich. How the FORTITUDE story was gradually filtered into the German consciousness was described in the (unpublished) post-war *History of Strategic Deception* by Major R.F. Hesketh, head of the 'special means' section of Ops B.[4] Hesketh measured its success by the *Abwehr* controllers' replies to the agents' transmissions and by evidence, secured after the war, of OKH's and OKW's acceptance of *Abwehr* deductions about Allied order of battle and intentions.

To think of what one would like the enemy to believe is easy, to find means capable of inducing him to believe it is far more difficult. Nevertheless this problem was solved with outstanding skill. To discover whether the enemy believes the falsehoods with which he is being fed and is acting accordingly, and to do this in time to profit from the knowledge, is a far more formidable task: surprising gaps in Hesketh's *History* seem to imply that Ops B was not much concerned with it or with adjusting its policy in the light of the enemy's revealed beliefs.

If he is to gain any benefit from it, the military commander who has commissioned a deception plan will need to know, before he begins his own operations,[5] whether the enemy has swallowed the proffered bait or not. How much of the disinformation has been received and accepted as genuine? What consequential moves has the enemy made? Have his suspicions been aroused? This means that if a deception plan is to be of any practical use there must exist in parallel with it an intelligence service capable of relaying news of the enemy's changing moods and measuring the degree of credence he is attaching to the false tale from day to day. Without this foreknowledge the hunter may unbalance his forces by dispersing some of them to inactive sectors of the front for insurance purposes, and thus lose the initiative to his intended prey. Kesselring repeatedly found this in Italy when he more than once vitiated his defensive purpose by setting his strongest divisions to guard coastal sectors which the Allies had no intention of assaulting, unaware that Ultra intelligence was keeping Alexander informed of the fact. Deception and intelligence complemented each other perfectly, and together formed an integral part of operational planning in the Mediterranean throughout 1943 and 1944. Was this co-operation reproduced at SHAEF and 21 Army Group? Was Ops B involved in the process? It is almost impossible to believe that it was not reproduced for so vital an operation as OVERLORD, yet the present state of the evidence makes proof equally impossible – and indeed much of it suggests the contrary.

I

Except in the simplest cases, accurate and precisely dated records are indispensable to a historical demonstration that a commander received the intelligence which proved the success of his deception in time for it to determine what he did next. Without it, impressionistic conclusions may misrepresent causality and put the cart before the horse.

Manifestly, Joshua could see the garrison of Ai pursuing him before he raised his spear as a signal for the ambushing detachment to rush the now unguarded walls; similarly Malatesta da Verucchio in an almost identical stratagem of 1291 which established his dynasty in Rimini for nearly two centuries. William the Conqueror could see with his own eyes the success of his trick at Hastings when he decoyed a large body of Saxons away from their defences on Senlac Hill to chase the apparently fleeing Normans into the valley, and then suddenly loosed a squadron of cavalry on their flank to cut down the rash pursuers. Far greater problems face the commander, and will face the later historian, when the conflict is on a wider scale and the deception embraces strategy, for visual evidence will not suffice. How is this kind of intelligence to reach the commander secretly and in time? What exactly is the historian to make, for instance, of the contemporary accounts according to which

Batu Khan led three Mongol armies to ravage Russia and Europe from the Volga to Silesia and the Danube in 1237–41, so precisely directing their movements that he could recall one of them from a nine days' feigned flight to a perfectly-timed rendezvous with the others outside Budapest for the siege and destruction of the city? We should be compelled to dismiss the story out of hand as either the triumphalist legend of the victors (analogous, perhaps, to the collapse of the walls of Jericho at the sound of the trumpet) or the terrified imaginings of the vanquished embroidering a chance series of unconnected events into a logical cause-and-effect sequence, did not the proven mobility of the Mongol warriors and the 'arrow riders' who carried their generals' despatches entitle us hesitantly to credit a synchronisation which would otherwise seem to demand radio communications.

Only precisely dated – even precisely timed – information can satisfy the historian that a commander did *this* because he knew *that*. Even so, he will scarcely ever be able to discover how a commander reasoned on the basis of his knowledge, for the commander will seldom or never have committed this to writing amid the heat and fury of battle. The criteria for absolute historical certainty are too demanding, and the historian will almost always be reduced to approximations to the truth and intelligent guesswork – which, of course, he has a duty to admit.

II

Since the western Allies expended much effort (FORTITUDE) in trying to induce the Germans to believe that the Normandy landing (OVER-LORD) in June 1944 was only a diversion and that the main blow would be struck in the Pas de Calais in July, and since Ultra demonstrated that the false tale was being taken for truth and that a strong garrison was being retained in the wrong place, it has been assumed that the two were related as cause to effect and that Ultra was the connecting link between them. There has been plenty of good evidence to support this belief. In the revised edition of his autobiography, for instance, General Bradley wrote: 'Ultra was central to Fortitude's conception and execution and provided a continuous monitor on German reactions to it, telling us whether or not we were really fooling the Germans. ... Without Ultra to monitor its intricate and interlocking parts, Fortitude could not even have got off the ground'.[6] This view has recently received formal confirmation. The latest volume of the official history of *British Intelligence in the Second World War,* published in 1988, says that in

January 1944 'arrangements were made for the deception authorities to receive from GC & CS without delay all decrypts that might have a bearing on their work' so that they could *adjust their deception programme accordingly'* (my emphasis).[7] Exactly how the linkage was effected, and by means of what decrypts, is not stated, however. *British Intelligence* devotes some 500 pages to the first nine months of 1944, the period during which FORTITUDE influenced events, but does not provide a single example to illustrate the link or to show how the deception planners used the decrypts with which they were supplied. Because of this omission, and because a great deal of the relevant material cannot be consulted in the Public Record Office, thick darkness surrounds the central question of what intelligence was supplied to the deception planners and by whom, and in consequence a vital part of the explanation for OVERLORD's success is hidden from view.[8]

Hesketh deepens the mystery when he writes; 'Before the invasion Ultra told us very little of what the enemy believed our dispositions to be'.[9] Exactly what is meant by 'Ultra'? The term 'Ultra' (with which 'Most Secret Source' is usually taken to be synonymous) was coined in 1940 to describe the information derived from German radio messages encrypted on the Enigma machine. In fact, most of these messages originated with the German Navy, Army or Air Force.[10] Strictly, therefore, what is commonly called 'Ultra' should be called *'Wehrmacht* Ultra', for other authorities (the *Abwehr,* the police and the *Reichsbahn,* for instance) also used the Enigma machine, and their decrypted Enigma messages can also be called 'Ultra'. In what follows, 'Ultra' will always be used in the sense of *'Wehrmacht* Ultra'.

In the passage already quoted, Hesketh refers to the conversation of Baron Oshima, the Japanese ambassador in Berlin, with Hitler on 27 May 1944 and says that knowledge of it 'was obtained from Ultra (BJ 508 dated 28 May 1944)'. The prefix BJ signified a diplomatic intercept. From March 1944 onwards some Japanese diplomatic intercepts were given the prefix BAY and included in the Ultra series of signals where appropriate; this report was sent to the usual recipients of *Wehrmacht* Ultra as BAY/KV 179, for instance.[11] It almost looks as if Hesketh's knowledge of it was the result of an accidental lapse in the security arrangements for the circulation of sensitive material, since this appears to be an exception to a general rule prohibiting Hesketh's sub-section from knowing about Ultra; Hesketh does not mention (and therefore presumably did not see) three earlier BAY/KVs[12] which closely affected Ops B's work because they inclined to predict an Allied landing in the

FORTITUDE area, nor does he refer to much other, later, material from decrypts of Oshima's traffic which were sent out over the special secure radio link to SHAEF and 21 Army Group which was otherwise reserved for 'normal' *Wehrmacht* Ultra.

On several other occasions Hesketh equates 'Most Secret Source' with *Abwehr* traffic,[13] the medium in which Berlin corresponded with the controlled agents. This was at first entirely in hand-cypher, though by 1944 some *Abwehr* stations used Enigma.[14] The *Abwehr* Enigma decrypts were presumably entitled to the Ultra classification, but it is noteworthy that no information from them was ever included in the long series of signals based on *Wehrmacht* Enigma decrypts sent from Bletchley Park to commands abroad, and that to this extent at least it was kept separate from 'normal' Ultra. The crucial question, therefore, is when, where and how were the two brought together and integrated for the purpose of tailoring FORTITUDE? Lastly, not once does Hesketh quote or refer to intelligence derived from *Wehrmacht* Ultra decrypts or to the signals which convey intelligence (much of it directly affecting FORTITUDE) from them to SHAEF and 21 (later, also 12) Army Group from January 1944 onwards.

Hesketh, therefore, cannot have been thinking either of *Wehrmacht* Ultra or of *Abwehr* Ultra when he wrote 'Ultra told us very little'. It must therefore be presumed that he did not know about either (it can hardly be supposed that he knew them but deliberately suppressed all mention of them when he wrote his *History* four years after the end of the war, for the *History* was intended only for 'in house' circulation). Was he deliberately kept in ignorance of Ultra by his superiors? It is possible (but in view of his duties very difficult to credit) that he was purposely excluded from the Ultra circle if we first suppose a remarkably severe application of the 'need to know' principle – on the ground, perhaps, that if he saw Ultra regularly a message inspired by him and drafted by the case officer of one of the agents through whom Ops B worked might one day inadvertently include some detail which could make German intelligence (which was then considered to be far better than we now know it to have been) suspect that Enigma had been broken, and that in view of the high stakes for which the Allies were then playing even this slight risk was considered too great to run. Since his immediate superior, Colonel Noel Wild (hitherto Dudley Clarke's second-in-command, who had been posted to England and put in charge of Ops B so that it should benefit from the practical experience which 'A' Force had gained in the Middle East),[15] had long been familiar with Ultra, it is necessary to suppose a knowledge-barrier erected between Wild and Hesketh. The obvious clumsiness of such an arrangement is a measure of our present ignorance of the way things actually worked. It seems calculated to cause awkward relations between the two men and also between Ops B and G(R) at 21 Army Group, which was fully briefed about Ultra and worked in close conjunction with the high-powered intelligence department there, but it can – just – be reconciled with the statement in *British Intelligence*. It cannot be disproved from information at present available, but the suspicion that it is incorrect or at least seriously incomplete is hard to resist.[16]

III

Strangely enough, the very first of the Ultra signals relevant to FORTITUDE bears directly on this question. This signal (the German original was dated 9 January 1944, but it was not decrypted until the 26th) reported that the German Y Service had recently identified several American formations in England, including 1 US Army Group, which was believed to have been still in the United States in early November but was now probably somewhere in the area of the British Southern Command.[17] These apparently routine order of battle identifications were in fact of greater significance for the whole FORTITUDE operation than Ops B could realise at the time or than has been recognised since. Neither Hesketh nor Masterman mentions it, of course, and *British Intelligence* dismisses it quite briefly.[18] Yet this signal offered Ops B, unsought and without effort on its own part, what proved to be the foundation upon which a great deal of its plan to mislead the enemy would come to rest: for it showed that the Germans were, of their own volition and without prompting, already disposed to credit the existence and even the approximate location of their later bugbear, FUSAG. In January 1944, however, the First United States Army Group, though real enough, had as yet only a nebulous existence (1 US Army, which had also been identified by German Y and reported in the same signal, was already well established by the same date). It had been set up in skeleton form in October 1943, and was scheduled eventually to take command of the US forces for the Normandy invasion.

In January 1944, then, enemy intelligence was deluding itself into belief in the substantial existence of a large formation which was in reality only a shadow or a skeleton: an intelligence error of major proportions, an error on a scale which any experienced deception staff would have been proud to induce. Yet no one had induced it; the FUSAG deception was not to be launched for another two months.

It is now generally recognised that a deception plan has little hope of success unless its intended dupe is already inclined to believe something of the kind – that is to say, unless it plays on existing fears. Such a predisposition can be powerfully reinforced by suitable procedures, but it is almost impossible to implant new fears by external means. Hesketh recognised this when he wrote 'We owed our flying start to German predispositions',[19] and Wild, with his memories of the Mediterranean, could have added that only a few months earlier MINCEMEAT had owed its success largely to similarly favourable circumstances – the imagined presence of Dudley Clarke's 'notional' divisions in the Middle East. Had Hesketh known about the Ultra signal of 26 January, he would surely have mentioned it in his *History,* because it gave him exactly the *point d'appui* which Ops B was going to need for its plan – in which, of course, FUSAG was to play a cardinal role.

Piquancy is lent to the timing of the 26 January signal, and to the reflection that Ops B apparently set out on the most crucial stage of its task without access to Ultra, when it is remembered that it was only on the previous day (and therefore without knowledge of the 26 January signal) that de Guingand had decided to vary the COSSAC plan so that the threat to the Pas de Calais should in future be represented as the main operation, to take place after D-Day in Normandy. Since 21 Army Group could not plausibly be depicted as controlling two major operations at the same time, this necessitated the creation of a second army group: 12 Army Group now took the place 1 Army Group was to have occupied. From this decision arose FUSAG's key role (first adumbrated in early February but not fully unfolded until its 'notional' order of battle was promulgated on 30 March) and the switch from passive or representational (camouflage) to active (radio) deception.[20]

The fortuitous coincidence in time of two unrelated happenings which wonderfully complemented each other (though in the theoretical sense they occurred in the wrong order) greatly enhanced the deception plan's chances of success, for it was now clear that its seed would fall on fertile ground. If Ops B was in fact denied knowledge of one of them, then its activities must seen as more dependent on 21 Army Group's direction than has hitherto been realised.[21]

FUSAG appeared in Ultra only three more times (all of them were intercepts of Paris Y Service reports) before D-Day: once each in March, April and May, always without any indication of where its headquarters were believed to be.[22] On the last two of these occasions the identification was said to be doubtful (strangely enough, these were the only two which post-dated Ops B's full use of FUSAG for deception purposes). The infrequency and vagueness of the references to FUSAG were presumably the consequence in part of the slow unfolding of its 'notional' existence and in part – notably during the crisis which followed the arrest of 'Artist' in Lisbon on 29 April[23] – of the realisation that, because natural prudence would obviously dictate at least some German preparations in the Pas de Calais, it was imperative not to overdo the threat to that part of the coast too soon, for fear that it might lead the enemy to deduce the opposite and suppose that the real invasion was likely to come somewhere else, probably in Normandy. No serious attempt to use the controlled agents to suggest the part FUSAG was destined to play seems to have been made until May, when 'Brutus' was 'notionally' posted to the FUSAG staff (with the unexpected result that the *Abwehr* became anxious to know more about the composition of 21 Army Group!), and until Second TAF staged a heavy raid on the Pas de Calais on 29 May in order to concentrate attention there.[24] Ultra had, however, by that time recorded a second bonus point for the future with an OKH report of 22 March that General Patton, the bogey-man about whose whereabouts and employment there was to be so much speculation in the early summer, had returned to England from the Mediterranean and 'been given command of another army'.[25]

In these circumstances it was natural that Ultra should provide evidence in conformity with the policy which Ops B was then pursuing – to suggest that British and American troops were being concentrated in south-east England, in the hope that the Germans would deduce an intention to land in the Calais area for themselves. The formations named in the nine further pre-D-Day Ultra signals[26] (half of which originated with either OKH/Fremde Heere West or OB West) covering order of battle overlap very little with those mentioned in Hesketh's Appendix III, 'British controlled agents' share in compiling German intelligence reports', over the same period. While this may suggest that the controlled agents were less successful in planting information than Hesketh implies, it is also important to note the large number of German errors the signals reveal: among several correct identifications (1 Canadian Army – important because Ops B could 'notionally' detach it from 21 Army Group, to which it really belonged, and place it under FUSAG without shifting its assembly area – XIX US Corps, 29 British Division and the total of six Allied airborne divisions, for instance) were at least as many which were neither under 21 Army Group for the Normandy assault nor in the bogus FUSAG set-up. This certainly showed that in this respect Ultra was not giving much helpful feedback on the Pas de Calais deception[27] – only the last of the nine signals, on 1 June, suggested it with emphatic reference to 'an unquestionable *Schwerpunkt*' in the south-east – but it also revealed unmistakably the ineffectiveness of German Y and direction-finding, and reinforced the suspicion that German intelligence was not up to its job.

In contrast with the order of battle items, several Ultra reports of German defensive measures in May showed signs of anxiety over the Pas de Calais area, and therefore presumably also of the controlled agents' efforts to suggest it. An exercise carried out between 8 and 10 May, with naval authorities in Calais, Dunkirk and Ostend as participants, assumed a successful Allied landing between Ostend and Bruges, together with heavy air and sea attacks.[28] This closely coincided with the views of the Japanese military attaché in Berlin, who toured the defences of northern France about this time and told Tokyo that the Germans expected the main Allied landing between Boulogne and Ostend, with diversionary feints between Le Havre and Cherbourg.[29] An OB West appreciation, written just before this, saw the outlook rather differently.[30] Having said that agents had recently provided no special information, but instead 'a plethora of invasion dates', Rundstedt set out his belief that Allied preparations were centred on Portsmouth and Southampton and that this suggested that the main assault was likely to be delivered between Boulogne and Cherbourg. From the Allies' point of view, the logic of this conclusion (which, though sound as far as it went, was geographically too wide to be of much operational use for defensive purposes) was offset by two manifest and very revealing errors: first, that it was essential for the Allies to capture large ports, particularly Le Havre and Cherbourg – thus proving that no hint of the Mulberries had crossed the Channel – and secondly that the Allies had shipping-space enough to lift the 20 or more divisions he expected them to use in the first wave (a threefold exaggeration). Lastly, an exercise which assumed an Allied landing between Isigny and Ouistreham (an almost exact forecast)[31] was less alarming when seen in the context of Rundstedt's mistakes, Luftflotte 3's prediction of the Dieppe–Seine area, and another Calais–Ostend exercise between 21 and 27 May.[32] The fact that the Isigny–Ouistreham exercise was only one among many carried out in a variety of places tended to confirm that the accidental interception of Exercise Tiger, which took place on similar beaches in

Devon in April, had still not led the Germans to useful deductions about the landing area.

Two other matters deserve a brief mention. At the end of the first week in May, German Y picked up Exercise Fabius, the wireless pattern of which had been set to resemble that which would be used on D-Day very closely, so that the latter might for a crucial hour or so be interpreted as only another exercise. Ultra showed that this hope was not realised, for Rundstedt saw Fabius as simply an experiment with new landing techniques.[33]

FORTITUDE NORTH, the plan to suggest an Allied invasion of Norway, appears to have followed the same pattern as FORTITUDE SOUTH, as far as Ultra was concerned. The possibility of such an operation was mentioned once, on 5 March, when OKM cited OKH's appreciation that there were four, five or six British divisions in Scotland, plus two US divisions in Iceland, and that they might all be used 'for operations in the northern area', probably in central or southern Norway; adequate shipping and air cover could be provided.[34] This corresponded well with Ops B's purpose, but OKH's appreciation must have been based on recollections of Operation TINDALL, which had been designed to the same end in September 1943, for the new wireless programme to suggest FORTITUDE NORTH did not come into operation until 22 March, a fortnight after OKH's appreciation was composed.[35] The revival of FORTITUDE NORTH before D-Day was reflected in a signal of 27 May,[36] but there seems no reason to disagree with Hesketh's conclusion that in spite of all the effort put into it FORTITUDE NORTH had no discernible effect because Hitler was so convinced of a threat to Norway that he had already stationed an unnecessary number of troops there and did not need to reinforce them in 1944.

IV

The output of Ultra, restricted during the spring by the Germans' natural preference for land-lines, rose dramatically from the moment of the invasion – an average of six or seven signals a day in the week preceding 6 June became 20 or 30 immediately afterwards and continued to climb – so that opportunities to discover how deeply the threat to the Pas de Calais had become embedded in the enemy's consciousness and how far it was distorting his appreciation of events became correspondingly greater. First signs were not encouraging. At 1500 hours on 6 June Naval Gruppe West's preliminary reaction was that the disposition of Allied Forces pointed to a further major operation, but during the night extra flak protection was ordered for the Quilleboeuf ferry over the Seine, which seemed to presage its use by troops of 15 Army *en route* for Normandy.[37] Further landings were predicted in Norway as well as Belgium,[38] and intermittently for ten days from 7 June onwards the army demanded air reconnaissance of the Dutch and Belgian coasts because new landings and a 'thrust towards Belgium' were to be expected, but the vital question was whether armour would move from 15 Army to 7 Army, in what strength and how soon.

There were three Panzer divisions in 15 Army: 1 SS Panzer (Belgium, recently strengthened by some 70 tanks), 116 Panzer (along the Seine between Paris and the sea, at barely half strength) and 19 Panzer (Holland, still being set up).[39] The issue on 7 June of new cover-names to 1 SS Panzer, 2 SS Panzer (Toulouse) and 17 SS Panzergrenadier (south of the Loire) was evidently in preparation for a move to Normandy by all three.[40] The last two soon started off (2 SS, harried by the *maquis,* committing the massacre at Oradour-sur-Glane on the way), and 2 Panzer soon followed, but 1 SS Panzer remained in Belgium, under orders to move towards the coast north of Brussels to replace 19 GAF Division (which was going to Italy), and 116 Panzer remained stationary too.[41] Since apprehensions about a landing in Belgium or on the Channel coast continued to be lively,[42] it was easy to suppose that it was this fear which had halted the two Panzer divisions. Confirmation of this came from a decrypt of 11 June: OKH, still grossly overestimating the strength of 21 Army Group, hesitantly endorsed OKL's forecast (which was not backed by captured documents, Y service or *Abwehr,* as OKH well knew) that FUSAG would shortly land between Seine and Somme so that the two army groups could concert measures for a drive on Paris via St Quentin – the strategy it had long expected the Allies to adopt.[43]

None of this need be seen as denying the merit of the long-planned, carefully-phrased and beautifully timed message 'Garbo' sent to his *Abwehr* control at midnight 8/9 June, which forms the showpiece of Hesketh's collection and which has usually been taken to be the reason why 1 SS and 116 Panzer remained where they were:[44] 'These operations are a diversionary manoeuvre designed to draw off enemy reserves in order to make a decisive attack in another place ... probably the Pas de Calais'. Garbo's message was passed by Keitel to Hitler, who in consequence cancelled the proposed move of the two divisions. But it was not until Keitel was interrogated in April 1946, and his somewhat grudging and impatient admission that it was this message which caused the change of plan, that the cause-and-effect relationship between the two was known. It is noteworthy that all Hesketh's footnotes in the lengthy passage dealing with this incident refer to material which he was not able to see until the war was over, not to feedback by the *Abwehr* to Garbo in June 1944.[45]

Ultra, on the other hand, continued to provide *current* evidence that German apprehensions of a landing in the 15 Army area were still too lively for them to risk transferring armour to Normandy. The OKH appreciation of 11 June was not decrypted until just after midnight 15/16 June, but before then there were strong indications that German defence policy was unchanged, in the shape of news that 116 Pz was still under 15 Army on the eleventh and had not moved further south than the Somme two days later.[46] Close surveillance of 116 Pz was maintained for the next fortnight (it moved frenziedly back and forth several times, but never south of Dieppe). 1 SS unfortunately disappeared from view for a few days, but was still only preparing to move to Normandy on 19 June.[47]

The interdependence of deception and intelligence is vividly illustrated by this episode. Ops B had invested many months of dedicated effort to build up its agents' credit in the hope that when the decisive moment came they would be able to mislead the enemy into holding some of his armour back from Normandy to meet an imaginary second landing. The event proved that they had not laboured in vain. Allied anxieties about the security of the beachhead would undoubtedly have been many times greater during and just after the four days' storm of 20–24 June had Eisenhower and Montgomery not been kept constantly informed that they would not have to face a new and massive armoured onslaught while their supply lines were still half strangled in the aftermath of the damage done by wind and waves. Ultra provided this information almost at once, while it was even more urgently needed than could have been foreseen when FORTITUDE was devised. The intelligence staffs at 21 Army Group received this vital information and passed it on to Operations; but in the present state of knowledge there is no avoiding the conclusion that Ops B remained ignorant of its own success until after the war was over.

The FORTITUDE plan had called for the threat of a second landing to be kept alive for three weeks after D-Day. By the end of June however, 15 Army was still strong, and the slow Allied advance – Caen was not captured until the second week in July – made it desirable to hold its formations away from the bridgehead for a longer period.[48] A new plan, FORTITUDE SOUTH II, was devised for the purpose; it accounted for the appearance of many of the original FORTITUDE divisions in France by creating two new armies, 4 British and 14 American (both 'notional') under FUSAG in south-east England.

A Foreign Armies West appreciation of 22 June showed that the new plan had a good chance of achieving its aim. FUSAG was still in south-east England, it stated, 20 or more divisions strong (the same as 21 Army Group) and ready for an amphibious assault. No specific target was named, though the Pas de Calais was obviously implied; but, as Hesketh says, 'It mattered little to us where the Germans expected the second landing to take place so long as it dissuaded them from sending 15 Army to Normandy'. Hesketh quotes this appreciation from the Lagebericht West for 22 June, but it was also put out in Enigma and, although decrypted with some unavoidable delay, was in the hands of Eisenhower and Montgomery on the 29th.[49] On 26 June OB West had been expecting FUSAG to land astride the Somme and drive towards the Seine, co-operating with 21 Army Group in a pincer movement on Paris against weak opposition.[50] On the last day of June, Foreign Armies West pointed to a diversionary operation in Belgium as the likely objective of 'Army Group Patton' (Ultra's first definite association of Patton with FUSAG),[51] which would probably attempt a landing in late July but might choose an earlier date; an alternative, mentioned only in passing, was a descent on Jutland, where the slowing down of fortification work was thought to invite an assault.[52]

Rumours of imminent landings continued to be frequent in late June and early July: Brest on 22 June, Ostend on the 23rd, St Nazaire on the 29th, Flanders on the 30th, Belgium on 2 July (two reports, one from 'agents' who seem not to have been under Ops B's control), Le Havre–Scheldt on 4 July[53] – all evidence either that FORTITUDE SOUTH II was having the desired effect or that the same end was being achieved through German fears that the Allies could exploit the advantage they were gradually gaining in Normandy by making a second landing, probably further east than Calais.

An appreciation by the new OB West, von Kluge, drawn up directly he took over from Rundstedt on 17 July, accepted the FUSAG story in its entirety: As soon as the boundary of the bridgehead ran from the lower Orne to Avranches and enough Germans had been attracted thither, FUSAG would be launched against 15 Army. A couple of days later Foreign Armies West agreed: FUSAG, under Patton and up to 35 or more divisions strong, would seek a decision in the Franco-Belgian frontier area.[54] These were perhaps the first two signals about FORTITUDE to suffer decryption delays long enough to diminish their strategic value seriously: the first could not be transmitted until 8 August, just as the Mortain battle was about to erupt, and the second not until 12 October, by which time it had of course only historical value.

'When the German line was stabilized at the end of September, the day of strategic deception was over', wrote Hesketh. Masterman preferred 25 October, when the Japanese military attaché in Stockholm reported to Tokyo that FUSAG had been broken up (OKH had already dated this the 21st).[55] After the great advance across northern France, the over-running of the V-weapon sites, and Arnhem, there was plainly less scope for surprise moves by the Allies and thus for plausible ways to disguise them. Until then, however, it was clear from Ultra that FORTITUDE SOUTH II, together with the brute fact that their seaward flank always lay open to the superior Allied air and naval forces, retained such a firm hold upon the German imagination that it was easy to prolong the threat. Indeed, self-mystification about the number and location of the Allied airborne divisions appears to have been rife in OKH well before Ops B began to play with them in order to suggest that MARKET GARDEN would take place a good deal further east than Arnhem. GOC Netherlands predicted just this on 11 September, two days after the correct target had been identified by an unspecified source; news of both was in the hands of all concerned 48 or more hours before the first Allied airdrop.[56] Foreign Armies West had counted ten airborne divisions (six British, four American – twice the real number) a month earlier, believed that they had recently been reinforced, and was still apprehensive about 14 Army; on 7 September the GAF was convinced that FUSAG controlled these divisions and would use them to launch an attack on the North German coast, Denmark or southern Norway.[57] Fears of air-landings in Jutland or Kiel Bay and on the Dutch coast as far east as the Friesian islands – the latter on the day after MARKET GARDEN began – were only available after they had lost all operational value.[58]

V

Ops B's primary method of work was to put out, through the controlled agents, false locations for Allied corps and divisions, hoping thereby to induce the enemy to make wrong deductions about Allied strategy.

When he examined German records after the war, Hesketh found evidence to show the success of this ploy. Ultra, on the other hand, lends little support to the effectiveness of order-of-battle items, and its merit (as already indicated) lies rather in revealing some of the more general appreciations into which OKH's and OB West's intelligence staffs digested the information they gathered from all the sources open to them.

None the less, Ultra was able to show that several real formations had been identified before D-Day, some belonging to FUSAG, and others which were entirely fictional.[59] Hesketh's party would no doubt have profited in two ways from knowing the numbers of the 20 or so Allied formations thus identified before D-Day and the many more thereafter. Except for what they could infer from the questions asked of the agents by their regular correspondents, the *Abwehr* control stations in Hamburg and Madrid (and these could only be treated as authoritative on the large assumption that in spite of successive convulsions in the German intelligence establishment the reputation of the *Abwehr* remained high), Ops B had no means of knowing whether their fictional story had been believed or not; and secondly, errors by the Germans might sometimes be as instructive as correct reasoning. The 'knowledge-barrier' which, it was suggested above (see p. 176) separated Hesketh from Wild, evidently denied him this information. The remarkable success of FORTITUDE obscures the fact that Hesketh could have used Ultra's revelations to sharpen his technique and thus have made the deception more effective still.

None of this category of Ultra information lived up to the promise of the early Ultra about FUSAG, however. This being so, and in view of the largely disappointing nature of Hesketh's Appendix XIII (which lists the agents' contribution to German intelligence) – as well as the fact that none of it was available to him until 1946 – it is permissible to wonder whether a considerable amount of the patient care over precise order-of-battle detail was not wasted effort and whether, had Hesketh and his colleagues been able to see and analyse Ultra, they might not have redirected some of their efforts into more profitable channels[60] (the trouble they took over 1 Canadian Army does not seem to have been worth while, for instance). Given that they had to credit German intelligence with greater abilities than we now know it possessed, and given that they apparently had scarcely any means of discovering whether the seeds they had sown were taking root, their actions were prudent and right. Masterman was nearer the truth than perhaps he realised when he wrote (though in a slightly different context), 'It is probable ... that we erred on the side of over-elaboration and excess'.[61]

The cancellation of FORTITUDE NORTH in July and the transfer of its notional troops from Scotland to Sussex and then to East Anglia shows Ultra in a more helpful light. The fictitious British 4 Army, which sup-posedly moved south in mid-July, appeared in Ultra on the 24th, only a week after the story was first put out by agents; 14 US Army, its imagi-nary partner, followed a month behind, together with several of its com-ponent divisions. Acceptance of this piece of disinformation must have been one reason why FORTITUDE survived so long – far longer than had been bargained for – but its usefulness to the Allies will have been restricted by the delay in its availability: the news about 14 Army could not be signalled until 9 August.[62] The delay may well have been due in part to the huge quantity of urgent operational material – to which priority of handling had of course to be given – which deluged Hut 3 between COBRA at the end of July and the capture of Antwerp on 3 September, but decryption difficulties will probably also have been partly responsible.[63]

VI

A firm, if of necessity only provisional, conclusion follows from all this: the interrelation of Ultra and FORTITUDE, and the influence of FORTITUDE upon events, are both far less clear than has been supposed.

That information from Most Secret sources was made available to the FORTITUDE planners cannot be doubted: the manifest absurdity of not doing so, together with the authoritative testimony quoted above, makes this certain. But what intelligence? If *Wehrmacht* Ultra, why is there so little trace of its having been used? On *Abwehr* Ultra, including the messages from the double agents' German controllers, no useful comment can be made in the absence of all documentation. These must have been the two prime sources, but the contrast between them must be prominently borne in mind: subject to familiar problems of under-standing and interpretation, *Wehrmacht* Ultra was 'hard' information, reflecting the actions or intentions of operational commanders or their subordinates; *Abwehr* decrypts, on the other hand, like all information from every state's secret services and their agents, bore no known or constant relation to action. There could be no certainty that Garbo's message of 8 June would be passed on by the *Abwehr* to OKW, still less that OKW would regard it as reliable or that Hitler would act upon it; nor could Garbo's controller guarantee this in his reply.

On the Allied side information is lacking about how (incoming) intelligence was utilised in the framing of (outgoing) strategy and tactics. Speculation – guesswork – has to replace rational deduction from evidence, and so inevitably risks errors of unknown magnitude. Hesketh focused on one aspect of risk when he wrote, 'It is always tempting for those who set out to deceive, and who see their projects fulfilled, to claim the credit for their attainment when in fact the motive force lay in another quarter. ... At all times the writer has kept before him the boast of Aesop's fly as he sat upon the axle-tree'.[64] But can the fly's mistake ever be wholly avoided? The desired result came about. Did the one cause the other? For proof that it did, Hesketh relied on the Garbo message of 8 June[65] and on Keitel's reluctant admission that the Panzer divisions' move westward was cancelled because of it. Keitel made the admission to a single interrogator, Roger Hesketh's brother Cuthbert, on 18 April 1946,[66] halfway through the Nuremberg trials at a time when he had reason to fear that the death sentence might be pronounced against him. His mind was focused on his own future fate, not on past history, and he was hardly in a frame of mind to review his recollections objectively, especially to an interrogator who clearly hoped for a particular answer. His words are a very slender thread to support the weighty conclusion that Garbo and FORTITUDE alone kept the Panzer divisions back.

Garbo, moreover, has a rival who should not be underestimated. As keeper of the OKW War Diary, the distinguished medieval historian, Professor Percy-Ernst Schramm, saw a great many intelligence reports and was privy to some, though not all, discussions at the *Fuehrerhaupt quartier.* Schramm singled out 'Josephine' (the brainchild of a journalist living in Stockholm whose reports were based on nothing but open sources and his own lively imagination) as of particular merit and dismissed all the other agents as tools of the Allies.[67] How much weight should we attach to so well-placed a witness?

Behind the agents' reports and Hitler's intuition lay the sound rational calculation that the invasion convoys could be guaranteed the greatest protection if they took the shortest sea crossing. In late 1943 Jodl plotted all the invasion-sites predicted by agents on a six-foot-long map of Europe, and found that he had left scarcely an inch of the coast blank between northern Norway and the Franco-Spanish frontier.[68] In circumstances of such uncertainty, would not fundamental strategic principles have become even more prominent than usual? They pointed (as COSSAC discovered that same autumn) to Normandy and the Pas

187

de Calais as the best places for a landing. Precisely because deception must attach itself like a parasite to a body already sick, it cannot later claim to be the sole cause of the patient's death. There is a good deal less cogency to a claim that FORTITUDE alone kept reinforcements away from Normandy than to a claim that MINCEMEAT alone kept them away from Sicily, for there the cause/effect relationship can be much more firmly established.[69]

In the past, attention has usually been mainly directed towards answering the question: did Fortitude achieve its purpose? It is plain that the available evidence does not entitle us to answer with a completely confident affirmative. Another question of at least equal importance has been given far less attention: how soon did SHAEF know how much of FORTITUDE's purpose was being achieved, and what use was made of the knowledge? Yet the answer to this second question mattered supremely at the time to the commanders engaged, and even the historian writing many years later needs to know the answer to it if he is to assess the commanders' actions fairly. For deception is nothing but the handmaid of operations, as Dudley Clarke constantly emphasised: an indispensable handmaid perhaps, but one with no independent life of her own. Deception has no other purpose than to secure practical benefits.

NOTES

An earlier version of this paper was presented to the Third International Conference on Intelligence and Military Operations at the Army War College, Carlisle Barracks, Pennsylvania, in May 1988. I am grateful to those who took part in the discussion, particularly Professor Michael Handel and Mr Tom Cubbage, for helpful suggestions.

1. According to David Mure, it was an axiom of Dudley Clarke, the founding father of Second World War deception, that 'intelligence is not a weapon which is fully effective in defence' (D. Mure, *Master of Deception* (London: Kimber, 1980), p. 85).

2. The Russians' use of deception is only now becoming known. See David M. Glantz, 'The Red Mask: The Nature and Legacy of Soviet Military Deception in the Second World War', *Intelligence and National Security*, Vol.2, No.3 (1987), pp. 175–259.

3. The command organisation may be briefly summarised as follows: Ops B was set up as part of COSSAC in April 1943 to deal with all deception measures, physical as well as 'special means' (we are concerned here only with the latter). Ops B presented its 'special means' proposals to the LCS, which then

prescribed the appropriate channel by which they should be passed to the enemy. Soon after Ops B was absorbed into SHAEF on the latter's formation in January 1944, LCS cut out a stage in the process by arranging for Ops B to work direct to B1A, a section of MI5 which managed controlled agents. When Eisenhower delegated invasion planning to 21 Army Group in February, Ops B came under 21 Army Group's authority; henceforward 21 Army Group had to approve every piece of information it proposed to 'leak' through the controlled agents. Ops B's immediate contact at 21 Army Group was an intelligence section entitled G(R).

4. See T.L. Cubbage, 'The Success of Operation Fortitude: Hesketh's History of Strategic Deception', *Intelligence and National Security,* Vol.2, No.3 (1987), pp. 327–46. The Hesketh report is not mentioned in either the text or the bibliography of F.H. Hinsley *et al., British Intelligence in the Second World War,* 3 vols (London: HMSO, 1979–88).

5. This seemingly obvious precaution, which had always been taken by Dudley Clarke – to whom 'The value of intelligence is in exact proportion to its operational value' (Mure, p. 180) – seems to have lost prominence in the eyes of some modern theorists, distracted from practical realities by an earnest but misconceived search for a general theory of deception: see, for instance, D.C. Daniel and K.L. Herbig, 'Propositions on Military Deception', in John Gooch and Amos Perlmutter (eds), *Military Deception and Surprise* (London: Frank Cass, 1982), pp. 155–77.

6. Omar N. Bradley and Clay Blair, *A General's Life* (London: Sidgwick & Jackson, 1983), pp. 219–20.

    Others had written in the same sense earlier, but with less authority, and none had made any attempt to explain how intelligence and deception were integrated: for instance, Mure, pp. 98, 101; C. Cruickshank, *Deception in World War II* (Oxford: 1979), p. 213; R. Lewin, *Ultra Goes to War* (London: Hutchinson, 1978), pp. 316–19 (in this passage Lewin uses 'Ultra' to mean both *Abwehr* and *Wehrmacht* Ultra, and quotes *Abwehr* messages in inverted commas without indicating where he saw them).

7. Hinsley *et al., British Intelligence,* Vol.iii, 2 (1988), p. 45; cf. 177–8.

8. It is plain from Hinsley that a good deal of high grade non-CX/MSS Sigint material bearing on Fortitude was passed over the normal Ultra signals channels. This material seems to have consisted mainly of Japanese diplomatic decrypts, the contents of which were classed as Ultra and signalled at first as AWLs and from March 1944 as BAY/KVs (Hinsley *et al., British Intelligence,* Vol.iii, 2, p. 50n). In addition some CX/MSS material seems to have been signalled in the pre-invasion months as AWLs, although the main body was passed as KVs (this seems a legitimate inference from the footnotes in Hinsley).

    Ops B, however, dealt with agents belonging to the *Abwehr.* Their controllers in Hamburg and elsewhere sent them instructions and commented on their replies. Some at least of this correspondence will have been included in the *Abwehr* traffic (some Enigma, some hand-cypher) decrypted at Bletchley as ISOS and ISK. By 1943 3000 of these decrypts were being handled weekly (Hinsley, *British Intelligence,* Vol.ii, p. 20, cf. Vol.iii, 1, p. 141). There is very little mention of this traffic in Hinsley, and the decrypts are not in the Public Record Office.

9. Hesketh, p. 95n.
10. Translations of these decrypts were given CX/MSS (earlier CX/JQ) serial numbers; signals to commands based on them were transmitted as KV, XL, etc. By 1944 messages decrypted on the Geheimschreiber (Lorenz) machine were also classified as Ultra.
11. Hinsley, Vol.iii, 2, pp. 50n, 61.
12. BAY/KVs 97, 103 and 123, printed in full in Hinsley, Vol.iii, 2, pp. 787–92.
13. Hesketh, pp. 70n, 92, etc.
14. Hinsley, Vol.iii, p. 20, cf. Vol.iii, 1, p. 141. It is worth noting that there is very little mention of *Abwehr* decrypts (known in Bletchley jargon as ISOS and ISK) and information from them in Hinsley, although by 1943 some 3000 decrypts were being handled every week.
15. Hesketh, Introduction, p. 2; Mure, Foreword (by Noel Wild), pp. 242–3; D. Wheatley, *The Deception Planners* (London: Hutchinson, 1980), pp. 179–81, 187.
16. In a (regrettably fruitless) endeavour to unravel the mystery surrounding the use of Ultra in Fortitude, I have corresponded with some of those intimately concerned. My correspondence with Major Hesketh was cut short by his death after a first formal exchange of letters. Colonel (now the Revd Canon) Strangeways, formerly head of G(R) at 21 Army Group, was not confident of the accuracy of his memory after more than 40 years, and consequently preferred not to give me an answer. I am grateful to them for their friendly response to inquiries from a total stranger.

    Over 100 signals bearing directly on Fortitude had been passed to SHAEF and 21 Army Group by the time the advance slowed down after Arnhem: 25 or 30 before D-Day, between 50 and 60 in June, 30 more by the end of September. Most of the thousands of other signals passed to Western commands during the same months were relevant in one way or another. Since the Germans preferred to use land-lines when possible, there were far fewer intercepts in April and May than later: the pre-D-Day intercepts must therefore be regarded as rather a chance selection, put out in Enigma by radio when bombing or sabotage had interrupted other means of communication.
17. VL 4834. I drew attention to this signal ten years ago in my *Ultra in the West* (London: Hutchinson, 1979), p. 53, but lacking knowledge then of the 'notional' Allied order of battle, did not recognise its full significance.
18. Hinsley, Vol.iii, 2, pp. 48–9. Hesketh, writing in 1949, indeed comments on the Oshima decrypt already cited in these words: 'This conversation provided us with one of the *rare instances* where we obtained, before D-Day, a really valuable insight into the enemy's thoughts' (Hesketh, p. 95n; my emphasis). Note that the Oshima decrypt in question referred to a conversation of 27 May, *five months after* the January signal mentioned in the text above.
19. Hesketh, p. 81.
20. Hesketh, pp. 46–51.
21. This dependence accorded, however, with the first of Dudley Clarke's ground rules (Mure, p. 273).
22. KVs 190, 3067, 3372.
23. Hesketh, p. 57.
24. Hesketh, pp. 61, 63.

25. VL 9732. Hesketh (p. 90), it may be noted, quotes this only from the Lage-bericht West, which he did not see until after the war. Ops B began to present Patton as commanding FUSAG much later, on 31 May (Hesketh, p. 64). Once more, German apprehensions antedated Ops B's attempts to induce them, and Ultra had revealed them long before Ops B exploited them.
26. VLs 6878, 9017, KVs 190, 353, 3067, 3372, 5792.
27. *Abwehr* decrypts may, of course, have given more, but they cannot be consulted at present. Hesketh mentions none in his Appendix XIII, relying instead entirely on documents captured after May 1945 as an index of the extent to which the agents' reports penetrated the German intelligence system.
28. KVs 3434, 3552, 3382.
29. BAY/KVs 97, 103, 123, signalled between 8 and 13 May, Hinsley iii/2 787–792. Luftflotte 3 was predicting a landing between Le Havre and Cherbourg at this time: KVs 3242, 3281. There seems to have been specially lively debate about probable invasion sites and corresponding defence measures during the first half of May. It was now that Rommel told Rundstedt that Normandy could not be reinforced by drawing in troops stationed on either flank because there were not enough of them, and asked for operational control over the OKW reserve, a request that was refused. Hitler was at this time expecting the first landings to aim to capture Cherbourg and Brest; he later preferred Normandy (Oberkommando der Wehrmacht, *Kriegstagebuch* (OKW/KTB) iii/2 301–3).
30. KV 3763, signalled 14 May. KVs 773, 5689 are also relevant.
31. It is important to remember that, in the absence of evidence to the contrary, precautions like these are likely to have been the consequence of strategic prudence based on topographical probability rather than on specific intelligence, genuine or planted. Similar caution is required in order to avoid hindsight in interpreting certain items of intelligence.
32. KVs 2273, 4728, 5446. Ops B had, in fact, firmly planted the threat from southeast England in the German mind by now, but of course this could not be known to them, to SHAEF or to 21 Army Group with any degree of certainty.
33. KVs 3372, 3763. Hesketh (p. 93) arrives at the same conclusion.
34. VL 9126.
35. Hesketh, pp. 33–42, 75–83.
36. KV 5406.
37. KVs 6635, 6822.
38. KVs 6724, 6834, 7364, 7381, 7431, 7535, 8415, Hesketh, pp. 69–70.
39. OKW/KTB iv. 301.
40. KVs 6933, 6958.
41. KVs 7593, 7986, 8024.
42. KVs 6724, 7071, 7305, 7312, 7535.
43. KV 8250. This was an extraordinarily maladroit assessment. The COSSAC planners, though unable to inspect any of the possible landing sites, had at an early stage ruled out all the beaches but those in Normandy and the Pas de Calais as quite unsuitable for large-scale landing operations. The German staffs, able to visit them at leisure, seem not to have realised that the stretch of coast between Somme and Seine was unfitted for the purpose they were assigning to it, as indeed the Dieppe raid of 1942 had demonstrated. The absurdity of the forecast quoted in the text was presumably at once apparent

to SHAEF and 21 Army Group (L.F. Ellis, *Victory in the West* (London, 1962), Vol.i, pp. 15–16;Hesketh, p. 115). An equally ridiculous error was made during the last stages of the war in Italy. At the end of March 1945, OB Southwest moved one of his best divisions to stand guard against a landing north of the River Po, an action which, by weakening his centre, simplified the final Allied breakthrough which overwhelmed him. The Allied deception planners had sought to suggest such a landing. Alexander's naval advisers had told him – what the Germans apparently did not realise – that the water was too shallow for a landing (Alexander, *Despatch* (in *London Gazette* 12 June 1950), p. 2959n.

44   Hesketh, pp. 55, 100–4.
45   Hesketh, Introduction, pp. 5–6, 102–4. In a footnote on page 78 of his report, Hesketh wrote: 'The daily OKH Lageberichte provide by far the most valuable evidence for the progress of Fortitude'. See also Lewin, p. 318.
46.   KVs 7592, 7982
47.   KVs 8881, 9058.
48.   Hesketh, pp. 116–18.
49.   Hesketh, p. 114, XL 103.
50.   XL 356, signalled 1 July.
51.   'Josephine', the fictional agent invented by Dr Kraemer, a German journalist living in Stockholm, had named Patton as commander of FUSAG on 19 June (Hesketh, p. 146).
52.   XL 688. The German military attaché in Stockholm had already suggested Denmark (XL 690).
53.   XV 9329, XLs 103, 202, 322, 498, 500, 502, 2287, 3921.
54.   XL 5226, HP 3119.
55.   Hesketh, pp. 153, 157; J.C. Masterman, *The Double Cross System* (Yale, 1972), p. 158. Physical (i.e. tactical) deception measures became effective once more in consequence, as in the desert. They had not proved of much value for Fortitude hitherto, because the decline of the Luftwaffe meant that they were not likely to be noticed from the air. In the west the GAF was 'virtually unable to carry out overland reconnaissance in 1944', and had done very little since 1941, so that no amount of physical deception – tents, dumps, 'Big Bobs' (inflatable dummy landing craft) and so on – could suggest FUSAG. Nevertheless, SHAEF would run no risks in March, and OKW believed that 'a single photo reconnaissance flight over the ports of embarkation could give more information than a whole group of agents' (Hinsley, Vol.iii, 2, p. 43; Hesketh, p. 44, OKW/KTB iv, 1800).
56.   HPs 242, 461; Hesketh, p. 147.
57.   XLs 7215, 7540, 9503.
58.   HPs 1376, 1459.
59.   VL 9017 of 3 March – V and VIII US Corps, 2 Canadian, 28 and 52 British Divisions, for instance; KV 5792 of 7 May – 10 US Division.
60.   Masterman, pp. 28–9. If this is so, then Dudley Clarke's maxim that the building-up of a false order of battle 'must be the first task of all for a deception staff, and it must go on unceasingly' (Mure, p. 274) would need revision. For straightforward intelligence work, to discover the enemy's actual order of battle was of course always a primary and essential task.
61.   Masterman, p. 28. All such speculation is confused, however, by the mystery

which still surrounds the *Abwehr* decrypts. What did they have to say? To whom was the information from them imparted? How, and by whom, was it amalgamated with other intelligence? Final judgement must of necessity be postponed until these things are known.

62. XLs 6212, 8937, 9540, HP 513.

63. One other feature of the late summer and early autumn attracted much attention at the time. The great majority of German Y Service reports were derived from intercepts of the radio traffic of American formations, which suggested lax security on their part and gave needless assistance to German intelligence; the same phenomenon had long been evident in Italy.

64. The fly boasted that he, and not the wheels of the chariot, raised the cloud of dust.

65. The message bears upon its face proof that Hitler saw it, but none of his subsequent actions.

66. Cubbage (p. 334) prints Cuthbert Hesketh's account of the interview.

67. OKW/KTB iv, 1798. On Josephine, see Horst Boog, 'Josephine and the Northern Flank' in *Intelligence and National Security*, Vol.4, No.1 (January 1989), pp. 137–60. Drawing on the vast resources of the *Militärgeschichtliches Forschungsamt* in Freiburg, Dr Boog shows convincingly that in Norway, even more than in France, German moves to counter threats of invasion were occasioned more by Hitler's convictions and by naval and military strategic considerations than by London-based deception, of which they were virtually independent. (Unless Josephine was indeed a controlled agent, despite Hesketh's denials. At one point (p. 152) Dr Boog uncharacteristically abandons his usual rigid documentary technique for a 'must have been' to suggest this. He cites no concrete evidence to support his suggestion.) German apprehensions, it appears, were at their most acute in autumn and winter 1944/45; yet Fortitude North was effectively ended in July, and finally wound up in September (Hesketh, p. 77). By that time, some German intelligence circles had begun to question Josephine's credibility, Dr Boog shows, but naval and military authorities were more apprehensive than ever of an invasion of Norway. His greater familiarity (because of his position at Führerhaupt-quartier) with official apprehensions than with the scepticism of a few may account for Schramm's opinion.

68. OKW/KTB iv, 1798.

69. See Chapter 9 of my *Ultra and Mediterranean Strategy 1941–1945* (London: Hamish Hamilton/New York: William Morrow, 1989), pp. 222–7.

Two additions to the above notes may appropriately be made now (1995):

Notes 14, 61: Michael Howard: *Strategic Deception* (published in 1990, two years after my essay was written) pp. 185–200, throws no light on the problems I raised. But the statement on p. 190 that 'Enough of the FHW situation reports were decrypted to give the deception authorities a very good idea of the success of their plans' seems to imply that Hesketh saw them. If this was the case, then Hesketh's use of only the Lageberichte West as proofs of the success becomes a deliberate evasion and impossible to understand (cf pp. 175–6, above).

Note 58: But now see *A Footnote to Fortitude*, below p. 194. While many of the questions asked above have still not been given satisfactory answers, this paper (written in 1988) bears the marks of its age because more relevant information is now becoming available.

A FOOTNOTE TO FORTITUDE

Mr Donald Gurrey has kindly drawn my attention to the document translated below, which he found in the Bundesarchiv, Koblenz. It illustrates the persistence, long after the Allies had ceased to promote them, of German fears of an Allied landing on the North Sea coast of Europe, and also underlines the astonishing credulity of German intelligence during the last months of the war, after Himmler had taken over the *Abwehr.*

Der Reichsführer SS, RSHA
Kdo. M. München, Meldekopf ZENO

Kdo. Meldegebiet München, Meldekopf ZENO, sends the following report on England:
2079 reports on 19.1.45 from Milan by W/T (Source: informant ORSO from one of General Eisenhower's staff officers):

Enemy intention of landing on the Danish coast

Landing intention on Danish coast. English east coast harbours 400 000 men ready. Landing docks ready. On standby for past six weeks. Landing to take place simultaneously with Kurland offensive. Delayed by German offensive in the west. Eisenhower currently in England to prepare for Denmark landing. This landing last Allied landing on continent of Europe.

Meldegebiet München was the former Abwehrstelle München, renamed after Himmler took over the *Abwehr* in March 1944. Meldekopf ZENO was an outstation of Meldegebiet München, located in north Italy. It specialised in training spies and dropping them by parachute, preparing stay-behind agents and recruiting sources in the Italian resistance.

'Landing docks' are presumably Mulberries, none of which had been built since D-Day.

By passing it on to its superiors without comment, Meldegebiet München showed that it believed the report worth taking seriously; yet it is astonishing that a senior German regional intelligence centre could believe, as late as January 1945, that the Allies – who had been fighting hard since mid-December to recover the territory that had been lost to the Ardennes offensive – could have afforded to keep 400,000 men idle in England for the past six weeks in preparation for a landing in Denmark.

It would be natural to count the report as evidence of successful Allied deception were it not for the fact that Fortitude South II had been cancelled four months earlier, on 8 September 1944, mainly on the ground that the Germans were already so hard-pressed that they were unlikely to respond to any deception at all. In any case, what deception officer worth his salt would suppose the Germans gullible enough to accept 'one of General Eisenhower's staff officers' as a credible source for a report originating in Italy at a time when all the world knew that Eisenhower was directing operations in France?

The document is of interest mainly as an intelligence curiosity, but it also forms a footnote to my article from *Intelligence and National Security,* Vol. 4, No. 3 (July 1989), pp. 170–93 above.

10

Ultra and Crete

The narrative of events during the Battle of Crete is plain enough, though dismal to contemplate 50 years later. It is the intelligence, and still more the use that was made of it, which is in dispute. Here I must at once 'declare an interest': as an army officer in Hut 3 at Bletchley Park I wrote some of the signals that were sent to General Freyberg, commanding the defence force, and was fully aware of those sent while I was not on duty. It is upon them, and upon their relevance to events upon the ground, that I shall concentrate.

But first it is essential to be quite clear what these Ultra signals were, why they were sent, and by what security regulations they were governed. By the end of the war, about 150 varieties of Enigma had been discovered, intercepted and decrypted, but there were at most only half a dozen in 1941, at the time of the battle of Crete. The most operationally useful were two Luftwaffe varieties, known to us as Red and Light Blue. Since the assault on the island was to be mainly from the air and under the command of an air force general, Student, orders for it were transmitted in the local Mediterranean Enigma key, Light Blue. Fortunately, this could be decrypted fairly currently.

What proportion of the Crete orders was decrypted and read at Bletchley was, and still remains, uncertain. It was certainly great, but certainly not exhaustive. Ultra was never more than a random selection of the enemy's correspondence; it included most of what he put on the air, but no more. This was probably not fully enough realised at the time, and is sometimes overlooked even now. The Germans had captured Athens on 26 April. On 20 May, only three weeks later, they launched the attack on Crete. Landline communications in Greece were inadequate, and there had been no time for a military network to be established. They believed Enigma to be unbreakable, so they used the

195

air freely. Nevertheless, some important arrangements were made either by telephone or by courier – e.g. the substitution of 5 Mountain Division for 22 Airborne Division in the assault phase, and the downgrading of the attacking element in the seaborne landing.[1]

With few exceptions, however, Ultra gave a remarkably clear picture of strategic plan and tactical appreciation. Only on three or four other occasions was it able to repeat the performance.[2] But these were much later and in very different circumstances. Crete was an exceptional situation, therefore, and it happened at a very early stage in the exploitation of Enigma and the birth of Ultra. This carried with it certain disadvantages.

The extreme novelty of the situation became suddenly clear when, to universal surprise, towards the end of April Hut 3 was instructed to send operational information about Crete to GHQ Cairo. There were precedents of a sort: signals about Rommel's advance in the desert had been sent since the middle of March, and about the fighting in Greece and Jugoslavia soon afterwards (the German attack there began on 6 April), but there was one distinctive feature of the Cretan situation. Since Crete was an island, it was improbable that much useful intelligence could come from any source other than radio. Advance warning depended on Ultra, and very likely the conduct of operations too. In consequence, everyone concerned in the production of Ultra was suddenly compelled to run before he had learned to walk. As yet Hut 3 lacked experience (most of us had been in uniform only a few weeks, and were totally ignorant of military ways and military vocabulary); there was no speedy and secure wireless channel exclusive to Ultra; MI6 had not yet formulated security rules for a source it had never controlled before and which could deliver news far quicker than the agents to whom it was accustomed; and the commanders in the field, unused to red hot intelligence which was absolutely reliable, distrusted it and did not know how to use it. All these limitations were to appear in some measure during the Crete campaign.

When the imminence of an attack became clear in early May 1941, only six weeks had passed since the first Ultra signal of all had gone out on 13 March.

In the spring of 1941 no one in Whitehall, in Bletchley or in the Mediterranean had any ready-made idea of how the consequences of the revolutionary breakthrough the cryptographers had made should be handled. All were fumbling in the dark, forced by the pace of unfolding events to do whatever seemed best in the haste of the moment. No suspicion of the prominent part Ultra intelligence would play in future planning had dawned in anyone's mind: simply a feeling that Ultra's potential was so vast that the secret should be guarded with the utmost care. Later, when experience had brought enlightenment, rules of all kinds were gradually formulated . A backward glance shows up glaring faults, faults which had not been apparent at the time – looseness of wording, security risks which should never have been taken. From its vantage point years later, hindsight makes for clear and perfectly focused rear vision, but hindsight is a cheat and can lead to unfairly harsh judgements of men and erroneous conclusions about events. At all costs, historians must avoid using hindsight; it makes history-writing easy, but distorts the truth; it can even make us forget that the most perfect intelligence cannot add a single gun or tank to an army's strength.

Hindsight has bedevilled much of the controversy about Crete, and my main purpose here is to correct it on certain points of intelligence and interpretation. Actors in an event are not necessarily the best judges of it, and I make no claim to appraise the campaign better than others simply because I had a hand in the intelligence about it. Nevertheless, the man who was driving the car when the accident happened knows what it felt like; the judge and jury have to rely on their imagination. An example will show what I mean.

One of the central documents concerning Crete is OL 302.[3] It was compiled by Group Captain Humphreys, one of the few older members of the army/air intelligence staff; he spoke with great authority to younger men like myself. He wrote OL 302 with his own hand, and described its origins in a paper he composed[4] for the Air Ministry in October 1945. 'On the Prime Minister's insistence', he wrote, 'the Bletchley Park air intelligence section produced a paper purporting to be a compendium of German documents obtained through Secret Service channels from German GHQ in Athens, the summary being couched in terms consistent with such an alibi. This was then signalled to Crete.'

If Churchill gave such instructions, then it can only have been the consequence either of forgetfulness or muddled thinking.[5] OL 302 was transmitted at 1745 on 13 May. But Churchill certainly knew that on or before 30 April – a fortnight previously – he had ordered Wavell (GOC Middle East) to tell Freyberg, when he appointed him GOC Crete, that he would be receiving Ultra, and that Wavell had explained exactly what Ultra was.[6] There was therefore no need to feed Freyberg with the cover-story about an omniscient agent a fortnight later.

197

Humphreys also knew, and so surely did Churchill, that almost everything in OL 302 had already been sent to Freyberg, a week earlier, on 6 May, as OL 2167, without any of the disguise which mars OL 302.[7] The essence of the two signals is the same,[8] though 302 embodies a few new scraps of information gathered in the week between the two dates. But there is one important difference between them. OL 2167 is factual; there is no element of interpretation or comment in it; it reads like a telegraphese version of a translation from the German. This is exactly what Ultra signals were, and this is the impression which reading them gives. That OL 2167 was in fact this was confirmed by OL 2170, sent next day (7 May); it is confessedly an Air Ministry comment on 2167. OL 2170 was an authoritative estimate of the scale of coming operations; OL 2167, on the other hand, was not 'a first formal estimate from London'[9] but a factual statement derived from an intercept. By contrast OL 302 contains elements of interpretation and comment mingled with fact in such a way that it is hard to determine where the one ends and the other begins. The mingling confused the intelligence picture, of course; how much came from German sources, how much from Humphreys' (intelligent and well-meaning) imagination? To overcome the problem, before long a strict rule was introduced: in future fact and comment were to be clearly separated: the facts were to be given first, then anything that needed to be said by way of elucidation, prefaced by the word 'Comment'. The first example I have found is dated 3 September, four months after Crete. Here is a clear indication that the Cretan campaign was still within the learning period.

To resume: by 6 May, then, clear warning of an impending attack had been given, although some details were a little imprecise. Just under a fortnight was available to make preparations to repel the invaders. Here we reach what has become – needlessly, in my opinion – a major controversy. The main blow would come by air, it was quite plain. This was not a new idea; the first British garrison commander had forecast, back in late 1940, that any German attempt to capture Crete would be delivered by air, and this had been abundantly confirmed when a menacing assemblage of bombers, fighters, transport aircraft and gliders on Greek airfields under Fliegerkorps XI had become known from 21 April onwards.[10] However, when seen in the context of the two signals just quoted, this posed the threat of a huge air landing, an almost unprecedented form of attack, on a totally unprecedented scale (the operations in Belgium and Holland in 1940 had been much smaller). But would the attack be *exclusively* from the air?

Over the years, Freyberg has been severely criticised for under-estimating the scale of air attack and for making inadequate prepara-tions to meet it, while at the same time overestimating the danger from the sea. That he made mistakes about the air danger cannot be denied, but this is hardly surprising in view of the fact that nothing like it had ever happened before, so that there was no precedent to guide him.

But the sea is another matter. The evidence has not been accorded the weight it deserves, nor has it been viewed in its true historical context. On the morning of 7 May, less than twelve hours after OL 2167, a correction was sent.[11] It ran: 'Flak, further troops and supplies men-tioned in OL 2167 are to proceed by sea', and suggested that 'three mountain regiments' was a more likely rendering of the German than '3rd mountain regiment' as in the text of OL 2167. Upon this there has been erected an edifice of 'wrong ideas' on the part of Freyberg,[12] as well as by the War Office, and the Air Ministry. But the word-order in OL 2167 already implied that all were to come by sea. I cannot see how a theory that Freyberg exaggerated the seaborne threat can rest on so flimsy a foundation.

It is more important to note that all these were *offensive* forces for which no provision had yet been made in the air drop. Did not they too threaten an attack, therefore? A week later OL 302 added the new information that roughly two-thirds of the total effort would be from the air and one-third from the sea. Further, Ultra had already announ-ced, on 11 May,[13] that 12 ships totalling 27,000 tons were assembling at Naples and in Sicily for the Crete operation: *some* would carry rations and ammunition. What the rest would carry was not stated, but it would surely have been exceedingly rash of Freyberg to assume that they would *not* be carrying assault troops? And in fact this is just what they would have carried if they had landed on the night of 20/21 May, a point that is often overlooked. The intended routes and timings of these ships were reported in four more signals right up to 19 May,[14] just 24 hours before the airborne attack began. Why this miniature armada was replaced by the fleet of caiques which the navy destroyed the same night remained obscure. (No doubt the change of plan was arranged by telephone; unexplained gaps in Ultra were always capable of confusing the intelli-gence picture at short notice – as happened notably before the battle of Kasserine in February 1943.)

In order to appreciate fairly the intelligence value of the information at Freyberg's disposal before the attack began, it is essential to bear in mind that, whatever later events showed, there was nothing to suggest to him that the air was the only assault route and the sea merely the back-up and supply route. All the evidence pointed the other way, and the word 'attack' was used to describe the sea landing as late as 21 May.[15] Freyberg would therefore have grossly neglected his duty if he had not taken steps to repel attack from the sea. Admittedly, he did not set on foot a study of the beaches to discover whether a landing was feasible – but neither did those who, with far more leisure and deliberation, planned the Dieppe raid in August 1942. It is hardly fair to blame Freyberg for making the same error a year earlier.

Most commentators have forgotten one thing. Fear of a threat from the sea did not originate from the Ultra signals; it came from something far older. No island had, in the whole history of the world, ever been captured except from the sea. Another method was technically possible now, though its validity was as yet unproven, since it had never been tried on so large a scale. Therefore anyone whose duty it was to defend an island was bound by his background and training to take the seaborne threat seriously and to prepare to meet it. Here again hindsight rears its ugly head. It is only too easy today to be too clever by half, to see things – consciously or unconsciously – with modern eyes, eyes which the actors in the drama could not possibly have had. Freyberg no doubt thought too much about the sea and too little about the air, but he could hardly have avoided doing so except by the exercise of a prescience far ahead of his contemporaries. Neither the War Office nor the Air Ministry possessed a crystal ball, nor do I recall that we in Hut 3 thought at the time that a sea landing was out of the question.

It is usually conceded that, brave as he undoubtedly was, Freyberg was not in the first flight of thinking generals and no strategist, though an excellent divisional commander and an outstanding trainer of troops. But few were otherwise in 1941 – Wavell, Brooke, Montgomery ... and who else? The pre-war British army, still reeling from the shock of Dunkirk, but still unchanged a year later, was far too lacking in mental alertness to cope with German professional skill and speed of thought and reaction. Most others would have acted as Freyberg did, and he must not bear the sins of his generation alone.

Moreover, a glance at the chaotic state of security concerning Ultra goes some way towards exonerating Freyberg from the more extreme charges levelled against him.

He was given Ultra on the highest authority, but forbidden to use it unless corroborated[16] – and in the peculiar nature of the Cretan situation corroboration was unlikely. Why this self-defeating contradiction? No one knows. It has been suggested that Stewart Menzies, 'C', the head of SIS, imposed the ban without telling Churchill, overriding the Prime Minister's instructions in the interests of security to preserve a secret which might prove of inestimable value in the future. (Had the Germans discovered that we had broken Enigma, they might have adopted a cipher which we could not break.) This is pure speculation, but it is at least plausible.

Other anomalies can be fully documented. General Wilson had been given Ultra in Greece and had not been forbidden to use it. Why? No one knows. Later on, there were two rigid rules about the dissemination of Ultra: no one to get it who could not use it – the famous 'value not interest' rule which governed our lives – and Ultra never to be sent to anyone who might possibly fall into enemy hands. In practice, this meant not to any command below army level. Yet neither Wilson nor Freyberg commanded an army, but an *ad hoc* force assembled in haste. (The 1st Airborne Division did not receive Ultra at Arnhem.) Moreover, both Wilson and Freyberg might well have been captured. Most surprising of all: for a week after the German invasion of Jugoslavia in April 1941 Ultra signals (44 in all) were sent to the British Military Attaché in Belgrade, who commanded no troops and so could not conceivably use the information – and who did eventually fall into enemy hands. All this defies logical explanation. It does show, however, that to ask why Freyberg was forbidden to use Ultra is a question which could not in 1941, and cannot now, receive a satisfactory answer. The prohibition imposed on him weighed heavily on Freyberg, but he was bound to obey it even though it tied his hands militarily.

This conclusion throws a clear light on the 'second thoughts' which caused him to cancel the move of the Greek battalion to protect the western bank of the Tavronitis river, which bordered Maleme airfield, and not to.take other steps to improve his dispositions in the light of intelligence received. It does not, however, allow him to escape the charge of making less than the best dispositions *before* he received any Ultra, i.e. in the first six days of May and before the arrival of OL 2167 in the early hours of 7 May. He is said to have thought that the steepness of the Tavronitis valley and the roughness of the ground would preclude the landing of aircraft and gliders – a failure of imagination, no doubt, but again there was nothing to guide him. The 11 gliders who had taken Fort Eben Emael on the night of 10/11 May 1940 (but did he even know about them?) had landed on the flat top surface of the fort.

What neither Menzies (if it was indeed he who imposed the ban) nor Freyberg could realise was that no improvement to the all-round protection of an airfield could possibly give away any intelligence source, so obvious a precaution was it. This needless prohibition, like (from the opposite point of view) Freyberg's near-repetition of an Ultra signal in one of his Orders of the Day,[17] simply reveals how primitive and irrational was the current understanding of the demands on security.

The Germans captured Maleme airfield on 21 May and could then fly in enough men to overwhelm the defence. Why did Freyberg not realise what was happening, and organise an immediate counter-attack? The answer is that during the critical hours he did not always know what was going on. Ultra had little of importance to say once battle was joined, but it does throw some light on Freyberg's difficulties. At midday on 20 May, the Germans signalled a claim to have captured the airfield (the claim was a little premature, but that hardly affects the question). OL 385 conveyed the claim at 4.30pm. At midnight, Freyberg signalled Wavell that as far as he knew the defence of Maleme still held. He would hardly have done so if he had known that the garrison had evacuated the airfield earlier that evening, or if he had received OL 385 by then. His own communications were handicapped by a crippling shortage of radio sets, and the radio link between London and Crete had been subject to interruptions (several OLs refer to this), one of which presumably accounts for the delay in delivering OL 385.

To write sound history requires strict attention to the mental as well as to the material equipment of the actors in the drama. This is doubly true of the intelligence history of recent times, where the former can be much more fully recreated than in the past. To forget this is to allow faulty analysis to obscure the causes of events. It is entirely appropriate to point out mistakes made by Freyberg and by Whitehall, though most of them have long been recognised, but it is not appropriate to read the intelligence available to them in the light of things they did not know or to criticise them for not possessing powers of divination and second sight. They did not know, for instance, that 5 Mountain Division had replaced 22 Airlanding Division in Student's plans, simply because the Balkan railways were so jammed with traffic that the latter could not get through in time; no argument based on any other supposition can therefore hold water.

Two approaches to the loss of Crete are admissible: either, using wisdom after the event, to point out things which might have been done better, or, by sticking closely to the relationship between knowledge and action at the time, to investigate the probable impact of the one upon the other.

But the two methods cannot be practised together and at the same time. Mr Beevor's book is fatally flawed by his persistence in doing so. By attempting to combine them, he has, in effect, sought to square the circle.

NOTES

1. See p. 196 above.
2. The battle of Alam Halfa in September 1942 was the first.
3. OL was the bigram denoting the first Ultra signals.
4. PRO. AIR 40/2323.
5. Both can of course easily be understood at a time when *Bismarck* was loose in the Atlantic and Britain's whole position in the Middle East appeared to be disintegrating.
6. Paul Freyberg: *Bernard Freyberg, V.C.* (London, 1991), p. 268.
7. The numbering suggests that 2167 must have been subsequent to 302. This was not so. The numbering system was designed to distinguish between addresses. It proved cumbersome and was abandoned.
8. That is, that on 17 May (later changed to 20 May) an air landing would seize Maleme, Heraklion and Rethymo airfields. Reinforcements, supplies, etc., would follow, some by air and some by sea.
9. As Anthony Beevor: *Crete, the Battle and the Resistance* (London, 1991), p. 89, calls it.
10. OLs 114, 164, 174.
11. OL 2168.
12. Beevor 90
13. OL 278.
14. OLs 340, 351, 361, 373.
15. OL 389.
16. Freyberg, p. 268.
17. Ralph Bennett: *Ultra and Mediterranean Strategy* (London, 1989), p. 57n.